Kaleidoscope

LENSES ON REALITY

Kaleidoscope

LENSES ON REALITY

Edited by Robert F. Lawson & Carol S. Lawson

CHRYSALIS BOOKS / *Swedenborg Foundation Publishers*

THE CHRYSALIS READER is a book series that examines themes related to the universal quest for wisdom. Inspired by the concepts of Emanuel Swedenborg, each volume presents art with original short stories, essays, and poetry that explore the spiritual dimensions of a chosen theme. Works are selected by the series editors. For information on future themes or submission of original writings, contact Editor Carol S. Lawson, 1745 Gravel Hill Road, Dillwyn, Virginia 23936.

LIBRARY OF CONGRESS CATALOGING-IN-PUBLICATION DATA
Kaleidoscope: lenses on reality / edited by
Robert F. Lawson and Carol S. Lawson.
p. cm.—(Chrysalis reader; 16)
ISBN 978-0-87785-240-7 (alk. paper)
1. Perception (Philosophy)—Literary collections. 2. American literature—21st century. I. Lawson, Carol S. II. Lawson, Robert F., 1948–

PS509.P43K35 2009
810.9'384—dc22
2009029169

CHRYSALIS BOOKS
Swedenborg Foundation Publishers
320 North Church Street
West Chester, Pennsylvania 19380

Contents

Detail from the fountain in Lincoln Park, Portland, Maine. The park was designed by civil engineer Charles Goodall and the fountain installed at its center in 1871. Photograph by Vincent DeCarolis, 2009.

Frontispiece

What is Man!

The Suns Light when he unfolds it
Depends on the Organ that beholds it

Published by W Blake 17 May 1793

EDITOR'S NOTE: ROBERT F. LAWSON

The Better to See You

TEN MINUTES INTO A PSYCHOLOGY CLASS, the door bangs open and a disheveled college student storms into the classroom, tells the teacher what he thinks of a difficult assignment, throws his overdue paper on the teacher's desk, and charges out. The instructor tells the shocked audience to not speak but record in detail what has just happened. He collects the students' eyewitness accounts and begins to read them to the class. Not one report agrees on the details. Was the enraged student wearing a blue sweater; was that a red kerchief around his neck; what was it he said? The incident had been staged, but the lesson is clear: how we perceive things is determined by our peculiar lens, our personal, distinctive filter. So much for factual reporting, and in the murky waters of internal perception of feelings and motives, determining where the truth lies is even less clear. William Blake, an early reader of the writings of Emanuel Swedenborg, illustrated the point:

> The sun's light when he unfolds it
> depends on the organ that beholds it.

In 1759, en route from London to Stockholm, Emanuel Swedenborg—renowned scientist-philosopher and esteemed member of Sweden's House of Lords—had an extraordinary experience. Dining in Gothenburg at the home of an acquaintance, he suddenly left the party of fifteen guests and went out of the room. He returned, pale and alarmed, and explained that a fire had just broken out in Stockholm (405 kilometers away) near his neighborhood and that it was spreading very fast. He was restless and left the table several times to monitor the situation, reporting the fire's progress upon his re-

Opposite: William Blake (English, 1757–1827). Frontispiece, Plate I, from *For the Children: The Gates of Paradise,* 1793. Blake etched in intaglio 18 plates for this work. The engravings have inscriptions of single words or brief aphorisms. He illustrated the course of human life from birth to death from a psychological perspective. Lessing J. Rosenwald Collection, 1813, Library of Congress.

turn. At eight o'clock he announced with joy and relief, "Thank God! The fire is extinguished, the third door from my house."

Three days later, official reports of the fire came in, corroborating every detail of Swedenborg's account. The visiting scientist-statesman was quickly the talk of Gothenburg. But the truth is, the cat was merely out of the bag. Swedenborg had been having telepathic or clairvoyant experiences for years. If asked, he would calmly add that he could converse with the dead. Now, however, he was under the lens of his fellow countrymen. Was he a madman, a crank, or was it possible that what he reported from "the other side" was true?

Swedenborg said that we are on earth for a purpose—to exercise our free will to grow into our own unique angel-hood. He would suggest that the lens is truth and helps us on our evolution to angelhood. Truth is what enables us to see what is good in others; and he would undoubtedly complete the equation by saying that truth and good combined are the whole lens—the binoculars that bring into focus our spiritual wisdom and wholeness, giving depth to our spiritual field. In a series of paired pieces, the stories, essays, and poetry of *Kaleidoscope: Lenses on Reality* explore this phenomenon of individualized perception.

This collection's preface sets the stage, identifying two ways of using a camera lens: one by a photographer, stepping out of a building into late afternoon sunlight, intent on using a newly acquired lens to capture the city's beauty; the other by a photographer in his studio who is making a family portrait through the controlled use of light and shadow.

The writers in *Kaleidoscope* remind us again and again of reality's deceptive nature. What, on first glance, may appear to be ordinary, on closer examination—or in some cases, when seen from afar—becomes extraordinary.

- In the first pair of stories (Secret Message), the mysterious inscriptions in a Knights' Templar chapel become clear when explained in the context of the knights' spiritual journeys. In the other story, a cryptic prophecy from nature takes on different meaning after being internalized by a shepherd.
- In the fourth pair of stories (Boxing Day), we discover the resourcefulness of individuals transitioning out of a way of life, of moving from the familiar and letting go of years of well-loved objects.
- In the Mirror, Mirror on the Wall pairing, unique angles of vision become transformative agents and radically set individuals apart from family and community. In one lens, we see up close the microscopic response of family members to a woman who is spiritually awakened. The other lens is fo-

cused on a mystic, centuries after his life, through the telescopic view of his countrymen, and like starlight, his reputation and wisdom remain a vibrant point of reference.

After university graduation, in 1709, Swedenborg had made the traditional first European tour. He spent time in Leiden, where he studied science and scientific equipment at the university. In exchange for his help, the young student was taught by his landlord the craft of grinding lenses. With this knowledge and a newly acquired skill in brass-instrument making, Swedenborg built his own microscope. Modeled after a 20-power version he had seen in the famous scientist Antonie van Leeuwenhoek's lab, and not to be outdone, youthful Swedenborg's microscope was 42-power.

Swedenborg's original focus on unlocking the secrets of nature was eventually turned inward as he explored the secrets of spiritual realms. To do this work, he learned to discern the truth through a divine lens—a lens Swedenborg would certainly concede has the ultimate, higher power. He explained the distinctive way that people see into the spiritual world as follows:

> People today have no idea what perception is. It is an inner feeling for whether a thing is true and good . . . . The sensation is so clear for angels that it gives them awareness and recognition of what is true and what is good, of what comes from the Divine and what comes from themselves. In addition, perception enables them to detect the character of anyone they meet simply from the person's manner of approach or from a single one of his or her ideas. (*Secrets of Heaven,* paragraph 104)

Swedenborg, if alive today, might suggest that we experience life in a hologram, in a convergence of earthly and spiritual worlds with an ever-changing focal point, depending on our receptive state to the light of truth. He was speaking of our sensitivity to what is happening around us. Depending on our levels of energy and awareness, we can shift our view of the spiritual landscape from lower to higher perspectives. And as described by the authors in *Kaleidoscope,* we understand and perceive the world around us in our own distinctive way. We have the freedom to move into our own angel-hood by means of the lenses of divinity with a multiplicity of interesting directions before us, and— with the potential of ever-improving vision—the sky's the limit.

DANIEL POLIKOFF

Water Lilies

1914–1917

They look like a raft
of roses—red

heads sticking out of the blue-green
pond as if afraid

of drowning, of
drinking too deeply with their painted

lips.
I know

Monet didn't mean any such thing—they're
not ladies, after all, not

roses, even, but
lilies with tough stethoscope stems

reaching down and feeling
the beat of what's below the shimmering

surface he half-
pretended to paint.

DANIEL POLIKOFF has published two collections of poetry, *Dragon Ship* (Tebot Bach Press, 2007), and *The Hands of Stars* (Conflux Press, 2008), as well as a translation of a dramatic version of the Grail myth *(Parzival/ Gawain: Two Plays)*. His poetry and translations have appeared in over sixty literary journals, including *Nimrod, Gulf Coast,* and *The Literary Review.* Daniel teaches literature in the Bay Area, and is presently completing a book on Rilke and archetypal psychology titled *In the Image of Orpheus: Rilke—A Soul History.*

Quiet City

THE PICTURE NEVER CHANGES ONCE IT'S TAKEN. That's why I remember Harry Luxman, as he was, in his building on a street that glowed in the afternoon. It was a perfect name, Luxman, considering his occupation—studio photographer. I'm not even sure he saw the connection when I brought it up.

"*Lux* is Latin for light," I mentioned. He showed no interest.

I admired Harry. He had a certain presence, something about him that inspired trust. He was solid, of medium height, and he walked with his head and shoulders thrust forward as if leaning into a stiff breeze. As for his clothes, he favored tweed sport coats and wingtip shoes—the expensive kind, genuine Cordovan leather. He had a different pair to go with whatever combination of jacket and pants he happened to be wearing, and I admired the way they carried him when he stepped out for lunch or started down the sidewalk on an errand.

If I could paint, it would be a picture of Harry in front of his building, emerging from the shadows cast by the pillars that stood left and right of the entrance. Or perhaps I'd have him heading up the street, toward where old Longfellow sits, just being himself in that theater of color and brooding light.

"These are your better wingtips," he once told me, pointing to his shoes. It was on an afternoon when I'd come by to look at a lens he had for sale. "I'll resole them three, four times before they're finished." I looked down at my own shoes, crepe walkers, worn and formless, but it didn't bother me. I knew Harry's remark was simply a statement of something he always did because he believed in doing it. Nothing more.

Then he unfolded a sturdy tripod and went about securing his Hasselblad while I examined the lens he had for sale. I checked the barrel for dings, scrutinized the glass. The thing was flawless. "Will you take two hundred?" I asked. He nodded that he would but kept his attention on the umbrellas he was setting up for an afternoon sitting. "Here it is," I said, giving him four, fifty-dollar bills evenly fanned so he could see each one. He slipped them into his pocket without looking. "I think I'm going to like this," I added.

"I think you will, too," he replied. "I wouldn't have sold it if I hadn't decided to change over." By that I guess he meant he was now working exclusively with his elegant Hasselblads, cameras that to me were the photographic equivalent of his handsome wingtip shoes. "But for a guy like you . . ." he observed. "Whose interests . . ." Just then a woman in a red, two-piece suit appeared in the doorway. She looked first at me.

"Mr. Luxman?" I shook my head, backpedaled a bit and pointed to Harry. Two little boys came next, followed by a man who was clearly their father. "Come in . . . come in," Harry said. "You're right on time."

The handsome couple appeared unsure of themselves. Harry sensed it and turned to me. "Stan," he said cordially. "These are the Robinsons." The couple looked at me and smiled. "Out in the kitchen, in the refrigerator . . . I've got some nice grapes and a pitcher of ice water," he told the little boys. They had blonde hair and wore matching blue blazers. "I'll bet you like grapes," he added, making it sound as if it were almost a dare. One nodded yes. The other looked at his mother. "Fix'em up a nice tray," Harry commanded brightly, sending me off with a wave. "My studio man," I heard him. I wanted to laugh but played along.

In the kitchen, if an old refrigerator and a workbench constitute a kitchen, I assembled the refreshments and rejoined them. I set the tray on the table normally reserved for equipment, and the family gravitated toward it. Suddenly I took it upon myself to fill the plastic cups, which I did in the way I imagined a competent waiter might. Harry busied himself with the lights and the screens and paid no attention to me. The boys went straight for the grapes while their mother watched to make sure they didn't soil their white shirts. "Okay, then . . . I guess I'm off," I said, checking my watch. Harry looked at me as if to approve. I picked up the lens, offered the Robinsons a courteous smile and walked out.

My footsteps were soft and quiet as I made my way across the marble tiles that lined the foyer of Harry's building. When I reached the big, glass doors, I cradled the lens to protect it and stepped on to the sidewalk. The sun was low in the afternoon, warming the storefronts, causing the taller buildings to loom. I walked into it, into a scene of a timeless city that would soon be forming in the pool of perfect glass I held to my chest.

Opposite: Statue of the American poet Henry Wadsworth Longfellow (1807–1882) by the sculptor Franklin Simmons (1839–1913). It is located at Longfellow Square in Portland, Maine, the poet's birthplace and childhood home. Photograph by Vincent DeCarolis, 2009.

Cars passed, but they were fewer now, as were the number of people on the sidewalks. "This is how it must have been fifty years ago," I thought. Above me, the rapid beating of a pigeon's wings merged with the sound of tires rolling to a stop. I crossed the street and thought about Harry back in his studio. Just about then he was probably leaning over his camera. Within the frame, a mother, father, and two boys were smiling on cue. Harry would never be able to understand what I could do with this lens or how and what I saw around me. But then, I could never handle myself the way Harry did. He knew how to make a family look like real patricians. I imagined the Robinsons at a dining room table, the little boys seated with their hands in their laps. On the wall, above tall candles glowing in the foreground, hung their new portrait in an expensive frame. Harry had deepened the greens and reds to flatter them just a little. He always did his best, and no one ever looked worse for the work he did.

So I walked on, feeling behind the lens, behind my ribs against which it rested, how the colors were warming in me now, too, but not in the way they did for Harry. This was the world as I would frame it, a place the sun has never touched from overhead, a place where the present lingers like a memory in the silent longing of the light.

VINCENT DECAROLIS lives in Freeport, Maine, and devotes most of his time to writing poetry and fiction. His lifelong scholarly interests have centered mostly around James Joyce and C. G. Jung. His interest in cameras and photography, beginning long ago with a Kodak Brownie-Hawkeye, continues into the digital age.

TIM MAYO

The Three-Dimensional Man

After the pain, after the rays
carrying their invisible poison,

after the MRI, you realize
a certain virtuality of yourself,

and in the metaphor of your shoulder,
its rotator cuff writhing this way and that
at the mere whim of a mouse, you see
a part of you you've never seen before.

You, too, are under a thumb. You cry out,

Heal me, Doctor, for I have moved
the wrong way. And then you see

how your heart could look like this: a self,

its many shades of gray muscling
against the limits of black and white.

TIM MAYO's poems have appeared in *Atlanta Review, Avatar Review, Babel Fruit, Del Sol Review, 5 AM, Inertia Magazine, Mannequin Envy, Poet Lore, The Rose & Thorn Literary E-zine, Verse Daily,* and *The Writer's Almanac.* In 2000 he was a semifinalist in the "Discovery"/*The Nation* Poetry Contest. He recently completed his first full-length collection, *The Kingdom of Possibilities* (Mayapple Press, 2009).

Lenses I
Secret Message

Ben Shahn (American, 1898–1969).
Portrait of Walker Evans.
Gouache on paper, mounted on board, 24 x 18½ in., 1931.
Williams College Museum of Art, Williamstown, Massachusetts.
Gift of Barbara and Arthur A. Gold, MD,
parents of Joseph B. Gold, MD, Class of 1975. (96.4)

KAREN ASCHENBRENNER

This Is Summer

THE SHARP NORTH WIND SWUNG AROUND MY BODY, biting my face like Nessie, the Loch Ness Monster, come to life as I stepped off the bus onto a pebbled side street in the small Midlothian burgh of Roslin, Scotland. My hand slipped. I dropped my digital camera onto the smooth stones lining the narrow street.

Breathing the country air, I loped up a promontory, a ross, for which the village was named, orienting myself to the freshness, having come from Edinburgh's bustling, debris-strewn, gated streets and the clinging smell of cigarette smoke, automobile fumes, and vinegar. I brushed off the camera and peered through its lens. Maybe I was, but the camera, at least, wasn't broken.

I draped my scarf tightly around my neck, having discovered in the Highlands it was a necessity, not a decorative adornment as worn in my Wisconsin hometown. My feet wobbled as they often did, but I pushed slowly on, reveling in the freedom of being a tourist on a Tuesday afternoon. Heartier women and men ran from their lunch hours to office buildings a block away in short skirts or loose jackets.

As I stretched out on Roslin Glen, I envied their physical prowess. At twenty-three, I had quit my first real job in December due to an unknown source of temporary foot paralysis. The uncertainty of my future was worse than my inability to comfortably move my feet. Sometimes the pain would keep me hobbling for a week. Other times, my tendons would loosen by afternoon.

Since I had been born with one hand, I never took my limbs for granted. My uncertain health led me to conclude that though I could not control what fate had in store for me, I could control, to a point, what I allowed to happen to me. I wanted to see Scotland, and walk it with my own feet. Without worrying about the price, I went.

I savored every moment. Here on the Glen, I stared fascinated at the orange-red bracken lit through a dark, purple-gray skyline, both eerie and alluring. It was too cold to stay still for long, but the pain in my ankles kept me contemplating an ancient chapel before me.

An older man approached wearing a striped button-up shirt and toting a large ring binder brimming with notes. He nodded to me. "Did you see the Templar mark there?"

I shook my head, confused by the question. In a rare moment of trust, I followed him to the left side of the chapel's entryway, weaving through the tarp-draped scaffolding that prevented sun damage to the edifice.

Inside, I marveled at the columns and the wall-to-wall carved caricatures. My newfound companion shoved back his bowler hat, opened his binder, and showed me his project. "I've been studying this building for seven years. I have three more binders like this one at home. I live a short walk from here."

A "short walk" in Scotland could be anywhere from a minute's jog to sixteen miles. I raised my brow, wondering which it was for him, as I viewed the pages he flipped through. He had diagrams showing the Star of David that aligned with the columns along with photos of each carving from every angle and in different lighting. It revealed a love I could appreciate.

He gave an overview of the place with an artist's proprietary air, waving his arms this way, then that, explaining what could be understood and what could not. "That one, the Apprentice Pillar, the Prince's Pillar. That's a story. The master artisan didn't think he could do it, so he . . ." While he talked, I pointed my camera at the pillar around which wrapped an intricate design, a stone replica of Yggdrasil, the Norse tree of life.

"It's the only place where carvings touch the ground," he went on, watching me with dour disapproval take picture after picture. I kept clicking away, frustrated I couldn't capture the things worth keeping—the artisan's love etched into the stone storybook, the lines on my companion's face, the hope in my eyes.

"When the knights reached this last chapel on their journey to become a Knight Templar, they had heard bits of the story along the way, and here, it all combined. They came in the back way, there, where there aren't any carvings. That's winter. Up here, this is summer," he pointed.

As he talked, I kept clicking, fervently wanting to recall everything, to untangle the barriers between my Midwestern prejudice and his seemingly thick brogue, and to record it all in megapixels. I made it an afternoon's work to capture seven years' research. As he warily eyed my camera lens with a hand covering his face, I persisted.

I was used to people underestimating me. When I was little, doctors predicted lots of insurmountable obstacles for my future. But I hurdled over each one. Peers told me I wouldn't last two weeks in a "normal" high school. I graduated in the top five percent of my class. People told me you need two hands to write. I learned how to type faster than anyone else in my ninth-grade year from an encouraging computer instructor, who helped me memorize the keyboard and feel my way through hunt-and-peck methods. I wasn't afraid of obstacles, man-made or otherwise, but I was terrified for my feet.

Two days before, I had limped through the door to my hotel room in Edinburgh. A kindly porter with whom I'd previously conversed asked, bewildered, "What did you do?"

I plopped onto a chair and caught my breath before beaming, "Everything."

Under my bravado, I felt my own Nessie rear its ugly head. Terrified that this challenge was the blow I wouldn't be able to take and angry with myself for letting it be, I walked onto Princes Street and watched the large, square slabs beneath my feet. Each slab I crossed over would be a victory. Line by line. I took each step one at a time. As I leaned against a shop window, looking over to Edinburgh Castle through the sleet-like rain, I wondered what victory was.

At Rosslyn Chapel, I took another photo and waited impatiently for it to show on screen. Try as I might, I couldn't get the camera lens to capture what I was seeing. *It's too dark,* I thought. My guide, who had not introduced himself by name, motioned me to put the camera down. Obliging, I let it dangle around my neck. He pointed up to a Latin inscription carved across the awning. I craned my neck to see it, itching to grab the camera.

With a discerning look, he says, "What are pictures? Don't take a picture. You have to know the story behind it. The whole story behind it."

I glanced down at my booted feet and felt a knot loosen in my chest as I exited into the flowerless gardens. My erstwhile companion disappeared behind an archway. I never saw him again.

There are a lot of things I will never see again—friends and colleagues, for one. Society can shut you out when you symbolize unspoken fears. I have been unable to find employment for two years now. I am losing motion in my one hand from the strain of a world set online, and yet, I know that someday, I will be given a chance to be a teacher. I will be as good a teacher as any out there. I will tell my students stories that cannot end, and I will not use a single picture.

Sometimes, when the coldest Wisconsin winter winds blow, I hear that nameless man's wisdom resonating, ". . . the whole story."

KAREN ASCHENBRENNER is a Midwestern writer working toward teaching certification.

JASON M. SCHOSSLER

Tree Frog

That August I finally trapped one in a Sanka can,
and by no means an easy catch,
summer evenings spent crouching in shadow
by the overhang of willows,
skimming long after dusk at splashes.

Back home my mother looked up from stirring peppers
in a black pan, shrieked, *Not in the house,*
as he wriggled in my cupped hands,
penny heart beating through thin underside.

So out in the garage, a dog barking far off,
I snatched a fishing bucket,
tossed in grass cuttings, a squashed caterpillar,
and watched as he perched on his belly,
tongue clicking from olive lips,
the way he likely was before I came along,
pure and unnoticed, a mystery of song
between moon and sun.

It took a minute, maybe two,
before he tried getting out,
and then often, springing for the edge,
eyes set on that sphere of sky,
twice landing on his back, legs kicking,
throat speckled brown like the sprig-choked water
that gurgled under the footbridge.

My plan was to return him to the creek before dark,
but when I looked away, maybe it was the catcher's mitt
hanging from the Louisiana Thumper
or the clang of Lickety's Ice Cream truck
that made me leave him behind with the lawn mower and rakes,
forgetting for the rest of the evening,
night hovering, a sparrow warbling in the bush.

Only later, after my mother had tucked me in
and I'd said my prayers, did I remember the bucket,
blinking awake as the attic, cooling after the day's heat,
creaked and ticked above my bed,
the wood falling back to where it'd been.

JASON SCHOSSLER is the winner of the 2009 Edwin Markham Prize in Poetry sponsored by *Reed Magazine.* He received an honorable mention in the 2008 *River Styx* Schlafly Beer Micro-Fiction Contest. His stories and poems have appeared in more than thirty magazines and journals, including *The Sun, North American Review, Rattle,* and *The Antioch Review,* and he has been awarded fellowships from the Ragdale Foundation, the Virginia Center for the Creative Arts, and Oberpfälzer Künstlerhaus in Germany. He works as a freelance correspondent for Thomson-Reuters and also teaches creative writing at Ursinus College.

DAVID S. RUBENSTEIN

The Shepherd of Shonto

CHARLIE ENDOCHEENY, squinting against the brilliance of the sky, watched the circling eagle with idle curiosity. *Idle* because three months in the high country without another human meant that any distraction, however small, was welcomed; and *curiosity* because eagles did not generally stray so close to people as this one.

Spread out before him on the green mountain slope were nine hundred sheep, give or take. *Give* the new lambs born into the late winter snow that were now kicking up their heels with the combined pleasures of youth and summer. *Take* the ones carried off by wolves, mountain lions, and coyotes, and then those the eagles had taken when they were small.

It was virtually impossible to protect them all from predators. There were just himself and his two dogs, Jake and Ramses, between all that fine mutton and the voracious hunger of the high country. It was an ongoing battle between him and nature, which he had ultimately come to accept as part of a natural ebb and flow of life in that wild range in which he had spent his last twenty-three summers.

In his youth, when his uncle first brought him up from the winter grazing lands near his hogan, he had fought fiercely and frantically to save each animal and could not understand his uncle's stoicism at a loss. To see a lamb he had carried in his arms across washes swollen with spring thaw, torn and bloody in the talons of an eagle or the jaws of a coyote, had been like a stake into his soul. But after he had spent a number of seasons with the flock and learned the rhythms of birth and death, he came to realize the shepherd could no more hold all predators at bay than could a sailor stem the tides.

So the speculating eagle did not anger him. For one thing, the lambs were all too big now to be carried away by even the most powerful bird, and for another, it had been a good spring. All the births were live, and the losses had been very low.

In fact, he had always admired the great bird, even in those strident days when he had felt it his mortal enemy. He imagined a shot with the 30-06 which stood nearby, cradled in the cleft of a boulder. He would line up the proud chest, just below the throat, in the crosshairs of his scope.

He'd miss, anyhow, and waste a good cartridge. He could see the bird eyeing him, calculating. *It knows I won't waste one at this distance,* he thought. *It knows me as I know it,* he suddenly realized with surprise.

Jake and Ramses were not so trusting, however, and they ranged below the soaring bird, watching for it to stray from its effortless gliding circle. The eagle floated away, riding the air currents further up the mountain. Charlie watched it dissolve into the whiteness of the distant sky, then shifted his attention to the clouds. *Might get some rain in the valley,* he speculated. *Bet they could use some.* His thoughts went to his home, where his father and sister would be thinking of him. He saw their faces turned toward him, and he smiled at the thought, and to tell them that he was all right.

When he returned to the present, he saw with a start a turkey buzzard perched on a rock not ten feet from him, locking him in its hideous gaze. He froze with momentary fear at the nearness of so wild and disturbing a creature. He returned its stare and calculated the distance to his rifle with his peripheral vision. The bird seemed almost to nod its ugly, bald head at the thought. No fear showed in its eyes or body language. *Where are the dogs?* Charlie wondered, speculating as to the possible damage the huge bird might do with its sharp beak and vicious talons. *Could probably scratch him up good, before he broke its ugly neck. Maybe that stick, which is a good five feet closer than the gun. . . .* But after a moment, when the initial shock had subsided, he told himself, *It's only a bird.* A sudden shout and waving of arms, and it would flee. But hold—a chance to study the creature up close.

His fear now subsided into curiosity. He held still and began to observe the bird with a critical eye. He could see that, despite its unattractive head and neck, it was a powerfully-built creature, not unlike the eagle. Its folded wings spoke of grace and duration, windriders. The chest was full and proud. The beak, hooked like a hawk's, appeared sharp and dangerous. The clawed feet were beautiful weapons of destruction. Charlie had always held disdain and disgust for the vulture, its ugly countenance in his mind a reflection of its ugly habits. But now, under close scrutiny, he came to tandem realizations simultaneously: the creature's sinister appearance was so perfect as to be attractive in its way, and it was clearly an important player in the cycle of life in the high country.

Then, as the bird held him in its gaze, the wind, a constant companion in the mountains, stopped suddenly, bringing an unaccustomed stillness. In the quiet, although Charlie struggled vainly to deny it, the bird spoke to him. It spoke in a hoarse, croaking voice, its raptor's beak mouthing the words. It said; *Beware the Higg's Boson at Waxahachie!*

Charlie, who had so recently feared for his physical safety, sank to his knees in fear for his mental health. He struggled with reality, knowing full well that a vulture cannot talk. As he knelt in muddled shock, the bird said again, as if to reinforce the fact of its speech, *Beware the Higg's Boson at Waxahachie!* Then, as the wind picked up, the bird turned into it. It spread its great wings and stepped off the rock. With barely a flap, it rose into the sky in gentle spirals. Charlie watched after it in dumb amazement.

A MONTH LATER, William Endocheeny, Charlie's uncle, came to the high pasture to bring him supplies and check on his well-being and that of the flock. Charlie, who had become less and less sure of the reality of the incident with the vulture over the passing time, said nothing about it to his uncle when he had asked about the past months. He spoke of the new lambs, the weather, and the eagles and the coyotes. He talked fondly of the two dogs and their health. He made no mention of the bird.

But that night, as they sat beside a smoldering fire, supper in their bellies and the night breeze blowing away the heat of the day, William said; "I have known you since your birth, Nephew. I brought you here for your first five summers. Something is troubling you. You will feel better if you share it." He looked closely into Charlie's stoic face.

"There is nothing that you could tell me that I would not accept," he encouraged. Charlie stirred the coals with a stick, watching the flames leap to the newly exposed wood.

His eyes, although turned to the fire, focused on that day some weeks ago when he finally spoke: "An eagle was circling the flock. Close, for me and the dogs being there. I watched it 'till it was gone. When I looked down, there was a vulture on a rock not ten feet from me." Here he paused. William waited politely for him to continue. "I did not hear it land," he said, shaking his head. "It seemed to appear from nowhere." He turned to his uncle. "Now I am not even sure that it was there." His uncle waited. "It spoke to me," Charlie said, his voice barely audible above the whisper of the wind. His uncle's face registered surprise, but still he did not speak. "It said, 'Beware of Higgs

Boson at Waxahachie.'" His uncle's eyes widened even more, but still he waited. When it appeared as though Charlie had spoken his piece, William spoke.

"A warning from a vulture. That is indeed strong medicine." Not for a moment did he doubt the story. He paused, searching his memory of the history of the Navajo for similar experiences. Recalling none, he asked, "Higgs Boson? Do you know of such a person?"

Charlie shook his head. "I've wracked my brain, thinking of everyone I ever knew; kids in school, teachers, people from the trading post, clan. No Higgs Boson."

"Waxahachie?" William asked.

"Nope. Never heard of the place. You?"

His uncle shook his head. "What happened then?"

"When?"

"After the bird spoke to you."

"Oh. It said it again. Then it flew away."

"Same words?"

"Uh huh." They were silent for some time, each turning the story over in his mind—for William, the first time of many; for Charlie, the ten thousandth time.

Finally William said, "I will tell the story to Old Man Denetsone up at Tuba City." He looked to Charlie for approval. Charlie thought for a moment, then nodded his agreement. Old Man Denetsone had been the family yitaalii since before he was born. He, like Uncle William, would not suspect Charlie of being crazy. He would tell them what the vision meant. Charlie nodded again, liking the idea.

IN OCTOBER, when William returned to help Charlie move the flock down to the winter grazing lands near their hogans, he told him what the shaman had said. "At first he said nothing. I went all the way to Tuba City, and he had nothing to say. Told me he would think about it, get back to me."

William was smoking a pipe, its pungent smoke mixing with the wood smoke from the fire. "Two weeks later, there was a letter for me at the trading post. From Denetsone. Said to come right away. He had talked to other yitaalii, he told me. None knew what the vision meant. But one, a Streams Come Together man, remembered a tale that his father had told him, which sounded similar. He said he would ask his father."

William continued, "The man had visited his father the next week and returned with this story. He says that in our spoken history, there have been several occurrences of a vulture speaking to a man of the diné. One spoke of a coming drought. It was said to one of the

Ancient Ones. Soon after, the rains ended, and the Ancient Ones had to return to the other world because they could not grow crops."

"The Anasazi?" Charlie asked. His uncle shrugged, lifting his shoulders slightly and letting them fall.

"The next one the old man retold was a warning about a vast pale tribe coming from across the great waters. Just before Columbus, it turns out." Charlie nodded to himself.

"The last one was fairly recent. It was said to a Running Water man about fifty years ago. Nineteen forty. It was told by that man to this yitaalii. The bird said to that man, 'Beware of Fat Man and Little Boy at Los Alamos.'"

"What does that mean?"

"Don't know. Old Man Denetsone didn't know. The man who heard the words from the vulture didn't know either." They played with the words, turning them this way and that for the next hour but could not find the meaning.

"I'll ask my cousin Anna," Charlie finally said. His cousin taught high school at Ship Rock, and had been to college. His uncle, who distrusted Belagana education, preferring instead to consult with the wise men of his own people, neither approved nor disapproved. Anna was, of course, of the clan, but her knowledge was pure white man's.

A MONTH LATER, after they had moved the flock to the low country and there were other family members to help watch over it, Charlie took his pickup truck to Ship Rock to see his cousin.

"Hello, Anna," he said, surprising her as she sat in her classroom grading papers.

"Charlie!" she cried, and jumped up to give him a big hug. "Just back from the high country?"

"Got back last month." They chatted awhile. Then Charlie told her his story. Anna listened raptly while Charlie talked.

When he had finished, she said, "I know *Fat Man* and *Little Boy.* Those were the code names for the two atomic bombs that the United States dropped on Japan, and I think they were built at a place called Los Alamos." She frowned in concentration. "A vulture spoke that to a Navaho?"

"Yes. In 1940."

"And what happened?"

"Nothing, apparently. Nobody knew a *Fat Man* or *Little Boy,* or what to fear from them." They sat in silence for a moment, contemplating what they had just discovered.

"So," Charlie said, trying to make sense of what had happened to him, "the warning was to somehow stop the bombing of Japan or the development of nuclear weapons?" Anna shrugged.

"Maybe. But the thing is, some spirit told the diné to take precautions before some pretty cataclysmic events in our world. And evidently we were too ignorant or apathetic to heed the warnings."

"But what could we have done? Against drought? Against Columbus? Against nuclear weapons?"

"Plenty," Anna said, jumping to her feet and pacing rapidly, as Charlie guessed she did during her lectures. "Build reservoirs against the drought. Dig canals for irrigation. We knew how. The Aztecs did it not three hundred miles south of here. Unite all the tribes of North America against the Europeans. Shine the light of justice on Los Alamos. Something. If only we had understood the warnings."

"So why me?" Charlie asked in bewilderment. "I'm just an ignorant sheepherder. Why not appear to a great yitaalii, or someone with learning like yourself, who would understand?"

"You understood enough to come seeking guidance. Perhaps you are chosen to follow up on the warning."

Charlie thought about this carefully. He was gratified that others had apparently been delivered messages via the same medium. He'd worried about his sanity. But he had carried the message forward. In his more accepting moods, he saw himself a messenger, delivering the words and then returning to his flock. Anna's suggestion that he was somehow chosen to fight the fight—that thought hadn't occurred to him.

"So," he asked hesitantly, "how do we find out about this guy Higgs Boson?"

"We go to the library," Anna replied, and she immediately led him through the deserted hallways to the school library. Charlie stood watching as she went through various references, looking for *Boson, Higgs.*

"Try *Waxahachie,*" Charlie suggested after thirty minutes of failure. She did, and in the second *Reader's Guide to Periodic Literature,* she said quietly, "Bingo." Anna wrote down the dates of several magazines to which she knew the library subscribed and went into the archives. In a cabinet labeled "Newsweek," she found the issue on her slip of paper, pulled out a reading shelf, and opened the magazine on it. "Here it is. Oh!"

"What?" Charlie demanded, reading over her shoulder, but understanding little.

"The Superconducting Super Collider! I thought that sounded familiar. That's where they're building the Super Collider! Waxahachie!"

"So?" Charlie asked, feeling stupid.

"An atom-smasher. Where they smash atoms together to try to find new pieces of matter. And the super collider is going to be the largest, most powerful atom smasher ever." Charlie began to feel more dread than ever. Here indeed was another possibly momentous event in human history, and he was somehow to become involved in stopping it. He looked at the pictures in the magazine, at the immense aerial view, and the cavernous underground tubes already dug. *What could one shepherd do against such powerful forces?* But Anna was reading on, skimming for mention of Higgs Boson. The first article did not mention it, so she returned the magazine and located a second. It, too, failed to discuss Higgs Boson, so she moved on to a third. An hour later, having exhausted the list of articles, she came to Charlie, who sat watching her at a reading table.

"No luck," she said needlessly.

"I'm starved," Charlie responded. "Let's go eat."

They didn't speak until the meal had been ordered. Then Charlie asked Anna, "Where do we go from here?" She frowned.

"I guess we ask Paul D'Orio. He's the physics teacher. I'm guessing that Higgs Boson has something to do with research planned for the Super Collider. If he does, Paul will know."

"And if not?" Charlie asked.

"If not, we look elsewhere," she assured him. "We'll find Mr. Boson." Her confidence bolstered him, and he ate with gusto.

That night Charlie slept on Anna's couch. In the morning they went together to school, and found Paul D'Orio in his classroom before the start of classes.

"Higgs Boson?" he asked, interested. "Sure. It's a theoretical particle, or force, which some think will tie together the universal theory of particle physics."

"It's a particle?" Anna asked, surprised. "Like an electron or proton or something?"

"Right. But smaller." Anna and Charlie exchanged looks of confusion.

"They hope to prove its existence with the new Super Collider," D'Orio added. The first period bell rang, and Anna glanced anxiously at the clock.

"Can you recommend a book or article that would explain the issue to a layperson?"

"Sure can," D'Orio said. He went to a shelf and quickly found a paperback book. "Here. You're welcome to borrow this."

Charlie and Anna thanked him and hurried into the hall.

"I'll read this," Charlie told her. "Pick you up after school." He walked toward the door, his nose already buried in the book.

After school, Anna went outside to where Charlie's pickup truck was parked, and when she approached, she found him oblivious to the world, still reading the book. The windows were open, letting the cool fall breeze ripple the pages.

"Charlie," she said gently, not wishing to startle him.

"Is it that time already? I'm sorry." He sat up, suddenly realizing the pain in his back. Wincing, he stretched it out. "I lost track of the time," he apologized.

"No problem," Anna said with amusement. "So what's with Mr. Higgs and his Boson?"

"Well," Charlie said, running his hand through his hair, "it's like Mr. D'Orio said, it's a theoretical particle that they think is going to finish up the nice little suite of pieces in the Big Puzzle."

Anna frowned. "So what could be wrong with finding the thing?"

Charlie shrugged. "Beats me. Maybe they can make some super duper new bomb from it. The Higgs bomb. Maybe one Higgs bomb can vaporize the world."

"Does the book suggest that such a thing is possible?"

"No. Doesn't mention any practical application . . . if a bomb can be considered practical."

Anna got into the truck and took the book. She sat staring at the cover.

"There is something . . ." Charlie said after a moment.

She looked at him, questioning.

"This Higg's Boson. It's one of those things they think could be a particle, could be a force field."

Anna nodded uncertainly.

"Well, the sense I get from reading about it, is that they think all the particles we know, the ones identified already, that make up everything in the universe, that they are all just places on waves of this Higgs force field. Just depending on where they are on the wave or where two waves cross."

Anna looked at him, not comprehending.

"It means to me that nothing is real," he said. "Even the hardest rock is no more than a jumble of invisible waves." He shook his head. "Its like . . . like, discovering that the Rocky Mountains are made of wind."

Anna sat silently, trying to imagine a world without substance. She looked instinctively toward the towering shape of Ship Rock, the formation that dominated the landscape to the southwest. She had been there several times, as had most Navajo, for it was an important symbol in their culture. *Wind?* She shook her head.

"No," she said suddenly. "The earth is here. It is solid and substantial. We can't let them take that away."

Charlie looked at her, surprised at her vehemence. "Yes," he agreed carefully, "but knowing or not knowing will not change things. Just because we understand, we don't make it so. We only . . . understand." He shrugged.

"But with the Belagana, understanding is the portal to perverting. If they learn its secrets, they will abuse it." She turned to him, suddenly panicked. "You've got to stop them!"

Charlie took her two hands, and spoke softly. "Stop who? From doing what? I can't stop learning. You, a teacher, couldn't really want that, anyway."

"But the message. The bird! Every time we failed to act on its warning, something catastrophic has happened."

"But do you really think we can stop progress? And if we can, at what cost?"

But Anna persisted stubbornly.

"You were given a directive from the spirits. You've got to do something!" Charlie was staring out the window, his mind in the high country.

"I'm a shepherd. I know sheep. I know nothing of atom smashers and particle theory. Sheep."

"We'll go to the yitaalii. They will tell you what you must do." She got out of the truck. "I'll finish up inside. Then we'll contact Hosteen Denetsone."

She turned to Charlie, leaning through the opened driver's side window. Her expression sought concurrence.

"I don't know," he said.

"Think about it," she said. "I'll meet you at my place in an hour." She was gone.

Charlie thought. He thought about droughts, and Columbus, and atom bombs. He thought about buzzards and eagles and sheep. He thought about the mountains and the wind. After many thoughts, he turned the ignition switch.

Later, when Anna pulled up to her house, she was concerned to see that Charlie's pickup truck was not there. But a note on her front door was visible from the street. Leaving her books in the car, its door ajar and key-alarm rasping, she hurried to the house and pulled the note from the door.

In Charlie's difficult print, it said simply, "To try to keep people from wanting to learn would be like trying to keep the eagle from wanting sheep. It's their nature. I'm going back to the hills."

She read the note again, then crumpled it up and threw it to the parched ground. A gust of wind picked it up and carried it away.

DAVID S. RUBENSTEIN is a painter and writer living in the American Midwest. His art and writings may be viewed at www.gruinard.com.

Lenses 2
Family Dance

COROT

M. GARRETT BAUMAN

Dancing with Deer

OUTSIDE THE OVAL WINDOW OF THE DC-9, a man in overalls waved a fluorescent orange baton. Despite grease stains and clunky work boots, his motions were ballet-like as he escorted the screaming jet to the runway. He skipped and swung his arms like a dancer leading a huge partner through her turns. The plane rumbled heavily, then found her lightness and leapt into the sky.

As we turned toward New Jersey, spring morning fog filled the river valleys. Soon only the tops of hills poked up like islands. Beneath the fog, these peaks joined the same earth, but from the air they had become scattered atolls in a vast, white ocean. The man beside me peered into his laptop screen. I wanted to tap his arm and tell him to glance outside to see how fantastic reality can be. But I did not kid myself. What you see is almost always more about yourself than the object you look at. His life lay in whatever computer game or e-mail he worked on; even if he shifted his eyes outside, he would not see what I saw. And what I saw was not really hilltops or islands but my daughters. Nor was I flying to New Jersey, but crossing an ocean.

The day before, as I packed for this trip, a herd of twenty deer had danced in our ten-acre field. A yearling raced the length of the field with pure exuberance at spring, circling and dashing among the others. Soon the field churned with running deer. They weren't going anywhere, just racing, feinting toward each other, and cutting away. Every fourth or fifth bound, each deer leaped high, white tail feathered out, and hung in the air for an instant. Several bounced stiff-legged toward grazing, older deer, bent their heads as if submitting, then suddenly dodged left and right to goad their elders to play. Many did join in. The deer ran to stay together and share the rush of spring

Opposite:
Jean-Baptiste-Camille Corot
(French, 1796–1875)
The Curious Little Girl.
Oil on wood,
16¼ x 11¼ in.,
1860–1864. The Metropolitan Museum of Art, New York. The Walter H. and Leonore Annenberg Collection. Gift of Walter H. and Leonore Annenberg, 1999. Bequest of Walter H. Annenberg, 2002. Photography © The Metropolitan Museum of Art. (1999.288.2)

life. They ran in five-acre circles, faster and faster, and strove for the ultimate jump that would keep them in the air forever. The grass was freshly greened, and the wintry fingers of cold and starvation had loosened from their throats. Young bucks with their first velvet horn nubs reared on hind legs and bumped chests, play that would become serious during fall mating dances. Life's cycles seemed well defined for them. This herd had probably shared genes over many generations. They were happy together. Today's dance was merely a few bars in the great dance they and their ancestors had performed for centuries in these hills above the Finger Lakes.

After watching for twenty minutes, I went outside, edged around the corner of the house, and stealthily stepped from tree to tree, then into the field. I wanted to enter their joy. In their play, the deer did not notice until I was perhaps fifty feet from the nearest one. As a dozen heads rotated to watch me, the bounding and racing ceased. I held still. Ten seconds. Twenty. One minute. Two. Several deer bent to nibble grass, eyes on me. One resumed cavorting. Perhaps I was a post after all. This was too sweet a day to focus on predators.

I sidled closer in micro-motions. Finally a doe stamped a hoof at me. I stamped back. She leaped sideways and glared at me. I hopped a few inches and flicked a hand back and forth to imitate a deer's tail. She answered with a wag of white tail. She snorted. I snorted. She bent her head as if about to eat grass. I bent. I mirrored each move in our dance.

If she and I shared genetic material, it was from way back, long before deer or humans evolved. Our common ancestor probably had not danced with joy but simply swayed mechanically or drummed its cold-blooded tail on the ground. She and I were family, but far-removed cousins who seldom gathered to tell old stories.

If I violated the boundary line she wanted between us, she raced a hundred feet away and stamped a hoof. To close the gap, we had to proceed through all the courtesies again. I have heard of people who so charmed a deer that they were able to touch it. I ached to do that. But my coy doe never allowed me within fifteen feet. Maybe she would have let me touch her if the disapproving eyes of the herd had not watched. Or maybe she knew exactly what I was and only toyed with me for spring amusement, as deer chase and tease cats, crows, and foxes. The doe and I continued this way another twenty minutes. Then the herd trotted into the next field, and she snorted and bounded after them without a single wistful glance back.

I WAS FLYING EAST TO HELP MY TWO DAUGHTERS MOVE. They lived ninety miles apart, but by happenstance picked the same weekend to move. Like the landscape below, we also were islands. In the beginning, they did not realize that I was restricted from always being with them by the custody rules of divorce. They only knew Dad was often not there. Dad had a happy family. Why did they not have a happy family in New Jersey? I had only recently learned that their stepfather, stepbrother, and live-in alcoholic step-grandmother had been verbally abusive, and that their house often crackled with cruelty and anger. To really dance—the kind where you touch—you need to know these things. You need to be there.

As they reached their teens, Beth and Sheridan found excuses to skip some visits. More upsetting, they seemed to "forget" happy vacations we shared and even created memories of upsetting incidents with my wife and I that I knew did not happen. I suspect now that these incidents occurred with their stepfamilies, and the children transposed them to us. They lived in two worlds with fuzzy boundaries.

Over time, our casual sense of belonging faded to mere duty. My youngest daughter, Sheridan, began to shrink when I patted her arm and to avoid eye contact with me. She announced that a friend's family called her their second daughter. She said it in such a way that my wife and I would know she wished she could make that happen.

Beth withdrew into a titanium shell. During visits, she sometimes slept twelve hours a day. One time she simply refused to open her eyes. We spoke to her, tapped her arm, and tugged, but she simply rolled over. We worried she was depressed, but she would chatter and giggle with my stepdaughter, Amelia, for hours in their bedroom. Rarely, something melted and the girls I knew reemerged. They would talk, laugh, and relax. We had some wonderful times. Then, without warning, as if a dead rat had dropped into the room, they would close off. When I asked openly what was wrong, they responded evasively and avoided me afterward. So I stopped asking. It kept the boundary marked between us, but it also kept them in sight. Should we have intruded more? Maybe. They have told me recently that they were ordered to keep their stepfamily's secrets, and my questions threatened them. Had I pressed harder, they might have opened up, and I could have helped them; however, they also might have fled for good. It was better to dance at a distance than not dance at all.

DEER DANCE WHEN A NEW FAWN IS BORN. The does often give birth in our field, and we have seen that miracle many times. Just after the birth, the yearlings and a few adults seem to celebrate by leaping around mother and fawn, dashing in and out, then prancing nearer with stiff legs until they bow slightly to nuzzle the wobbly new one. It's a welcome to the herd and the world.

Walking the field one June, my foot was about to come down on an odd brown lump when I stepped aside. It was a week-old fawn—white-spotted, long legs curled beneath it, ears and eyes absolutely unmoving. Does hide their fawns daily until they can outrun predators. I could not even see it breathe. Its ears were large and soft, and sun shone on its plush, chocolate fur. I could easily have bundled it into my arms. I wanted to let it know I was no enemy, that although I was different, my blood was warm and my heart beat, and I too welcomed it to life. But it would not look at me, would not move its eyes or even blink. Its only defenses against the dogs and coyotes of this world were silence and invisibility. Like my children who would not speak, it curled into itself silently, passively. This was how it had to be. You cannot convince fawns or children that you love them. You circle each other and wish.

Beth began living on her own when she started college. After Sheridan graduated high school, her mother moved out west. She expected Sheridan to accompany her, but my daughter surprised everyone—including Carol and me—by announcing she planned to live with us and attend my college. Infused with independence and determination we had not seen before, she earned honor grades and drove with me to college each day. Yet it barely altered our relationship. The long rides were often silent, her responses curt.

Finally, I said flat out, "You seem unhappy with me. Why did you want to live here?"

"I want to get to know you," she said. "I never had the chance to know my father." I did not, could not speak. Yes, we'd been apart sometimes for months, but how could she not know me? I'd known her eighteen years. What about those five weeks each year we lived together? The weekend visits? The phone calls. . . . No, that was how I saw it. I had to see through her eyes. What about the forty-seven other weeks and the one night she really wanted to talk to me that did not happen? So I said, "I want to know you better too. But you don't seem like you want to share yourself with me."

"It's hard, Dad."

"Well, let's start. Let's not put it off." That skimpy moment opened a crack in the wall between us. But only a crack. There were days of bonding talk, but still days when she seemed to will invisibility onto herself. College flew by. She took an apartment her last two years, chose a self-absorbed, glib young man and, after she graduated, moved to southern Jersey with him. She was gone—again.

Beth opened up more readily. We exchanged serious letters and long conversations about our relationship, the divorce, and its effects. When I asked why she had become so distant, she told me, "If I am distant, it's because I will not be part of the battle anymore. I'm not going to let you and Mom run my life."

"Run your life?" I could hardly speak. As with Sheridan, I felt as if I was in a different reality from my children. How could this be? I said to her, "I never tell you what to do. I don't say bad things about your mom. I bit my tongue a hundred times—"

"That doesn't mean I don't see it. No one ever talked to me about the divorce, do you know that? Not you or mom or grandma or my aunt and uncle. I thought I caused it. You let me hang while you were fighting." I wanted to tell her that I did not fight with her mother, that she picked arguments, and I kept most of my retorts to myself. I never told any of that to my daughters. Before I spoke, however, I tried to see it from her viewpoint. Did not retorting mean I was not fighting? Did that mean the children did not know what was going on? No. Parents hide far less than they imagine. None of us are invisible.

The weekend of my air flight, they seemed happy I was helping them move. Sheridan had driven north to help her sister and would then drive me to her place to help her. Beth had a gang of cheerful, boisterous friends, and we hefted her worldly goods and danced them into the truck, then from the truck to her new apartment. We shimmied past each other on stairs with boxes, held doors, signaled to lead each other's moves. Beth was the queen doe; she showed off her new boyfriend, and he had his arm familiarly around her, as if he had known her a lifetime.

When Beth and I hugged and kissed goodbye, I held her, let go, then kissed her again, and she pulled me tighter and relaxed against me, as if we had known each other a lifetime too. Something had thawed in her; we truly touched for the first time in a long, cold age. I still don't know why this moment among many others meant so much, but it did. If you're there long enough, it will happen.

ON THE TURNPIKE IN HER CAR, Sheridan drove through long gaps of silence. It was not companionable quiet but an emptiness that roared. The boyfriend she lived with had decided to date other women. That was when Sheridan had phoned to ask, "Dad, can I come live with you again? Just till I find a new job and place to stay." I felt horrible that her expectations were smashed, but at the same time my heart bubbled. We would have another chance.

"We'd love you here!" I said. We would rent a truck that I would drive back.

Sheridan, the soon-to-be ex-boyfriend, and I ate together, loaded the truck, watched a movie, and chatted about inconsequentials, evading the breakup. We danced stiffly around flesh and words. In the morning we packed the last few things, and the ex-boyfriend woodenly kissed her goodbye through the window of her car. On the eight-hour trip home, we flashed lights, honked and passed each other for diversion as we raced north. But these games were not enough. I wanted to hold her, tell her she was loved, and say that I would take care of her, but we rattled at sixty miles an hour in our wheeled islands. At the rest areas, we made small talk—the traffic, the accident ten miles back, the next stop. As I pushed the vibrating truck along the miles, the sense of my daughters' worldly goods uprooted recalled the dislocation years earlier, when the house was empty without them for the first time. A few tattered doll's clothes, a scrap of crayoned paper, and a stuffed bunny were all that remained in their room, like dried grasses from last summer.

JERRY LEE LEWIS USED TO SING, "There's a whole lotta shaking going on." And there is. The world is dancing. The universe is dancing. Particles vibrate in all of us, dance to a universal beat. It's not just people and deer. Molecules change partners and move on. Atomic research has discovered that no bond is absolute, that things really do not touch, and that particles, on even the smallest level, keep their distance in their tiny dances—attracted and repelled by a balance between positive and negative charges. Some quantum physicists say that substance itself may be an illusion—that the spaces between particles, not the particles, define objects. Perhaps that is true for people too. So it may be up and down the great chain of being. For nearly 1,500 years most scientists and philosophers believed in the cosmic dance of the planets—that the transparent spheres that held the stars at their proper distance from each other made music as they rotated, and the entire cosmos danced in a beautiful, perfect harmony we humans were too imperfect to hear. It was God's music, this music of the turning spheres. Everything, they thought, was ordered and related perfectly to everything else, and the harmony that unified it all was God's love. It was a beautiful landscape where everything had its place and danced together. Back then no one sat alone.

Today, with relativity, evolution, the uncertainty principle, and the knowledge that we live on a tiny planet in a universe in which galaxies speed away from each other at hundreds of thousands, perhaps millions, of miles per hour, the connections among things seems ever more tenuous. Our dance may be merely random, atonal vibrations. So many people seem not to know why they're here or who they are. What bond joins people into families or even holds one person together as an "I"? On a global level, we seem no nearer peace between nations than we were a hundred years ago. We do not acknowledge our shared genes. Yet we are all members of one herd grazing on this blue and white meadow in space.

Finally the truck bumped up our long dirt lane, and I backed it to the door. When the cargo door rattled up, the objects that surrounded and defined my daughter lay jammed together. Yet they seemed oddly detached, like a pile of debris, not a life. This was not her. She studied her stuff with me a moment, then leaned against me and cried. I pulled her close and patted her back. "Everything will be fine," I whispered. I rubbed her shoulder and cradled her as I'd wanted to for many years. Behind her the fresh spring grass rippled in the breeze, and I wondered if the deer were watching us.

These days M. GARRETT BAUMAN greatly enjoys his daughters' three children, Faith, Lucas, and Gabrielle, and contemplates the wondrous healing abilities of human beings and nature. He writes for *The Chronicle of Higher Education* and many literary journals, and is a 2008–2009 winner of the New Millennium Prize for Creative Nonfiction.

ROSS THURBER

Business Partners

Another morning.
He descends from the upper farm
House to the barn.

I watch him from the barn door
Survey the farmyard in morning light
As I let the first cows in.
His timing, his gait, and the mental tick I have to open
The first round of morning conversation are as routine
As putting the milk filter in the pipeline and carrying
The milking machines back to the barn.

Our sunrise salutation has all the hallmarks of a Yankee
Conversation with predictable introduction, body and conclusion.
For starters, we have settled on "Good Morning, How are you?"
We are always good.

Talk meanders across sports and weather.
Occasionally politics is permissible.
The economics of oil prices fall into this category.

But when it comes to farming particulars,
We need an ombudsman, to herd, to hone, to weed out
Our agenda. Because after we have finished chores,
Set up some fencing, mown a hayfield, changed
A tire on the hay tedder, hauled in a load of sugar wood
And checked on the dry cows—"There is one due on the 15th"—
The morning has spilled into Thursday and is threatening Friday.

I focus on the six cows that are waiting
To be milked. He heads out to the other barn to feed
The young stock. "We'll get there" he says, "We'll get there."

What I don't say but think is: Dad we're already there.

ROSS THURBER is a third-generation farmer in Vermont. His family, daily farm chores, and the foothills of the Green Mountains fuel his writing. He is influenced by the poetry of Robert Frost, Hayden Carruth, and Jane Kenyon.

MARY BETH LEYMASTER MATTEO

White Side of the Barn

RAY GOT RELIGION IN DETOX and goes to church every Sunday. Every now and then Grace accompanies him but doesn't like the feeling of hypocrisy. She is still stuck. When they settle into the pew, Ray jostles Lindsy on one knee (he refuses to leave her in the toddlers' room) and places his other hand on his wife's thigh. "You listen," he whispers, "This is good." Something to ease the pain, she supposes, sort of a Sunday quaalude. But the syrupy roll of the pipe organ and stained-glass windows hold her attention, the kaleidoscope of rose and amber sifting across her arms and hands. She's calmed by the way Lindsy rests her head on her Daddy's chest and looks up at her with wide brown eyes.

The preacher is talking about the Light. St. John's gospel. "Jesus said to them, 'The Light is with you for a little while; walk while you have the Light, so that the darkness may not overcome you.'" He must mean that Jesus is the Light and that the disciples should learn from him while they can, before he gets tacked to the cross. The preacher's humming voice dips low to keep the congregation's attention, then soars for emphasis, "he who walks in the darkness does not know where he goes." No kidding. A few weeks ago, on her walk at dusk, she wandered off the dirt path into the woods where the beech trees grow thick and close. It turned dark so quickly, she lost her bearings once she could no longer see the sky.

The preacher's voice doesn't keep Lindsy awake. Drifting off, her eyelids sinking heavily, she rummages around with her hand until she finds Grace's arm. She pats it, just the way her father does.

She chose not to think about what she was doing at the time, using Jack like Ecstasy. When he came into the shop, right from the start, he electrified her down to her toes. He was one of those men who, feature by feature, wasn't perfect—chin a little too receding, forehead a little too broad—but the way it got put together and the way he flashed that smile left her weak-kneed and wanting more.

After she finished shampooing his hair she said, "Do you like your shoulders rubbed?"

"You do that for all your customers?" His hair was black, threaded with silver, thick and wavy.

"Most like it." His shoulders were knotted. Kneading the thick muscles made a hot sensation slip through her, even though her mind was saying, *whoa, girl, you got Ray and Lindsy, and thirty-three years of trouble already—get a grip.* But he watched her intently in the mirror with those deep blue eyes, taking in what? She patted her hair to see if something was out of place. That afternoon, she took far too much time to cut his hair, her next customer waiting, noisily clearing her throat in the next room.

He told her his name was Jack and asked for hers. He smiled, "Grace? As in *amazing?*"

"I suppose so. My mother got religion and me about the same time."

"Lucky woman." His smile made the neon lights splinter and blink. The stylist next to her looked over from her customer's head, eyebrows raised, and motioned to the waiting room to let Grace know her two o'clock was getting impatient.

"Well, Amazing Grace, do you ever go out to dinner?"

"Only when I'm not cooking for my husband." It was her way of catching herself, when her mind was racing—do it, girl. He is so good looking. And sweet.

"No ring." He stared at her hand.

She'd hocked the ring before they'd even gotten married, for some meth and a night clubbing, back when she and Ray were ingesting anything they could put in their noses and mouths. Ray thought getting another ring, even if they could afford it, was bad luck. He wanted to wait until they'd conquered this thing.

Jack left her a five-dollar tip. "I'd like to see you next month, if you can fit me in."

She'd felt her face go hot and struggled to focus her attention on Lindsy, although her baby girl's face kept getting pushed aside by the intense gaze of this man. *He could do things to me,* she thought, and blushed again, this time turning her back so she could keep Lindsy's face in front of her.

THE SHRINK TOLD HER that walking would wear her out and keep her focused. The walks do help her notice things besides the thrumming in her head. You can tell which direction the wind's been blowing by where the leaves cling to the trees: the pin oaks have leaves on the west, the maples on the east; the black walnuts resemble bald men with beards, and the elms have top knots of leaves high up. Then, there's the Star Barn with its three silos and embossed star, bleached bone white on the side that faces the sun but charcoal gray on the side in shadow. Beside the willow, the stream is a mirror that reflects the mulberry. You see two versions: trees in the water and trees on land. Today, leaves float downstream, spinning in eddies, but in the reflection they float on air, gliding past the branches.

She especially likes how you see the big picture and the small details simultaneously. From a distance, the field looks like peppered salt pork where the crows are scavenging, but when you look at each bird as it flies east toward the sun, you notice specific things, like how their wings gleam copper in the light. Then there's Seth Kreider's place, with a picture frame of blue spruce planted on all four sides of his five-acre field: when you look closely, you notice that each tree has pine cones clustered at its top but none on its lower branches.

With Jack, she was counting only the cluster of cones, refusing to look at the larger landscape. Each thing she discovered—the curve of his back, the buttery soft flesh on the insides of his biceps, the steady grasp of his long fingers, the surprising silkiness of his beard—pine cones, but not full view of the field. When she woke each morning, the thought of him made her heart pound: the waiting, the anticipation. It wasn't the urgent couplings in his darkened apartment; it was the fullness of his attention, the way he cupped her hands in his and whispered, "Amazing Grace." She was weightless and able to fly; she didn't need coke or pills or booze—back on the high wire with no fear of falling.

She rationalized it with half-believed thin excuses. Because of Jack, she wasn't doing drugs. She didn't want drugs. Ray wanted her free, so she was at least half doing what he wanted—staying clean.

Ray had been in the life too. Who'd believe you met your husband in a ménage à trois with your girlfriend? That's the way they were in those days, but it took less than a month for them to decide to make it a twosome, just her and Ray, clubbing and getting high every night. A couple of times they got busted, but for the most part it was good—spectacular. But it didn't stay so hot after she got wasted that night and tried to saw off his toe with a steak knife, then match it with one of her own.

Before long Ray was saying things like, "Let's stay in," just as they were dressing to go out, a tape stuck on repeat. "We're going to end up dead or pulverized by some coke-head creep."

"We're fine."

"No we're not, Grace, and you know it. You have the guts to give this up? I don't want to do it alone, but I will."

"I can't talk about this."

"You're going to have to sooner or later."

Ray is lucky, she thinks. He's got Jesus to give him strength. What isn't fine is that he's traveled to some foreign place where she watches helplessly from a distance, feeling abandoned. Before she met Jack, as Ray dressed for work each morning, she panicked, terrified of what she might do in the house alone, not trusting herself with Lindsy. In the beginning, all she needed to know was that she could call Jack. Holding the phone in her hand, she could ignore the tightness in her throat and stomach. She could withstand anything. She could ignore the ATM card she always carried in her wallet, her account with five hundred dollars she kept secret from Ray to insure that if things started to crash, she could get a little help. After all, she was climbing a rock face without a rope.

EVERY MAN'S DREAM—wild, uncommitted sex. No strings. She'd handed it to Jack on a silver platter.

That morning, Jack stood with his back to her, silhouetted by the window. "I have to know your plans." In recent weeks, she'd been noticing how his shoulders had begun to droop, his neck had begun to sag forward, as though he were warding off blows to the back of the head. She'd been observing other things, too: the unwashed dishes, the unmade bed, the refrigerator all but empty.

"Are you going to leave him?"

"I didn't know that was part of the deal."

"This is not rocket science."

"I thought this was okay."

"I'm not big on hiding."

Picking up her shirt, she'd buttoned it slowly and slipped into her jeans. She could hear him breathing heavily, waiting.

"Grace, I want to see what you look like in daylight—it would help me decide if I love you."

The word *love* made her scalp itch. She hadn't uttered the word since the last time she was way gone on booze and pills and proclaimed from a bar stool that she loved the world. "I'm not good at love."

"That's a lie." Hands shoved deep in his pockets, now turned toward her, his face still lay in shadow. At the top of his head, spines of his hair shone silver with the light behind him.

"With Ray, I'm the one who's failed. With you, I'm on the winning side. If I give you up, it's my last hold."

"So?"

"But I won't leave my child. It's not a possibility."

"I didn't ask you to."

"We're a package, Jack."

"What's that supposed to mean?"

"You know, Jack. I know you do." She searched awkwardly for her handbag, her jacket, and shoved her arms in. She pulled out her key ring, stalling, removed the large brass one and placed it in his palm.

She refused to think about it until she was in the car and glanced back to memorize the outside of his apartment, watching him stand briefly at the window, then flick the blind shut. Knowing he would be able to forget her filled her with dread and sadness.

EVERY MUSCLE IN HER BODY ACHES; her calf muscles are burning. It's already three miles because she kept going when she reached the weeping willow. This morning she told Ray, "Abstinence and Jesus take all your energy. There's nothing left over for me."

"What's wrong?"

"Oh, I don't know, Ray. I feel like some bear with its foot caught in a trap, trying to decide if I should chew it off or just die."

"I have no clue what you're talking about. Look, Grace, I've got three hours of yard work—just tell me what's going on."

"Never mind. No point in both of us getting buried in this."

"Look, Grace, I do the best I can. Maybe you think it's not enough, but it's all I've got. "

When she hears the back door slam, she grabs her purse and makes for the bathroom. Rummaging in the cabinet, she locates her good shears on the second shelf and sticks them in her jeans pocket. She searches her purse for her wallet, finds the ATM card in the last slot, and shoves it in the other pocket. Jerking on her jacket, she heads out.

The autumn air is soothing. She knows she needs to forget the long view. Thinking about how vast the landscape is could kill you. Focus on the detail. She studies the starlings on the electric wires and tries to decide what they look like. Notes on a score of music, like a hymnal.

Trying to figure things out is like trying to decide whether the crows flying into the sun are black or copper. You know they're black, but they're also copper because you're seeing them with your own eyes as they catch the light. And, the Star Barn. In the sunshine, one side gleams like ice. But the part in shadow is charcoal gray. Light, or darkness? Same wood, same building, but the line of demarcation is razor sharp. It's about keeping to the side with the light. Like Ray and Jack or giving up secret stashes because if they're there, you'll use them. It's about having your foot jammed in the trap and hoping you can pull it out, your husband assuming you're clean and free, never suspecting you might bleed to death with the effort.

Her calves are knotting up now, her foot burning in the place where she gets a heel spur. She forces her mind to focus on the details. Bushong's field is rust colored stubble because he plowed it under during the drought, but straight through its middle runs a emerald ribbon that must be the path that leads up to the house. And then, beside the road, there's that weed on the crimson stalk bursting with purple berries, looking good enough to eat but probably poison. Over there, the doctor's place, Nolt Farms, where nothing is farmed, the barn and house painted burgundy, picture perfect against the turquoise sky, the man-made pond spilling noisily over the stone causeway and out into the fields.

Four miles. As she makes a wide circle at the Star Barn, she turns west into the afternoon sun. It warms her face and arms. She closes her eyes and lets the heat soak in.

Shoving her hand deep in her pocket, she fishes out the shears and the ATM card. Snipping the plastic into pieces, she tosses them into the sumac at the side of the road.

There's another hour of light left in the day, just enough to make it home. She forces herself to picture Lindsy, strawberry curls and brown eyes, head against her daddy's chest, and how her daughter's hand feels in church when she reaches over to pat her arm.

MARY BETH LEYMASTER MATTEO's short fiction has appeared in over a dozen literary and commercial publications, including *Nimrod International, Antietam Review, Snake Nation Review, Nebraska Review,* and *Liguorian.* She lives in Lancaster, Pennsylvania, and manages a family business program at Elizabethtown College.

Lenses 3
Village Life

ELLEN O'NEILL

Through the Cracks

OLD MAN CRAVETTS LIKED TO SLEEP IN HIS DINGHY by the shore, when the downeast nights were hot and steamy. A reclusive old coot, he was ornery as the shotgun he kept by his side.

Timothy was about six, with a face sweet and round as an altar boy's. His Momma had taken off with the train engineer six months back, no forwarding address. The town was looking after Timmy, shuttling him from home to home as the need arose and folks' schedules changed. The town loved the boy, but he wasn't always convenient.

So the Samsons and Clarks took him on alternate Tuesdays, and the Changs and MacLellans alternated Fridays, and every third Sunday he went to the Nordholms, and . . . well, it was complicated. But he didn't have to switch schools, thank goodness. Timmy went every weekday to Miss Jones's first-grade class down at PS 36, just as he ought to. A rolling, tumbling little stone he was, a boy who kept his possessions all folded up in a backpack. That was his life.

Edie managed all this as best she could, keeping track on a calendar down by the station. You could see it on the wall when you went to buy a ticket. She collected the tickets for the train and sold them, too. That was Edie's job.

Anyway, one night between the Clarks' and the MacLellans', a Wednesday I think, little Timothy just slipped right through the cracks like a nickel on the boardwalk down by the arcade. The Clarks thought he was at the Samsons', and the MacLellans just forgot about little Tim entirely.

This was the very same night that old man Cravetts woke up from one hell of a bender, stood upright in his boat, grabbed his shotgun,

Opposite:
Frank Duveneck
(American, 1848–1919).
The Whistling Boy.
Oil on canvas,
27⅞ x 21⅛ in., 1872.
Cincinnati Art Museum.
Gift of the Artist.
(1904.196)

shot it three times in the air, then fell back asleep like a babe in arms. The force of those returns, each one just a little, shoved that boat right off its mooring there by the water until that boat was set out to sea, the old man in it, sound asleep. Now Tim, he's watching all this, 'cause he's got no home that night but the stars above.

Morning comes, and no one notices anything except Miss Jones, when she goes to take roll in first grade, PS 36. One by one she calls the names of the girls and boys in the class, and each one says "Present, Miss Jones!" Except Timothy. Timothy wasn't there.

Miss Jones thinks this is odd, since Timmy rarely missed school, so she sends Jake, the custodian, over to the train station to find out where Timothy is supposed to be. Edie says he was at the Rivertons' last night because the Samsons had company, and the MacLellans were out of town. So Jake gets on his bicycle and rides over to the County Store, where Papa Joe Riverton works. Papa Joe says "Nope, nope, haven't seen Timmy, he wasn't with us last night. We traded with the Simpsons." Well, Jake was running all over town, sent from one family to the next, trying to track down who was looking after little Tim that day. As it turns out, no one was.

By noon they had a search party going, one group scouring the woods, another following the train tracks, a third splitting up between the shore and the sea. By nightfall they still hadn't found him, and you can bet lots of soul searching was going on by then. *How could we have been so careless with this boy,* they asked themselves. As each family found out who had had Timmy and when, they began to get a picture of how thoughtless they had been of him and how homeless the boy actually was.

Now they wanted nothing more than to find Timmy and bring him home—this time to a real home, one where he could stay. His own room, his own bed. No more life in a backpack. If they just had another chance, they'd make it right.

The search group down by the water discovers that old man Cravetts' boat is missing and they go berserk, thinking to themselves *Oh my God, that whiskey-drinking pervert! Sure as hell, he's taken the boy with nothing good on his mind.*

Everyone in town who's got a boat is out on the water quick as snow melts in summer. They're ready to lynch the old man soon as they find him. They search with their dinghies and lanterns, their fishing boats, too. They get the Coast Guard out, and the State Troopers to cover the roads. Pictures of Cravetts, looking like Jehovah, scraggly beard and all, are on the ten o'clock news, along with a snapshot of Timmy with his angelic smile.

Morning comes and still no break in the case. Classes have been interrupted, pupils kept occupied with games in the gym. The town's on its knees, wracked with remorse and fear. If only they could turn back the clock, and do it all over again. They'd love this boy better this time. They'd give him a home. They longed for a second chance.

No one even noticed the pair, the old man and the boy, walking into town toward the school, Cravetts using his gun as a walking stick. He was limping a little, leaning on the boy, small though he was, for support.

Miss Jones was the only one in the classroom, cleaning her blackboards and saying her prayers, at a loss for anything else to do, when the two walked in. "Miss Jones, Miss Jones," Timmy cried, "Look who I found!"

Timmy told her how Cravetts' boat had slipped out to sea, how he ran after it for a long time, 'til the moonlight faded and his legs gave out. He slept that night in an abandoned boathouse. Next morning he trudged through the woods, thinking to take a shortcut to town.

"But I got lost, Miss Jones. Everything looked different," he said. "I walked and walked. Then I came to this big river. It was too deep for me to get across, so I walked along it. Then I found Mr. Cravetts!" Timmy gave a big smile and looked over at the man, who by now had set himself down on a chair by Miss Jones's desk.

Turns out, the old man's boat got pulled by the tides into the estuary, where it ran up on some rocks. Busted the boat clean through and tossed the old man out like a leaf in winter. That's where Timmy found him, cold and wet. The two of them spent the night in the woods, 'cause Cravetts couldn't walk so well.

"He's hurt, and he needs a place to stay, Miss Jones. Do you think we could find him a one? I'll take care of him," Timmy said.

Miss Jones bent down and scooped little Timmy into her arms with tears of relief. Then she turned to Cravetts. "How about we get that leg of yours seen to, and then we figure things out?" Next she called Edie. Soon the medics, the Sheriff, coffee, and cocoa were on the way.

Miss Jones took them both home with her that day. But not 'til the town had hoisted Timmy on their shoulders and carried him up and down the schoolhouse steps.

Then she gave them each hot baths followed by scrambled eggs and hotcakes with maple syrup and butter. Finally she put them down for naps like babies.

It was supposed to be just temporary, while Miss Jones's fiancé was out of town. But the old man and the boy kind of grew on her, and the fiancé didn't. He wasn't so nice to the newcomers, which put him in a whole new light.

I think you can figure out the rest of the story. The two castaways came to live with Miss Jones permanent like. 'Course the town helped. They built a room for Cravetts off the kitchen, where he wouldn't have to climb any stairs and could come and go as he pleased. Built Timmy one above it, with a big, round window that looked out to sea. Old man Cravetts even dried out, except for the occasional bender. Timmy got five gold stars on his next report card at PS 36.

And the town—well, they got their second chance. They treated each other with a little more care after that; young, old, and in-between.

ELLEN O'NEILL lives in Santa Cruz County not far from the Pacific, off a dirt gravel road bordered by redwoods and a mountain stream. She is a career consultant to individuals who have lost jobs in the San Francisco Bay Area. Her news stories have appeared in newspapers, including *The Christian Science Monitor.*

WESLEY MCNAIR

Snowplow

Down the road
where street lamps

sift snow,
this smallest boat

comes closer, lifting
its long wave.

See how it pauses,
rolling its lights,

wiping its dark
eye. See

how it opens
the white wake

between these great
arks with tin roofs

and lit curtains,
anchored, floating.

WESLEY MCNAIR received a United States Artist Fellowship in poetry for 2006–2007. His book of selected poems, *Lovers of the Lost: New and Selected Poems,* is forthcoming in February 2010 from David R. Godine, Publisher.

SUSAN JOHNSON

Belle's Diner

The diner anchors one of the four corners of the Otisville Common. The common was just that—common—with a few trees of no distinction, scruffy grass, and in the center a bandstand that shed paint the way a tin barn roof sheds snow.

In Otisville the first frost comes before Labor Day, and lilacs don't bloom until June. The town sits in the shadows of the surrounding hills, the sun rising later and setting earlier than in any place in Vermont—or so townspeople liked to brag, there being so little else in Otisville to boast about.

Belle's husband, Howard, had died in fall 1962. He was mean-spirited and humorless, and he was stingy with his time and treasure. The town turned out for his funeral; most said they went to make sure the bastard was good and dead.

Within a few months of Howard's death, Belle sold the farm on North Mountain, cashed in his veteran's benefits, and bought the diner with the attached apartment. In a moment of financial frivolity and with the sweet taste of freedom still on her tongue, Belle had a fifteen-foot long sign erected with MISS BELLE'S written out in big red-metal letters. When it turned dark, which could be as early as three in afternoon on a late December day, a spotlight lit up the sign. She told people she wanted to forget all about that Mrs. business. No one blamed her a bit.

Townspeople talked among themselves about how dramatically Belle changed since she left North Mountain—careworn, stooped at only thirty-one—to take over the diner. She was not local born, so they never knew the girl with the quick smile and easy laugh. It is true that meanness can suck the life breath out of you.

In the diner, Belle became who she had been before she married. She served the regulars what they wanted before they asked and called everyone honey—man, woman, or child. When she called you honey, slow-like in a lilting sweet voice, it felt like a blessing bestowed and was more than worth the price of a cup of coffee. She was a rememberer of birthdays, an attendee of school plays, and the first to a troubled neighbor's back door with a covered dish. Belle was a woman you could count on.

Anna wasn't at the diner, and then one day she was. Belle's cousin twice removed on her mother's side vaguely from one of those coal-mining states. The customers were familiar with the unexpected landings of hard times, so they minded their own business and asked no further questions.

Anna became Belle's baker, her straight man, and second-in-command, although in truth the diner was never much more than a two-person operation. The two performed Abbott and Costello's "Whose on First" each year at the town's Annual Vaudeville Show to benefit the repainting of the bandstand. Anna was also Belle's thug. She once chucked a rolling pin at a smart-mouthed logger who was rude to Belle. Just winged him, but nevertheless polited him up some. Truth is, Anna would have thrown herself in front of a truck to save Belle.

In the late 1960s, the hippies started to move to town looking for the rural experience on the cheap, trying to change the world one joint at a time. They didn't stay more than five years or so; even LSD could not brighten the dreariness that hung over Otisville like smog. Although their stay was short, they left a legacy to the townspeople of long hair, pot cultivation (red Christmas tree bulbs on the plants to make them look like tomatoes), VW vans, and electric guitars. To Belle, they left a recipe for hash brownies and the realization that the use of Miss or Mrs. was just sucking up to "the man."

"Well, Ms. I'll be then," Belle exclaimed. "Nobody's business but my own if I'm married or single or, thank the lord, a widow, may that husband of mine rot in his grave for all eternity."

Ever after, well at least for a couple of years, she made a point of addressing her female customers by that appellation. The women actually preferred being called honey, not getting that kind of sweetness at home, but didn't want to hurt Belle's feelings by telling her so. Normally such a disregard of the norms of polite society would have been the cause of a great deal of harumping by the men, but they did love their pies, coffee, and meat loaf smothered with gravy, so Belle got no argument from them either about the Ms. business.

One day, about the time Nixon was on his way out, Anna and Belle returned to town from a shopping trip to Albany to find the sign had been changed from MISS BELLE'S to MS BELLE'S IS. The "IS" was left for no other reason than indecision by the pranksters and maybe a little unfounded worry that Belle might not be all that happy with the change. The IS stayed; as did the eternal unanswered question, IS what?

Back in the day, back before the satellite dish became the Vermont state flower, television watching was only for a few. If you lived in the hollow that passed as downtown Otisville, forget about it. With antennas that touched the sky and unfortunately attracted lightning or rabbit ears encased in aluminum foil, hill people were able to bring in a couple Albany stations.

Just before the Vietnam War ended, cable TV came to the village. Edgar Jones got permission from the selectmen to run cable wire along the electric poles and into the houses in town, plugging the whole deal into an antenna on top of the old forest fire watchtower. The town folk breathed a collective sigh of relief as they greeted the twentieth century.

How do decades pass in places like Otisville? Both as fast as a summer storm tearing across the sky, its thunderclaps so loud you duck for cover, and as slow as the frost lifting from the mud of the back roads in April. Years are marked by births, deaths, enormous snowstorms, floods, factory closings, collective sorrow, great pranks, comeuppances, and unimaginable feats of fecklessness.

In 1981, Belle, while topping off Bill Wright's coffee, died right on the spot, died right in the middle of suggesting to him the strawberry pie was particularly good that day. She was sixty-one. It was summer. How terrible to die at a time when, even in Otisville, the sun rises early, breaks through the morning mist, and makes promises you can almost believe will be kept.

SUSAN JOHNSON works as a victim advocate in a domestic-violence prosecution unit. A former newspaper reporter, she began writing fiction two years ago.

Lenses 4
Boxing Day

Grant Wood
(American, 1892–1942).
Daughters of Revolution.
Oil on masonite,
20 x 40 in., 1932.
Cincinnati Art Museum.
The Edwin and Virginia
Irwin Memorial.
(1959.46)

BAILEY PRIZE WINNER: CHERYL SEASE

Old Junk

THE STACK OF BOXES INSIDE THE FRONT DOOR began to resemble a cardboard hula dancer. Brian made a grab for its waist, but the toe of his loafer caught in the shag carpet, and he fell to a knee and then his hip. Inadvertently he bumped the stack behind him, then quickly threw his arms over his head when it shifted, because you never knew what was in one of these things. Could be Styrofoam. Could be a set of encyclopedias. Boxes rained to the floor. When the cave-in ended, Brian looked as though he had had jumped into a pool of cartons. They floated topsy-turvy around him.

"Darn it, Dad!" It shouldn't be this hard to visit. Brian sat amid the debris and waited to be acknowledged. Sunlight coursed into the living room from the kitchen window and draped his father's shadow across the mess. Brian twisted his head to try to see him. "Look at this!"

"Yeah, yeah. Don't worry. You didn't hurt anything." His father returned to the kitchen.

Brian didn't care whether the contents were priceless or breakable. He angrily shoved and kicked boxes aside and stood up. He swept his hands over his clothing to knock off the big pieces of debris from the carpet, then picked off hair from his black slacks that had belonged to the last homeowner's cat. Brian lifted up a box to begin to rebuild the stacks, then dropped it. The heck with it. Dad wouldn't even notice.

Norman was standing at the enamel kitchen table, books and papers and a pile of Post-it notepads nearly obliterating the green surface. He looked as though he might be watching a vertical tennis match as he quickly looked back and forth through his bifocals, first at some notes in his hands and then over the line at an open book on the table. A company of toy soldiers stood in loose formation in front of the book. Norman's bobbing head accentuated his scrawny neck.

He was stubble-faced, and his beaten green T-shirt sagged below his Adam's apple. One shoulder strap of his wrinkled, paint-splattered overalls hung off his waist, and the other held them up.

"A person could get killed trying to get through all those boxes. No wonder the girls won't come over here." Instead, his sisters, Susie and Jean, complained about their father to Brian and drilled him for details.

"You're crabby," Norman said. "Lori must have the kids this weekend."

Brian's mouth stiffened. "If I'm crabby, it's because of the mess I have to get past every time I come in."

Norman didn't look up from his task of putting small Post-it notes on each of the toy soldiers.

Brian scowled. He took a turn around the kitchen, hands in pockets. The disarray mirrored his feelings. It wouldn't do to have it looking this way today. He began to putter. He took the full bag from the trash can, tied it, and dropped it carefully near the door. An unidentified liquid made finger-like tracks on the inside of the white plastic. Next he found a new bag and began to fill it with detritus from the counter. TV dinner boxes, bread wrappers with moldy heels in them, empty pork-and-bean cans, lids still attached by a nubbin. He saved scraping leftovers from plates and pans into the bag until last.

"You could take out the garbage at least."

"Huh?" Norman looked up. "Oh. I've been meaning to get to that."

"What happened to the housekeeper I hired? Why hasn't she cleaned this up?"

"I fired her."

"What? Why, for heaven's sake?"

"She broke a plate."

"Was it priceless or something?" Brian asked sarcastically.

"Hey." Norman stabbed Brian with his gaze, briefly but long enough that Brian looked away. It had always worked when Brian was sixteen, too, and it dredged up an old adolescent grudge about Norman's unfairness.

"Too much money anyway. A housekeeper. It shouldn't cost that much to wash a dish."

"Maybe she thought of it as battle pay."

"Maybe she wanted to buy a helmet."

Brian's shoulder's sagged in defeat. He couldn't keep his mouth from quirking in a half grin. He retreated to fight another day, as usual. "Those anything special?" Brian nodded at the small, painted figures on the table.

"Picked'em up at a sale Thursday night. They ought to be worth something if I can find the missing piece."

Some people played the lottery to strike it rich. Some invested in the stock market. A year ago, Norman Sorenson had started looking for his fortune at the bottom of a cardboard auction box marked miscellaneous. In pursuit of that goal, the house had become his staging area. Apart from dirty dishes, unopened mail, and car keys, every available surface in the kitchen was devoted to Norman's big finds.

Depression glass was arranged on the counter next to the refrigerator. On another counter were cookie jars, all more than thirty years old. A flimsy office envelope box bent to the whim of an enormous pile of old silverware that resided in it. A serving cart held a menagerie of copper coffeepots. Apart from the silverware, each item was adorned by a Post-it with notations of item and value, plus the name of the reference book where Norman had found the information.

"You haven't marked the silver," Brian said.

"I need room to spread it out. I need to make a space."

Brian glanced around the room. Not a single horizontal surface showed up beneath the collections. "I guess there's always the floor," Brian mumbled. At least it was controlled chaos. Kitchen and dining items stayed in the kitchen. Lamps, old paintings, and clocks in the living room. All the furniture was in the basement. Brian knew, because he'd helped to carry much of it down.

"You could sort them in the basement. On that walnut dining table we took down a few weeks ago."

"Oh sure."

Brian began to restack a jumbled pile of dirty dishes on the same space they had occupied and ran hot water in the sink. "Where's the dish soap?" He looked on the counter, then dug in the cupboard underneath. Once he found a bottle, he squirted the tiny bit of remaining soap into the water.

"There a reason you're doing my housework?" Norman asked.

Brian didn't answer.

"The girls are coming over, aren't they? You only worry about how the house looks if your sisters are coming."

"I'm cleaning up so I don't have to listen to them complain."

"They haven't been here in weeks, either of them. What's going on?"

Brian looked at him, and he felt warmth invade his face. His lips parted to speak, but Norman cut him off.

"You told them about the attic, didn't you? I asked you not to. Cripes, they think I'm nuts as it is."

"Dad, *I* think you're nuts!"

"Thanks, boy. Thanks a lot."

"Dad. You sell the house, a perfectly nice house that you lived in for forty years, to buy this wreck. You put nearly all of your belongings in storage so you can have room in this house to fill it with the junk you buy, telling us you're going to make a killing and get rich. Tell me you didn't lose your retirement money somehow and now you're trying to make it up. Are you gambling on the side? Trying to keep a woman somewhere? What? And then, last Monday I find you in the attic taking it apart piece by piece."

"Sometimes these old houses have something valuable hidden behind the walls."

Brian rolled his eyes. "Look, Dad. This has to stop. Just tell me what's going on, because it's the only way I can help you. The girls are coming over because they had Phil draw up papers."

"Why would they need Susie's husband to draw up papers? Papers for what?"

"Psychiatric evaluation papers. They're going to force you to see a shrink."

"You're in on this too? This evaluation?"

"Dad, maybe it's a good idea."

"Maybe it's a good idea that you just head yourself out the door. I figured of all you kids, you'd understand."

"But I don't. Tell me what it is I'm supposed to understand."

The refrigerator hummed in the silence that followed, and several clocks in the living room ticked disjointedly. With jerking motions, Norman picked up an antiques book and yanked through the pages. Brian mentally traveled the house and the contents that seemed to shroud his father, hiding him from his children.

The house was engorged with bric-a-brac. It was as if like items had been grouped and encouraged to breed. In the living room were walls of cardboard boxes with a single walking path from the front door that split near the kitchen. At the end of the right fork was a couch with one space reserved for a guest, normally Brian. Snugged up against the couch was Norman's recliner and side table, piled high with newspaper ads for auctions and the remote for the old RCA that faced the chair.

Norman slept in a double bed made single by a line of old radios on one side. The other bedroom was declared the music room and reserved for old sheet music and an upright piano with missing keys and scarred cabinet. It ought to be worth something. It all would, according to Norman. He watched *Antiques Road Show* from his recliner with a gleam of anticipation for the day he would appear on camera and be told his something-or-other was worth a hundred grand.

Until then, Brian and his two sisters endured their father's peculiarity and kept it secret from everyone outside the family. It wasn't the only thing Norman did that was odd, but Brian wasn't up to thinking about the attic today. He was already overwhelmed. His sisters were coming, and they were going to do something about Dad.

Brian went to the sink and stood before it, intending to wash dishes but unable to do anything but stare at the suds. When Norman dropped the book with a thud, Brian finally blinked and sighed. His eyes traveled to a glass vase displayed on a shelf installed in front of the window over the sink. Dust motes hovered above their comrades already resting on the vase's surface. The vase was a swirl of different colors, bright and fanciful. Brian's curiosity piqued. It had no post-it. A new addition and one of a kind. He picked up the vase and turned it over. Norman appeared at his elbow and plucked the vase from Brian's hand. He blew some dust from it and rubbed it against his T-shirt before carefully replacing the vase on the shelf.

"Leave that there," Norman said. He didn't immediately move away.

"That the moneymaker? I break it, I pay for it?" Norman didn't respond, and for a moment, Brian thought his father might be ill. His complexion looked pasty.

THE VASE WAS IN HER HANDS. Garish red, blues, and greens flowed in a river over the bulbous base to a trickle that teased its way under the gold-edged rim. Nell's hands were becoming wrinkled, and a few brown age spots dotted the back of them. Her fingers were still graceful but looked purposeful because of plain blunt nails. She rubbed her thumb against the smooth glass and tipped the bottom up.

"Is there a mark?" Norman asked his wife.

"Yes, but I don't recognize it."

"How much?"

"Fifty cents."

They grinned at each other then, as they stood in a damp, musty garage amid old dishes, endless piles of baby clothes, and eight-track tapes, the third garage sale stop on a blindly sunny Saturday morning.

"Think it's worth something?" Norman asked.

"Surely a million dollars."

It was their standing joke. Sometime or another they would hit the antique lottery with a garage sale find and show everybody. Never did they expect it happen.

"Well, better buy it, then. Did you see the flower pots over there? You were looking for flower pots."

Nell clutched the vase to her chest and followed him through the maze of tables in the familiarity of their comfortable silence. The rest of the morning meandered on, companionably and slowly. Eventually, they returned home, and Nell put the vase on a shelf in their bedroom to look at while they changed to go to Brian's for supper.

"Darn thing will keep me awake, it's so loud," Norman groused good-naturedly.

Nell threw him a look, which was what Norman was after in the first place. If he had a dollar for all the ones she'd given him . . .

Then she fell abruptly, landing like a rag doll on the floor. He was at her side in a breath. By the time he lifted her into his arms, she was gone.

"ARE YOU ALL RIGHT?"

Norman's eyes came back to life and he looked at his son. "Miller glass. Made in 1849, England. One like it went for auction last year at Sotheby's for ten grand."

Brian's jaw went slack and he squinted. "Ten thousand dollars?"

"Your mother paid fifty cents for it at a garage sale."

"Dad . . . you did it!" A grin broke out on Brian's face, but his father remained sober.

"I thought of it, after I read about the Sotheby auction. I went to the storage unit and found the vase in the cedar chest. I put it there myself. Your mother bought it at the garage sale the day she dropped dead. After the funeral, I put it away. Couldn't look at it. But you're supposed to get over things, right? So I read about the vase and dug it out of storage. It made me laugh because that day we joked about it, that we got a million-dollar vase for fifty cents. Ten grand is as good as a million to us. But your mother wouldn't have parted with it, and I won't either.

"Your mother and me. We were going to start an antique store when we retired but didn't get around to it. We were going to call it Old Junk, mostly because that's what we thought we were ourselves. Castoffs. Too old to be good for anything. We never saw much of you kids; you were so busy, and we thought it would give us something to do. We never wanted to travel, just piddle away our weekends collecting this stuff then reselling it."

A sheen covered Norman's eyes, and he looked directly at Brian. "I sold the house because I couldn't stand to be in it, and none of you seemed to care if I kept it. This place was cheap and could hold everything I needed it to. You and the girls, you think I'm crazy, well then go ahead, but we wanted that store, your mother and me, and I'm going to do it. I've got enough inventory now. I can open as soon as I find a building."

Norman pushed Brian aside and dropped his hands into the dishwater. He fished out a stained dishcloth with one corner unraveled and sloshed it against a plate. Brian blew out a breath, careful that it sounded measured and not like it was coming out over a washboard. He blinked until his eyes were clear of moisture. He was inches away from Norman, but he didn't reach out to him. Brian hardly remembered a time his father had touched him with anything more than an affectionate slap on the shoulder or bump with his elbow, once he had become a teenager. But then, Brian conceded, maybe he wouldn't have allowed it. So he didn't put his hand on Norman's back now, even though he wanted to. Instead he picked up a dishtowel and took the plate Norman had just rinsed under the tap.

It occurred to Brian that he and his sisters hadn't asked Norman about anything. Norman's obsession had begun over a year after their mother died, so surely it couldn't be because of that, they said to each other. They'd made their assumptions because they weren't sure Norman was upset about losing Nell, anyway. He was as stoic and distracted as he ever was. Absolutely normal. Brian felt a twist inside. Normal for a guy who never willingly spoke of or outwardly showed his feelings, but demonstrated them in other ways.... and Brian knew that.

"Dad."

Norman turned and then frowned. "What's wrong?"

Brian swallowed, lifted a hand, then dropped it back at his side. After a moment he spoke. "I could do the books, if you wanted. At your store."

The corner of Norman's mouth tugged up, and he nodded. "That's a fine idea. You're good with numbers." Norman handed him another plate. "But if you do the books, you should work in the place once in awhile, to get the feel for the business."

"Can I bring the kids when I have them?"

"Of course. Sure. But don't tell your sisters what the vase is worth. They'll think I'm crazy not to sell it."

"You want crazy? Jean bought herself a pig and has been walking it on a leash in her neighborhood."

Norman dropped the dishcloth in the water and looked at Brian. "A pig? A pig pig?"

"A pot-bellied pig. Her neighbors tried to sue her for having livestock in town. She had to hire Phil to get it all straightened out. I've got dirt on Susie, too."

"I'm not so worried about the attic anymore," Norman said, and his smile disintegrated into a fit of laughter that stopped short of a sob. Brian blinked and looked away. The sun infused the Miller vase with light and laid a kaleidoscope pattern across their bare arms as they began to work again.

"It's a pretty vase," Brian said.

"Yes." Norman looked hard at the vase. His hands stilled.

"Almost as pretty as Susie's new tattoo. The one she doesn't remember getting." Brian nudged his father's arm with his elbow.

CHERYL SEASE, a Des Moines resident and current English major at Grand View University, has been awarded the Swedenborg Foundation's 2009 Bailey Prize for fiction. Each year the Bailey Prize is open to nominations by instructors of undergraduate and graduate students in the arts and sciences for nonfiction, fiction, and poetry. By offering this annual publishing prize, the Swedenborg Foundation furthers the traditional Swedenborgian connection with the arts and celebrates the Chrysalis' Reader's more than twenty years of publishing established and emerging writers. Cheryl's short story was nominated by Dr. Paul Brooke, associate professor of English at Grand View University.

Family Car Trip

The mother is driving the car.
The father distracted, always distracted
lets the outdoors race through him
while two little girls in the backseat
watch him watching all but them.

In the rearview, a seagull interrupts the pattern
of streaming lines and steady streets.
Objects may be closer than they appear.
The bird folds into the distance like origami.

"You girls buckled in back there?"
The mother asks, not knowing how long
the belts have been undone, how far
the windows have been rolled down.

The daughters are gone.

MARISSA LA ROCCA recently completed a bachelor's degree in fine arts and creative writing at the State University of New York Purchase (SUNY) and was awarded the Swedenborg Foundation's 2009 Bailey Prize in poetry. Marissa extends thanks to Professor Kathleen McCormick at SUNY for entering her work in the Bailey Prize competition and for being an inspiration and role model that ignites minds and spirits.

PATRICK F. MURPHY

The Unopened Gift

HANNAH SHOVED PAST THE ATTIC COBWEBS. A stray ray of sunlight, filtered through the dusty, gabled window, had glinted off something, and caught her attention.

"What've you found?" demanded her older brother, crawling up beside her.

"Nothing, Bray. It's mine," Hannah said.

"Don't call me that," said Bray, who was called that because when he laughed he sounded like one of the donkeys on their grandfather's farm. "What is it?" he asked again.

Hannah cleared away the rest of the cobwebs. "It's a present," she squealed. "It's still wrapped up. It has a bow."

Bray took the package from his sister. He shook it, but there was no sound from within. "Wonder who it's for," he muttered, turning the box over in his hand. "There's no name on it."

"It's mine!" Hannah cried again, reaching for the package.

Bray jerked the box out of her reach. "No it's not," he said. "It belongs to Grandpa. It's his house."

From the floor below, the children heard Grandpa shouting at their mother. "I am not leaving," his muffled voice came through the floorboards. "This is my house, and you can't take me out. You might as well call her and tell her not to bother coming."

"Now, Dad," their mother said. "We've gone over this."

Hannah and Bray heard Grandpa's angry steps retreating from their mother. They looked at each other, trying to figure out the ways of adults.

Suddenly Bray ducked out of the corner and ran for the stairs. "Let's take it down and see what it is," he cried, still holding the package.

Hannah raced after her brother and caught up with him in the upstairs hallway. Bray was standing before their mother.

"What are you doing up there?" she asked, a cloth tied around her hair and a broom and dustpan in her hands. "I have too much work to do without keeping an eye on the two of you. Now quit making so much noise."

"We found something," Bray said, holding the package out for his mother.

"Put it with the other stuff," she said, brushing by her children. "I have two more bedrooms to clean before the realtor gets here." She paused to remind them, "Try to behave. This isn't easy on your grandpa. He's lived here since I was a little girl."

"Then why does he have to go?" Hannah asked.

Her mother's lips tightened into thin lines. "It's best," she said shortly.

"I'll keep an eye on Hannah," Bray said, stepping into the role of big brother.

Their mother smiled and nodded. "And Hannah," she said, "you keep an eye on Bray." She disappeared into a bedroom and returned to her cleaning.

"C'mon," Bray said, pulling at his sister's arm. "Let's go ask Grandpa what this is."

Hannah followed her brother down the stairs and into the kitchen. This had always been Hannah's favorite room. If she closed her eyes just right, she could still see Grandma standing at the stove. An apron was as much a part of any of Grandma's outfits as blouse or shoes. She could almost hear the sounds of pans banging or a spoon stirring, and it helped her not miss her so much.

Grandpa was sitting at the table, his eyes closed lightly. A hint of a smile touched his lips, and his nostrils opened and closed like there was some wonderful scent lingering in the air.

"Grandpa?" Bray said gently, tugging at the older man's sleeve.

The man started, then smiled broadly when he saw his grandchildren. "Eh?" he asked. "Sorry. Did you say something? I was just talking to your grandmother."

Bray's eyes darted to his sister, warning her not to say anything. Grandpa often said things like that. It was one of the reasons why their mother and father decided to move him into the apartment building with all the other old people.

"Look what we found in the attic," Bray said, holding up the box.

"I found it," Hannah protested. "Bray just took it from me."

"It doesn't matter," Bray said angrily to his sister. He turned to his grandfather. "What is it, Grandpa?"

Grandpa took the package carefully, and his eyes became young again. "Hannah," he sighed.

"Yes, Grandpa?" Hannah answered.

"Not you, dear," he said, wiping at his eyes. "Your grandmother was Hannah also. This is the gift she gave me on our second wedding anniversary."

"Didn't you ever open it?" Bray asked.

Grandpa ruffled his grandson's hair. "Nope," he said. "Unopened gifts are better than anything else in the world."

"Well, what's in it?" Hannah asked, climbing onto her grandfather's knee. Bray pulled a seat out from the table and scooted it close to Grandpa.

"It could be anything," Grandpa said when Bray had settled in. "That's the magic of an unopened present. Inside this box is anything I ever needed."

"Anything?" Hannah asked. Grandpa nodded.

"It couldn't hold anything," Bray argued. "It's not big enough to hold a tractor."

"It did once," Grandpa said.

"Is it magic, Grandpa?" Hannah whispered.

Grandpa's belly jumped around against Hannah's back as he laughed. "It is magic in a way," he said. "The year your grandmother gave this to me we were very poor. What little money our eggs were bringing in we had to use to buy feed for the other animals. We didn't have enough left over for things like presents.

"But that morning, when I got back from feeding the pigs and milking the cows, there it was on the breakfast table. Right beside my coffee," Grandpa said. His eyes were closed again.

Hannah closed her eyes so she could see too. There was her grandmother. Her hair was darker, and there weren't any wrinkles on her face. But the apron was there, so Hannah knew who it was. "She's pretty," Hannah said, and felt Grandpa give her a squeeze.

"Yes, she was," Grandpa said. "She didn't turn around or say a word. She just kept cooking breakfast like nothing was any different. 'Hannah,' I said, 'I know it's our anniversary. I haven't forgotten that. But I don't have a gift for you.' She kept right on cooking and said that was all right."

"You didn't have anything for her?" Bray broke in. "Boy! I'll bet she was mad."

"Not your grandmother," Grandpa shook his head. "She knew we didn't have any money. 'What's in here, Han?' I asked her. 'Whatever you want it to be,' she said."

"But how can that be, Grandpa," Bray asked, trying to understand.

"Because, son, we don't know what's in a box till we open it," Grandpa said. "So, as long as I left that box wrapped up in the pretty paper your grandmother saved from our wedding, it could hold anything in the world.

"One year, I remember, your grandmother wanted a new pair of shoes," Grandpa said, closing his eyes again. "They weren't too expensive, but they were dressy shoes, like for church. We could have gotten them, but she also needed a pair of shoes for working around the farm. She asked me which she should get, and I told her to get whichever pair would make her happy. When she came home, she had a new pair of work shoes she could never wear on Sunday. I asked her then why she didn't get the dressy pair. 'Because my life here with you is what makes me happy,' she said. 'And besides, maybe there's a new pair of Sunday shoes in the unopened gift.'"

Grandpa set the box on the table and tapped it with his finger. "Over the years, that box held everything we thought we wanted but didn't need, and some things we needed but couldn't get."

"A tractor?" Bray asked, looking at the box with new respect.

Grandpa nodded. "Once. It also held tickets to a movie, new clothes for your mama, rain for the crops when it was dry, and sunshine on a rainy picnic day."

Just then there was a knock at the door. Bray left to answer it and returned with a lady in a navy blue suit. "It's the realty lady," he said, frowning.

Grandpa nodded at her and told Bray to go get his mother. Bray ran from the room, and his footsteps pounded up the wooden stairs. A few moments later Hannah's mother came down, the cloth pulled from her hair and draped loosely around her neck.

"Hi, Ann," she said extending her hand. "I'm Joyce. You've talked with my husband."

"Of course," Ann said, smiling. "I'm glad to meet you." She looked around the room, but her eyes seemed to see beyond the walls and throughout the whole house.

Ann and Joyce spoke as if the children and Grandpa weren't there. Hannah was used to this sort of treatment, but Grandpa was not.

"It's my house," he said fiercely, defending his position. "Nobody has asked me if I want to sell."

Joyce shared a pained expression with Ann. The look was of one who has had to explain "why" too many times to a child. "Dad," she said. "Trey and I explained it to you. You're too old to be out here alone like this. We don't like to think about what might happen if you needed something and no one was around."

"It's my farm," Grandpa stated, "It's been mine through droughts, floods, early frosts, and times when no one wanted to buy my crops. It's mine, and I don't want to give it up. We worked too hard for it."

Joyce smiled thinly at Ann. "Why don't you go make yourself comfortable in the next room," she said. "Bray, take Ann into the front room."

As soon as Bray and Ann were out of sight, Joyce turned on her father. "Look Dad, we're not going to go through this again. Not in front of your granddaughter," she said, motioning to Hannah. Hannah hoped they would go through it again. She wanted her grandfather to keep fighting until her mother saw his side.

"You don't even work the farm anymore," Joyce continued. "You've rented the land out for the last six years. Now I don't want to hear another word about it. You're moving into the apartment." She turned on her heel and got as far as the doorway to the next room before turning around.

Hannah saw tears in her mother's eyes as she walked back across the linoleum flooring and put her arms around Grandpa's neck.

"Daddy," Joyce said, her face buried into her father's shirt collar. "I'm just doing this because I love you and worry about you."

Grandpa's large hand, rough from the years of tossing hay bales and wrestling plows, came up and cradled his daughter's head.

"I know, honey," he whispered, "but I can't go without a fight."

Joyce sniffed and choked on a laugh. "You old man," she smiled. She dabbed at her eyes with the cloth around her neck, straightened her hair, took a deep breath, and exhaled. "Well, I'd better go talk to Ann. Keep an eye on Hannah, will you?"

Grandpa winked at his granddaughter. "You bet," he said.

Joyce clicked out of the kitchen, and her muffled voice could be heard saying a cheery hello again to the realty lady. Hannah glanced at Grandpa and saw him touch his hanky to his eye. He stuffed the hanky back in his shirt pocket and patted his knee. Hannah had slid down when Ann came in so she could get a better look at her.

"Climb on up here," Grandpa said. "Let's you and me talk some more."

"About what?" Hannah asked, pulling herself up into his lap.

"Whatever you want," Grandpa said, looking out the window.

Hannah looked at the gift again. Still sitting on the edge of the table, she wanted Grandpa to open it and spill out its wonderful contents. "Tell me another story about the box," she said.

Grandpa's gaze seemed to drift further away, and his voice sounded as though it came from a place removed from Hannah both in time and space. "Well, there was the autumn when the roof blew off the barn," he said. "We had a late storm, a big one, and in the middle of the night your grandmother and I heard a loud crash, as if the Lord had reached down and smacked his palm against the earth. We didn't have the big light then, but there was enough lightning to see by for split seconds at a time. It was long enough to see the slate and timber that used to be a roof lying all over the barnyard."

Hannah felt her grandpa shudder like thunder, and she snuggled in closer to get out of the rain she could almost feel.

"I ran out there with a lantern to check on the animals," Grandpa continued. "Your grandmother went with me, even though she was scared to death of storms. On a farm, the animals come before our fears. We picked our way over the wreckage and got into the barn. One beam had fallen on our best milk cow, but the rest of the animals were all right, except for the fear," he added.

"We stayed out there with them the rest of the night, trying to calm them down. I had to get the cow out of there because the smell of death panics animals," Grandpa said. "The storm was gone by the time the sun broke out over the hills in the east, but we didn't have a roof, and winter wasn't going to wait.

"Your grandmother fixed us breakfast, and tried to keep my spirits up, but this time it looked like we were licked," Grandpa said. "We didn't have the money to get workers in, and I couldn't put a roof on by myself. 'Hannah,' I told her, 'looks like we're going to have to give it all back to the bank.' She just smiled and piled more eggs onto my plate. 'We could always cash in what's in the unopened gift,' she said." Grandpa chuckled at the memory.

"The way your grandmother figured it, as long as we had that unopened box, we had everything in the world we ever needed. She went into the bedroom and dug it out of the closet and set it on the table in front of me," Grandpa said. "And we both just looked at and started talking about what type of roof the box had in it."

"But Grandpa," Hannah protested. "That box isn't big enough to hold a roof."

"Don't you believe it," he replied quickly. "An unopened box is big enough to hold anything. We sat there at this very table and described the roof we wanted. It helped get rid of some of the gloom. We were concentrating so hard on the gift we didn't hear Kyle Neff pull up in his old Ford truck. Kyle was out driving around, seeing who all had been hit by the storm. He had already been past our farm and visited the neighbors."

Grandpa ran his finger along the edge of the box. "Kyle sat down and helped himself to a plate of breakfast and said everyone was on the way over. In less than two weeks our neighbors had put a roof back on the barn, just like the one Hannah, and I talked about."

"But that was your friends," Hannah pointed out. "It didn't come out of the box."

Grandpa shrugged. "I don't know," he said quietly. "I never told your grandmother this, but when Kyle showed up, I picked up the box to get it out of the way. And I mean to tell you that box was full of something. It was heavy. And once the roof was fixed, it was light as air again. Now I believe the roof was in the gift, but it took all our friends and neighbors to get it out."

Hannah stared wide eyed at the box. She was just about to ask for another story when Ann clicked noisily into the room. "Mr. Brice," she said, taking his hand. "You have a lovely home. I'm sure I can get a good price for it, even in today's market."

She stood there in her blue outfit, waiting for Grandpa to thank her. After a few moments of silence, she turned to smile at Joyce who had come in behind her. "Can you get your husband to stop by the office and sign the papers?" she asked.

"I'm sure that won't be a problem," Joyce said, shrugging an apology for her father. She walked Ann out to her car and waved as she drove off. When she came back into the house, she went through the kitchen without a word and went back to cleaning.

A few hours later she came back into the kitchen with her father's suitcase. "I'll just load this into the car, and we can go," she said.

As she walked past the table, her eyes fell on the box. "Is that going?" she asked wearily. Grandpa nodded silently. Joyce shifted the suitcase in one hand and took the box in the other. "Oomph," she grunted, hefting the small package. "What's in here? It must weigh a ton."

Grandpa glanced at Hannah. Hannah felt a cold rush race down her spine, and she shivered. "What's in the box now, Grandpa?" she breathed once her mother was out of sight.

"The same thing that's always been in it," Grandpa said, getting up out of the chair and slipping into his coat. "It's got everything I ever need."

PATRICK F. MURPHY has been a reporter and columnist. He now works as a graphic designer for an architectural/engineering firm based in Columbus, Ohio, but continues to write. Patrick lives in Zanesville, Ohio.

Lenses 5
Peak Experience

JEFF RASLEY

Himalayan Heroes

I WAS ON A CLIMBING EXPEDITION TEAM on Mera Peak, a twenty-one-thousand-foot mountain in the Khumbu region of the Nepal Himalaya, southwest of Mt. Everest. Our Nepalese crew included a guide or "sirdar," cook, "kitchen boys," and a crew of porters. In 1999, most Himalayan porters had no rain or severe cold-weather gear. They wore flip-flops or cheaply-made Chinese tennis shoes on their feet, even on snow-covered trails.

Porters are usually small and slight, standing five feet four to six inches and weighing between 125 and 135 pounds. Our sirdar, Seth Chetri, is large for a Nepalese; the Chetri are the warrior caste in Nepal. He was about five feet nine inches and 160 pounds. in his early twenties. He spoke English well and shared with me his dream to win a scholarship to the National Outdoor Leadership School in the U.S. He loved to practice his English telling and hearing dirty jokes.

Jid Baldoo was our senior porter. He is also tall for a Nepalese at about five feet eight inches, and probably weighed 140 pounds. Most of the porters on mountaineering expeditions are Tamang, one of the many distinct ethnic groups in Nepal. The Tamang have lived as peasant farmers for centuries on the great slopes of the Himalayas. Their ancestors were horsemen in Genghis Khan's army. Jid had worked his way up to senior porter and had recruited our staff of porters from his village. Although he spoke no English, I had gotten to know Jid from a previous expedition, and a special affection had grown between us. I gave him a rain jacket, making him the envy of other porters on the trail.

Above:
Jeff Rasley.
Photograph, 2004.
View from Langtang Valley trail outside of Kyanjin Village in the Langtang district of Nepal. The author was on an expedition to trek Langtang and climb Yala Peak with two friends and a Nepalese crew.

Opposite:
Standing Male Worshiper.
Alabaster (gypsum), shell, black limestone, bitumen, height 11½ in., Mesopotamia, Eshnunna (modern Tell Asmar), 2750–2600 BC, Early Dynastic I–II. The Metropolitan Museum of Art. Fletcher Fund, 1940. Photography © The Metropolitan Museum of Art. (40.156)

NOT ONE OF THE OTHER FIFTEEN CLIMBING TEAMS could successfully summit Mera that first week of October 1999. The conditions were too tough for climbing due to unrelenting snow and terrible visibility. It rained every day for two weeks below fourteen thousand feet and snowed every day above that altitude.

The eleven-day trek to Mera base camp was surrealistic, over high mountain passes, across rushing, glacier-fed streams, slipping and sliding through a muddy bamboo forest, and past a Sherpa village wiped out by an avalanche. We were soaking wet from rain every day the first week, and then slowed by deep snow as we neared our base camp. After four days of fighting the weather between base and high camps, our team gave up. I spent the last day on the mountain in a tent by myself, retching and wretched with altitude sickness.

The snow continued to fall as our defeated and bedraggled team finally hiked out of base camp. At sunrise on the second day of the hike out, my tent sagged with five inches of heavy snow, which had fallen overnight. It continued falling as we ate breakfast, packed gear, and then trudged 2,000 feet up the backside of Zatrwa La. This was the last high pass we had to cross to get out of the great white-capped peaks and back to civilization in Lukla Village, where a Twin Otter airplane was scheduled to pick us up and fly us back to Kathmandu. By the time we post-holed up to the crest of the pass, the fresh snow was over two feet deep.

Barely visible through the falling snow on a ridge above and behind us were splotches of red and yellow—down parkas of three Nepalese porters from another climbing expedition that was following us out of the mountains. The three porters were inching their way across the ridge, slowed by the blowing snow and the heavy loads they were carrying.

The conditions were perfect for an avalanche—fresh, deep, and unstable snow and warmer-than-usual temperatures. We were on top of a fifteen-thousand-foot pass with a four-thousand-foot descent.

We huddled together at the top of the pass. Heather wanted us to spread out for the descent, but Tom argued that the five of us ought to stay close to each other. We didn't rope up. All of a sudden, Heather yelped and took off running. Tom cursed. Seth bellowed, "Go!" And I heard the low, distant roar mountain climbers dread.

We started running after Heather. Judy cried out and fell down. Tom and Seth grabbed her arms, pulled her up, yelling in her face, "Run! Run!"

I saw them out of the corner of my eye as I pounded mechanically down the rocky, snow-covered slope, stumbling into and over boulders hidden by snow. With my mental capacity still impaired by altitude sickness, my only conscious thought was to keep going down to survive.

The spindrift came over us, stark white and opaque; I could barely see my gloves and boots. The avalanche petered out. We fell to our knees gasping. We looked back up into the vast whiteness of the mountain.

The three Nepalese porters from the other expedition had disappeared—vanished in the gigantic wave of the avalanche. We later learned that they were killed, along with four others who died in a series of avalanches across the Nepal-Tibetan Himalaya that week.

Seth instructed Heather, Tom, Judy, and me to catch up with the members of our crew who were ahead of us on the trail and to hike on to Lukla. We arrived in Lukla Village that night just after sundown. The worst part of that last ten-hour hike out of the mountains was just enduring it. The next worst part was wading across three glacier-fed streams. The water was freezing and running fast as the massive snowfall melted and ran off the sides of the mountains. We were all bone tired, wet, and emotionally drained.

At the Mera Lodge in Lukla, we sat by the wood-burning stove trying to warm ourselves. The night wore on, but Seth, Jid, and four of our porters didn't arrive at the lodge. We feared something had gone wrong for them.

Around midnight, Tom and Ram, our cook, hiked back to the nearest stream. They returned with the frightful report that it had become a raging river, neck high. When we had crossed around 6 PM, it was only knee deep.

We stayed up until exhaustion sent us into our sleeping bags on the lodge's cots. Before we went to bed we gathered in the kitchen to pray—Buddhists, Hindus, Christians, and agnostics—all united in our fervent hope and prayers for the safe return of Seth and our porters. Sick, wet, and exhausted as we were, we fought off the dread that was creeping around the edges of our minds with hopeful prayers.

After Seth had instructed us to hike on to Lukla, he began trudging back up the Zatrwa La to find the porters in our crew who had been following us. We watched Seth disappear back up into the blowing snow.

Seth found Jid and four other porters struggling halfway down the pass. The two youngest porters, Suk and Chandra, were hypothermic and too weak to descend under their own power. Seth and Jid carried Suk and Chandra the rest of the way to the bottom of the pass. Then, Seth and Jid climbed back up four thousand feet to the top of the pass and carried down the two seventy-pound *dokos* (carrying baskets) left behind by Suk and Chandra.

The ethics of Nepalese guides and senior porters do not allow them to abandon gear. They will risk their lives to preserve their company's tents and their climbing clients' personal gear. I have seen a sirdar dive off of a ridge with a one-thousand-foot drop to save a daypack carelessly dropped by a client.

After Seth and Jid carried the two *dokos* to the bottom of the Zatwra La, they divided the extra loads among themselves and with the two other porters who had the strength to carry. They all set off in the dark for Lukla.

When they reached the first stream, it was waist high. Seth tied a rope to a boulder, waded across, and tied the other end to a boulder on the other side. He helped Suk and Chandra cross the river as the others passed the gear across. They repeated the process at the second stream. The third stream was up to Seth's shoulders and running too fast to cross. They spent the rest of the night soaking wet beside the river at freezing temperatures.

Around nine in the morning we heard whistling coming up the lane outside the Mera Lodge. Suk and Chandra were barely walking, still suffering from hypothermia. But Seth was whistling as he walked into the lodge. He and Jid had brought the others out safely. Seth proudly announced that none of the gear was lost. He and Jid each carried 120 pounds over twenty miles on mountain trails and across three swollen-rushing streams in the dark while caring for Suk and Chandra.

SOME SIX MONTHS AFTER MY RETURN from the Mera Peak expedition, I was driving home from my office in downtown Indianapolis. Tears started streaming down my face, and I had to pull over to the side of the street. I was crying uncontrollably. I could no longer hold in the feeling of guilt and shame. The picture was seared in my mind of the three porters just before they disappeared in the white tsunami. I had done nothing, could do nothing, but it would not release me.

I called Tom in southern Indiana and Judy in Montana a few days later. Each had had similar symptoms. We were experiencing mild post traumatic stress disorder.

I had participated in four Himalayan expeditions in five years. I swore off mountaineering after Mera in 1999. It was no longer safe to visit Nepal, anyway. A violent Maoist revolution against the king had broken out, and there were shootings and bombs going off in Kathmandu.

Four years later in 2003, however, I felt beckoned back to Nepal. That year, 2003, was the golden jubilee of the first 1953 summit of Mt. Everest by Sir Edmund Hillary and Sherpa Tenzing Norgay. The country needed tourists to return, and the Maoists and government declared a truce. The Hillary family decided to use its resources to bring back tourists to Nepal. Sir Edmund would co-host with the King of Nepal a black-tie affair in Kathmandu, and Hillary's son, Peter, would co-host with the Incarnate Lama of Tengboche Monastery a celebration on the grounds of the monastery at eleven thousand, five hundred feet.

I heeded the call. I did not attempt to climb any mountains, but trekked through the Khumbu to Everest Base Camp at eighteen thousand feet and, as a freelance journalist, covered the world's highest party at Tengboche Monastery.

Since 2003, I have returned to Nepal to lead several Himalayan expeditions. I will often stop at a trail bend or take a rest cramponing up a glacier and reexperience that fateful 1999 expedition to Mera Peak without tears. I remember and honor the heroic strength and goodness of Seth Chetri, my guide and sirdar, and Jid Baldoo, a Buddhist peasant-farmer. I will not forget those three unnamed porters I saw disappear in the avalanche, and I honor them too. I will try to face the challenges life puts in my path inspired by the courage, strength, and kindness of Seth Chetri and Jid Baldoo, the two strongest men I know.

JEFF RASLEY holds a master's degree in divinity from Christian Theological Seminary, a law degree from Indiana University, and a bachelor of arts degree from the University of Chicago, where he majored in philosophy, religion, and politics. He lives in Indianapolis and is a practicing lawyer, when not practicing his other calling of world travel and adventure.

KATE GLEASON

Morning Walk on My Fiftieth Birthday

A pressure front
is blowing in,
storm clouds
skimming the fields
at such a clip
it's almost biblical,
almost enough
to believe in something
conveying them along
on a belt.

On the edge
of my orchard,
a few apple saplings,
their slender trunks
wrapped with silver tape
at the base
like the delicate ankles
of race horses.

Walking toward me:
my teenage niece
and her boyfriend,
who are just now
coming home
from the concert

in my neighbor's
field last night,
that ruckus that kept
disrupting my sleep.
They stop to kiss
against the trunk
of a Cortland
whose full limbs bend
and brush close
to the earth,
almost breaking
under the weight
of so much sweetness.

I remember once falling
for boys like him—hooded
eyes, high cheekbones—
not big on looks
but with a certain
indefinable something
like the dark matter
of the universe
and its baffling gravity:
with more pull
than there is substance
to account for it.

It seems like only
a moment ago
that my niece
was still in grade school,
boys the furthest thing
from her mind,
eager to show me
her science project:
the galaxies drawn
as dots on a balloon
she blew up to illustrate
how the universe
is expanding,
our Milky Way
pressing into the void
on a skin growing thinner
with each new breath.

It's hard to believe
she's the same person,
so different now
with her shocks
of henna-ed hair,
her multiple piercings,
her blue nail polish
with metallic flecks,
the color of star clusters.

I, too, have changed,
my hips stiffer today
when I bent to pick
the last batch of spinach
from my makeshift
cold frame,
a storm door
that closes on the earth.

Last night when I kept waking,
I read a little more
from a book on Edwin Hubble
who, middle-aged like me,
began measuring the dark
and was startled
to find the galaxies
out on the rim
shifting, in his scope,
toward the red end
of the spectrum, meaning
they were pushing
into the night
much more quickly
than those close by,
the equation he worked out
for the speed of their receding
changing how we look
at physics,
becoming a new constant
with his name on it.

Hubble's Constant,
his famous *redshift,*
the groundbreaking
finding of our time.
But haven't we
always known this
in our bones,
the speed of anything
being relative
to where we stand?
Take any of us
and place us
in relation
to our childhood:
The farther
we get from it,
the faster
we seem to go.

KATE GLEASON is the author of two chapbooks and a full-length collection of poetry, *Measuring the Dark* (Zone 3 Press). Her work has appeared in *Green Mountains Review, Best American Poetry, Los Angeles Times Book Review, Crab Orchard Review, Boomer Girls,* and elsewhere. She is a recipient of writing fellowships from the NEA (in conjunction with the Ragdale Foundation), the Vermont Studio Center, and the New Hampshire State Council on the Arts.

JACQUELINE ST. JOAN

Meeting the Dalai Lama in Tibet

DON'T TAKE PHOTOGRAPHS OF THE DALAI LAMA with you to Tibet, my friends advised—as did the U.S. State Department, the Free Tibet website, and my travel guidebook. Before the Chinese Cultural Revolution, photos of the Dalai Lama were as common on the streets of Lhasa as soldiers are today; then in 1994 a political crackdown resumed, and mere possession of images of the exiled Tibetan national leader meant treason, beatings, and imprisonment. When I asked my Buddhist teacher for advice about traveling in Tibet, he said: "Take your prayer book and use it."

In August, I am on a five-day road trip from Kathmandu, Nepal, to Lhasa, Tibet, along with twenty-one people and a travel guide. There is one other American in the group, whose name is also Jacqueline. She is twenty-eight years old, raised on Long Island, living in Hong Kong, and speaks Mandarin. An experienced Asian traveler, she is thoroughly competent at negotiating difficulties, and she is bold about going off the beaten path for small adventures. I have none of these qualities, but I do know one or two things about Buddhism, which she does not, so this knowledge makes me valuable to her.

First day out, I take photographs like a mad tourist. When we reach the bridge over the river between Nepal and Tibet, our guide waggles his finger and says, "No photos. Soon we will walk across and enter China." *It's Tibet, not China,* I think, but I say nothing. As the days ahead reveal, I am so wrong. Tibet is China, and China is Tibet, as inseparable as *samsara* (cycle of birth, misery, and death caused by karma) and *nirvana* (state of bliss that transcends all suffering).

At the border our two vehicles queue up so that officials can check our documents. We wait and wait. Local money-changers stick their friendly faces in our windows, asking, "Yuans for rupees? Yuans for rupees?" I finger the red protection cord given to me by the well-known Tibetan monk Thrangu Rinpoche and tied around my neck, as I respond. I point to my heart. "Tsering Longchen," I say, introducing myself with the Tibetan name I received on the day I took refuge. I feel slightly embarrassed to call myself "Melodious Long Life," but his sparkling eyes blink. He smiles and whispers the words I will hear again and again during this trip. "Dalai Lama, Dalai Lama," he repeats, giving me and then the others in the jeep the universal thumbs-up sign.

Over the next two days we visit the usual tourist stops—one of Milarepa's many caves, an eighteen-thousand-foot pass planted with prayer flags, and a local teahouse in a mountain town. The town is only a few blocks long (if you can call them blocks), with a few shops, horses tied to posts, and grinning, mucky children hiding in their mothers' skirts. The scene reminds me of sepia photos of Colorado mining towns, circa 1860. Hearing voices, I turn to see Jacqueline surrounded by several women who are laughing, lifting their aprons, and pointing at her. Jacqueline has transformed herself from a chic traveler into a modest Tibetan maiden. She is wearing a *chuba* (an ankle-length robe) with a striped apron, and her dark hair has been braided, woven with ribbons, and fastened to the top of her head. Later she tells me, "Oh, I do this wherever I go. It always draws people to me—to see a Western woman in their local dress. They love it. They always do." That night we are designated as roommates and despite our thirty-year age difference—we become devoted companions.

At Tashilhunpo Monastery (founded in 1447 by the first Dalai Lama) and the seat of the Panchen Lama (the second most important spiritual leader of Tibet), Jacqueline and I stand in line with fifty others waiting to enter. Most are tourists, but some are Tibetan pilgrims—very tall men with scarves tied around their heads, and women with long, dark hair, braided with rectangular pieces of coral, turquoise, and amber—three or four inches long. Inside, we follow their lead—touching holy objects, tossing money offerings, draping *khatas* (symbolic scarves), and scooping yak butter with spoons from oily bags to add to the plentiful, glowing lamps.

A Tibetan man with a young child stops me to hand me my *mala* (Buddhist prayer beads), which I had dropped. The boy points to my prayer book, a tattered notebook-sized collection of prayers, practices, and bright photographs from a retreat I attended in Colorado.

The notebook has an ink-drawn Sanskrit seed syllable, *Hung,* on a pale yellow cover and is held together by black plastic binding. The word *Hung* is part of the mantra of Dalai Lama and the national mantra of Tibet: *Om Mani Padme Hung. Om* is a universal sound. *Mani* means jewel. *Padmé,* or *pema,* means lotus. The meaning is that the jewel is in the lotus and that wisdom and compassion are within all of us, like pure seeds blossoming and unfolding within our hearts. I hand the book to the boy's father.

Quickly others gather around us, intently paging through the text. The man skips over the written chants searching for pictures. At each one he stops to absorb the colorful image pasted on the page. Are they disappointed not to find photos of the Dalai Lama inside? Do they know the names of these Buddhist icons? Have they had any Buddhist teaching in the past forty years of Chinese occupation?

"Guru Rinpoche," I say, pointing to one image after another. "Padmasambhava."

"Ohh," the man says.

"Chenresig," I say, and they all nod.

"Chenresig. Chenresig," they repeat to each other happily, seeming satisfied.

Later that afternoon Jacqueline and I leave the tourist path and follow two old monks to their living area, where brick buildings form a courtyard. One building has potted flowers in front of it. Pink hollyhocks peek over a garden wall, where I see a shaded place with a bench. I am happy to take a rest. A young monk is leaning out a window above us, watching. Jacqueline gestures with her camera to ask if we can take his photo. He signals "No," and disappears. But soon he is down in the garden with us, where he poses with her under the tree, while I take the shot. Jacqueline speaks to him in Chinese, but he does not respond.

The monk leads us inside the building and upstairs into his cell. The room is larger than I'd expected, but still, it is small. There is a shrine and books, and his clothes are folded in one corner. The room is not very clean, but it is well organized. He gestures for me to sit next to him on his prayer rug. When I show him my prayer book, he becomes very excited to see the picture of Chenresig. He looks back and forth at us, one to the other, and we wait for him to find a way to communicate without a common language. He points to his eye, then to the picture of Chenresig, and moves his hand over his head, as if indicating the past. He whispers, "Dalai Lama, Dalai Lama."

Is he telling us he has seen the Dalai Lama? Could that be? I have read that some monks do cross the Himalayas covertly, going back and forth into India, to visit family in Dharamsala and to hear the exiled Dalai Lama teach. I explain to Jacqueline that Tibetans consider the Dalai Lama to be a living, human manifestation of Chenresig, the mind of compassion, loving-kindness, and wisdom. As I am speaking, the monk becomes excited again. "Yes, yes," he says in Tibetan, giving us the nod of understanding.

The next day we drive through enormous valleys, passing villages and barley fields studded with prayer flags and *stupas* (mound-like monuments that represent the Buddha). We come upon a government work team painting a yellow line down the center of the road. Vehicles stop while the machines drip paint. Children gather at the car windows. "Hall-o. Hall-o," they call out. Our guide hands each one a cigarette, which they place between their lips triumphantly. Two hours later we reach Gyantse, home of the largest and most famous stupa, Kumbum.

The following day we visit Yamdrok-Tso Lake, one of the three largest sacred lakes in Tibet, with snow-capped mountains in the distance. Lakes are considered the dwelling places of protective deities. At about sixteen thousand feet, overlooking the Yamdrok-Tso Lake, we arrive at the Kamba-La pass. We see a Buddha carved into a wall, suffocated by colorful prayer flags and white *khatas.* We have reached the outskirts of Lhasa, which once was the capital of Tibet and seat of the Dalai Lama. Now it is the administrative capital of the Tibet Autonomous Region in the People's Republic of China. To Tibetans, it is the holiest center in Tibet.

My first impression of Lhasa is not the grand Potala Palace, but the ubiquitous, identical, white-tiled buildings that the Chinese government builds to line the streets. Our hotel, although modest, feels like a palace to me. The entrance is beautifully flowered, and we have our first sit-down toilet. I sleep long and deep until morning. After breakfast we climb the steep path to tour the Potala Palace, which was the chief residence of the Dalai Lama and now has been converted into a museum and tourist attraction. Along the way I catch my sleeve on a bush of nettles, and at once my arm and hand itch. While scratching furiously, I take the time to ask our guide if he has seen the film *Seven Years in Tibet.* He nods. "Here in Lhasa?" I ask. He nods again. "It was filmed here," I say, showing off my knowledge. Suddenly, his face hardens. "And many people were imprisoned because of it," he replies.

In one of the Potala's thousands of shrine rooms, I search again for old monks—on the theory that they are the ones most likely to be legitimate, trained, devoted. I find one sitting on the floor in silence, his prayer beads flowing through his fingers. I sit beside him, open my book and chant the hundred-syllable mantra quietly. Moments later, recognizing the prayer, he joins me. After a while, when I rejoin the tour, I give him a few coins. He smiles back and whispers, "Dalai Lama. Dalai Lama," both of his dirty, old thumbs pointing straight up.

I enter the large audience room where the Dalai Lama would have received guests. There are images of earlier Dalai Lamas, but none of the fourteenth. After six days, I have not seen one image of him in Tibet. In front of his wide, vacant chair, however, along a passage where pilgrims would have come to offer a *khata* and receive his blessing, a narrow tapestry is suspended, on which is printed the *Kalachakra*, the mantra of the Fourteenth Dalai Lama. The cloth is smudged and worn thin from all the fingers that have touched its skin. Pilgrims pass the empty chair—he is not there, they know—but they recognize the *Kalachakra* symbol as readily as they would know his grinning face.

In the afternoon we visit Sera Monastery, across the valley from the Potala. Red-robed monks are debating in the courtyard, the older ones circling the younger ones, who sit in the center quoting texts and making their arguments. It is difficult to know if this activity is for the tourists or for the monks' training. Probably both. On a back wall we see an ancient mural of a deity with a musical instrument. The mural has been battered mercilessly, and the head of each monk has been hammered out deliberately, one by one.

By late afternoon, I have had my fill of murals, statues, and butter lamps. I decide to wait for the tour bus while Jacqueline continues exploring without me. About twenty minutes later I see her running toward me, her apron flying, eyes red and wet. She's been crying.

"Come!" she calls out. "Come right away. You have to meet this man! Bring the prayer book!"

I gather my things and follow behind, up around in back, along a narrow wall, to an area outside a row of monk cells. I bend down to look into the room and there he is, sitting cross-legged by the window in a shaft of afternoon light. He is, or once was, a big man. Now he is bald, with a wide nose and what my mother would describe as "jug ears." He has straggly white hairs on his chin. He is smiling at us, his blue eyes bright and curious.

The lama extends his hand, invites us in. We have to more or less climb into the room. I have an urge to do prostrations, but I do not. I have no *khata*, no yak butter, nothing to offer. He gestures for me to sit in front of him, and I sit cross-legged, my knees a few feet away from his.

Jacqueline squats nearby. "Show him the book! Show him the book!" she says urgently, and I begin what has become our usual routine when we find an elderly monk. I show him my protection cord and tell him my teacher's name. I turn over my prayer book and offer it to him. When the lama sees the cover, he looks softly into my eyes, and says, reverently, "*Hung.*" I nod and repeat, "*Hung.*" We speak the word back and forth to each other several times as if we were naming our baby. Then I begin to turn the pages to show him the colorful image of Guru Rinpoche. He takes the book and moves it in closer to his eyes, and smiles when he recognizes the image. "*Om Ah Hung Benzra Guru Pema Siddhi Hung,*" he says to me, and I join his recitation. He smiles with enormous pleasure. But the second time I speak the mantra, his smile fades, his face tightens, and he repeats the mantra slowly, adding another syllable to it that I had dropped, emphasizing my error. I repeat it two or three times until I get it right, then he smiles, gesturing with an open palm toward Jacqueline. He wants me to teach the mantra to her! Jacqueline recognizes the nature of the moment, of the man, and readily repeats "*Om Ah Hung Benzra Guru Pema Siddhi Hung.*"

Observing us from several feet away, a young man seems to be amused—a security guard or perhaps an attendant? Jacqueline's mouth is twitching. "Pictures of D.L.," she mumbles through her teeth. "Over my shoulder." She throws her glance to the back wall. I am trying to see, but the wall is dark, and it seems rude to look away during this meditation. Suddenly, the lama nods toward the back wall, "Dalai Lama, Dalai Lama, Dalai Lama," he says, in a relaxed way, as if introducing another guest. No whispering. No hidden thumbs up. Just a simple, direct pointing to the dozen photos of the Dalai Lama taped on the wall—the Dalai Lama as a boy, young man, and old man. The lama is full of happiness and entirely unafraid. Something in the room grows stronger—something like a breeze, not warm, not cool, not even a breeze really, but something there.

The next day our group tour takes us to the Dalai Lama's summer palace, Norbulinka, where a few rooms are accessible to tourists. Our guide is a middle-aged man wearing round spectacles, a long black coat, and a soft hat with a brim. His English is very good. The murals in the first room depict the entire history of Buddhism, images of many of the great masters from the past sweeping across the wall. The very last picture in the far corner is of the young Fourteenth Dalai Lama. "The only public image of him that is permitted in Tibet," the guide tells.

Later, when we are the only tourists remaining, the guide tells us that he was once a monk. We walk together through a short hallway where there is no security camera. The guide touches my arm and lowers his voice, "We have no human rights in Tibet. Don't forget Tibet. Don't forget Tibet." The passageway ends, we enter the second room where we join the others, and suddenly he becomes merely a tour guide again.

To recall Tibet, I think about stones laid out on a hillside, mantras as daily reminders, cloths greasy with devotion, forbidden images pasted on a private wall, whispers, thumbs up, and the symbols of the enlightened mind. Over and over Tibetans let us know that the Dalai Lama lives, not only in Dharamsala, India, where his body now resides, but also in Tibet—in the minds of the people who wait for him still.

JACQUELINE ST. JOAN has won writing awards from the Colorado Council on the Arts, the Denver Press Club, the Rocky Mountain Women's Institute, the Clinical Legal Education Association, *Writers' Digest,* University of Colorado, the Rocky Mountain Modern Language Association, and *The Colorado Lawyer.* Her essays and poetry have been published in *Ms., The Bloomsbury Review, Empire, Tumblewords: Writers Reading the West, The Denver Quarterly, War, Literature and the Arts,* and *Texas Journal on Women and the Law.* Her human rights novel set in Pakistan, "My Daughter Made of Light," is currently seeking publication. She lives in Denver.

Lenses 6
Reality Check

vitz, Käthe

18.-

SARAH A. ODISHOO

Delivering Mary

Mel Gibson's *The Passion of the Christ*

IN *THE PASSION OF THE CHRIST,* Mel Gibson invents the character and behavior of Mary, the mother of Jesus. His imaginal depiction develops a "new" physiognomy for Christ's birth mother; she becomes a fusion of myth and a new realism—a wondrous heartbreakingly human mother. I use the word "imaginal" not as "fancy, a fantastic invention created by the mind," but more as an image we are born with, an archetype of the possible human capacity to reach incalculable limits.

It is through the figure of Mary (Maia Sternberg) that the audience is able to realize the poignancy of the human Christ, a figure who is generally perceived of as a divine being. She becomes the eyes and heart of the audience, so that through her, we see Jesus as child, young man, and most importantly, her son. He is no longer "simply" a personification of God; he is a man, who has a history with the woman who raised him, loved him, and struggled to make sense of her relationship with him. She knew, I think, he was meant for an "awakened" life, a life in search of metaphysical truths. As his mother, in Gibson's vision, she is the audience's gateway to see Jesus in his wholeness (holiness).

Opposite:
Käthe Kollwitz (German, 1867–1945). *Self-portrait with Hand to Forehead.* Etching, 1910. Harvard Art Museum, Fogg Art Museum. George R. Nutter Fund, M10077. Photography © Imaging Department, President and Fellows of Harvard College.

THIS ESSAY BEGAN AS A REFLECTION. I was looking for some meaning to my experience of the film. I realized that I can look deeply for meaning, invent it because I need to, or simply ignore the call to look. When cartographers mapped the known world, they would insert the words *"terra incognita,"* the unknown world, for what they hadn't discovered, for the formidable, the mystery of the nameless: beyond anything they could name! That's how I have felt writing this piece—identifying the *terra incognita.*

There is a *terra incognita* of our being—what calls our lonely hearts to discover our source. When we begin the journey through that land of stone and blood, we have to trust both our belief and our terrorizing disbelief, or all we have been will be lost.

When I watched *The Passion,* that's what I realized about my relationships with my daughters—they are the latitude and longitude of my heart. When I look into their eyes, I see through them—through their love—to the wellspring of an immense, inarticulate Source—one that binds us in and beyond the love I "see."

When I watched Mary in her relationship to Jesus, I "saw" my own uncertainty and disbelief, and the terrible price of that knowledge—one I didn't know if I could pay. With Jesus, I was able to recognize that someone consciously "knew" and willed himself to pay, and that knowledge shook me with shame. With Mary, I saw more personally a woman's devotion to her son and the instinct to protect and defend "the flesh of her flesh" dissolve as her knowledge of her God and her son's relationship to some higher order made her submit to his will, to his destiny. She could do nothing—in some ways, more hopeless and despairing than the victim's trials. She must live out her life reliving the tortures.

She was the one who had me sobbing uncontrollably as I considered my own relations to my children and how they remain "children" into adulthood. Their parallel lives, the child within the adult, inflict a double pain on me. Although I can sense the call—the "twinning" (more accurately, intuit because they don't always know exactly what it is they need and they don't know what to ask in the way of help), I know that they feel defenseless and vulnerable and in pain. I cannot answer the call to respond because I know there is nothing I can do (or as Samuel Beckett says in *Waiting for Godot,* "nothing to be done"). Only they can act on their own behalf, in their own sense of what is necessary. I must watch.

All the women I have spoken to about this painful situation have reiterated the same collective response: uncontrollable sobbing—*terra incognita.* I began to write this.

MARY, BY AND LARGE GIBSON'S CREATION, is intuitive, compassionate, fearless, and invariably silent. He characterized her as a woman with a distinct, devoted character, signaled by her eyes, gestures, intentions, and her silence.

Sternberg, as Mary, holds an indefatigable motherliness sustained superhumanly over the span of the film. Her astonishing silence reveals an innate spiritual stoicism thinly disguising the tenderness and scarcely graspable depth of compassion that flashes across her face and in her gestures; but it is in her eyes that her two natures interpenetrate so thoroughly that she is the conduit to the divine for the audience. Sternberg's mastery of her body unveils a language no film director ever imagined for Mary's character before Gibson for her anguish and the accompanying impotence that is a mother's. She becomes the audience's access to Christ's suffering, to the violence and violations he is subjected to. Through her eyes, the audience perceives Jesus both as a babe and a man, a child and an adult, an innocent and guiltless, fated and choosing.

But Gibson's use of Mary as mother taps an unexpected resonance in the audience to Jesus, the historical man. She mirrors him, revealing a doubled suffering—as he is tortured, she suffers the dread and horror of the crimes committed against him; he greets his persecution and torment with the same silence she draws on. His silent anguish at the uprushes of violence one might call "adversaries of the soul." She knows his responses; they are hers.

This is mother-love, this "twinning" of emotions, this the most moving and unforgettable experiences of our lives, the mysterious root of all human growth. As mother, she is creator and steward, one who maintains and sustains the life of her creation through love. Carl Jung says it as well as anyone when he says the mother-image "carries that inborn image of the *mater natura* and *mater spiritualis* of the totality of life of which we are a small and helpless part."

Because of that role and the circumstances that evolve, Mary is the only reliable witness to the crucifixion—she is the bridge between knowing and unknowing, the known and the unknown, the loving and the unloving.

Mary, in Gibson's version, receives and remains actively receptive to the numinous, consciously enduring her son's agony and her own, as well as the savagery perpetrated against him. Simultaneously, she intuits the outcome and the dark abyss of power and destruction he must endure.

Through her moral and spiritual concentration on her son's visible destiny she is led to another world—one she recognizes to be an older, truer source—a divine destiny, inexplicable and unthinkable—one she is powerless to stop or even to ease.

She becomes an observer, heartbreakingly watching her son, the rabbi, subjected to the brutality and savagery of man's indissoluble hate, its blinding power, and mass delirium. As a woman and mother, she is powerless except as she can accompany him, be there, and accept, as he does, what his life needs, and what he perceives God requires. Besides Jesus, she is alone in accepting Jesus' adversaries, his betrayers, his pain, and his journey toward death as necessary.

The disciples, the men, who had vowed to stay with him, protect him, if necessary with their lives, had scattered; fearful and terror-stricken, they had abandoned the very one who had given new meaning to their lives. His trial and its terrible injustice reached their core, "and they were sore afraid." Afraid for him, for their own lives, and for the lives of their families, they ran as "good" men often do when a single event has the capacity to freeze the marrow and crack open the mind—choking on its injustice and burning fear into their eyes.

MARY IS INTRODUCED when one of the disciples breaks through the door to her house and says, "They have seized him."

"It has begun," she responds more to herself than to him.

Her reaction indicates her knowledge of the future, that which has been ordained, his birth and his death, the beginning of the end. As a mother who knows her child and his history, his inclinations, she understands intuitively the events that will close the distance between being and meaning, between his life and his freely accepting his death, between fear and trust, between his destiny and his free will, and between his will and her acceptance of his will. And although she loves him deeper than her own life, she is also aware of his "other" life, one she cannot grasp wholly and one that lays beyond the realm of sense. Although helpless to alter events, she can identify the onset.

The phrase, "it has begun," is not in the Bible; in fact, the words she speaks are almost entirely fictionalized. But they are apt, according to what little is attributed to her in the Bible. More pointedly, Gibson depicts what a mother of such a man might experience and express at such a time. Again, Gibson gives voice to a woman who has been silent for two thousand years. Mary's role as mother becomes her voice in the film and invests that silence with meaning.

When Jesus is condemned by Caiaphus and taken to the dungeon beneath the temple floor, in a stroke of genius, Gibson has Mary enter the now-emptied room in the temple where Jesus had been tried. She seems to be searching for something, and even the audience is at a loss as to what she is doing. When she finally drops to the floor, fingering the stone tiles with her hands, she finds a place near the pillar where she freezes—she has found what she was looking for.

The camera takes us through the rough floor to the ceiling beneath where Jesus is chained and staring up, sensing his mother's presence as she senses his.

Their visions of the other give form and meaning to the word "Spirit." With acuity for the elusive frequencies of the human heart, Gibson gives these two characters "ears to hear, eyes to see," and souls to sense the insensible. They feel the other's love—the spirit more sensible to them than the chains and stone that separate them, and as inescapable.

Gibson's Mary gives "voice" to the eons of accumulated memory and intelligible emotions of the archetypal mother when he inserts the following two scenes. The first is Jesus' flashback during the trial reseeing himself sanding a table he has constructed in the courtyard of his mother's house, and, as she assesses it, he humorously cajoles and hugs her and makes her laugh, she the beloved of her son.

In this scene, we are given a personal moment of a mother and son's intimacy and loving joy in one another's company. The penetration into a private world of the mythic Jesus is one that gives his humanness a relational history, albeit a fictional one, but one that would fit a pattern of a man who had been loved and loved well.

The second scene culminates the first as Mary, following the mob, attempts to get closer to Jesus as he carries the cross through the streets of Jerusalem. From an intersecting alley, she waits, watching for him until he drags the cross into view, then, as if fated, he stumbles and falls at that juncture, dropping the cross, and sprawling across the cobbled street. In that fall, Mary recalls in her flashback another time she saw Jesus fall.

Suddenly, the child Jesus, playing in that same open courtyard, falls, and she, frightened, turns, running to him to protect, soothe, and finally, kiss his injured hand.

In that flashback, both child and man fall. Then her grown son pits her memory of the child falling against the futility of this fall. She recognizes that she can do nothing for him this time. That he must suffer both a divine and a human fate, so interpenetrated are his two natures that to separate them would be to mutilate both. Her lot too so interwoven with the human and the mystical that what stands out clearly is her love for him, her recognition of his love for humankind, and a larger force at work they both recognize.

In this moment, she sees as Christ sees—what she sees is that "very darkness from which God split himself off when he became man." She sees with Christ "the spirit of God itself, which blows through the weak mortal frame and again demands man's fear of the unfathomable Godhead" (Jung) and something else. Both his destiny and hers are locked in this moment of revelation as they look at each other and resign themselves separately and as one to grasping the ungraspable.

Both figures recognize in that moment the fear of God and the love of God, in tandem, as the burden of oppositeness that is mankind's destiny—to suffer irreconcilable, insoluble conflicts until they "know" that "all opposites are of God." Both Mary and Jesus must bend to this burden consciously, and by doing so, both are reincarnated.

In this version, Mary is Christ's only human companion—the only one who shares his life, his joy, his spiritual call, and his pain.

FINALLY AT THE CROSS, Mary remains a witness—witness in its original sense, one who has the intuitive comprehension to give a firsthand account of the truth, a sign for all the ages to remember. She stays, watches what was unwatchable, she endures his unbearable suffering and brutalizing death for him, for herself, and for something else.

Jesus recognizes her vision, her farsightedness, her spirit, when he commends her to his disciple. He makes her the mother of those who believe but who couldn't stay, witness, and "see" his reasons for this sacrifice and its necessity. She does.

WHAT MEL GIBSON DOES with the figure and character of Mary is to reconfigure the possible woman—to give her a similar mystery of spirit, strength, a sense of her own destiny, knowing even in her unknowing. Gibson acknowledges her mythical history (as in sacred historical context), then proceeds to actualize her humanness in the familiar: her persistence, faithfulness, the blood-of-my-blood anguish and joy, and the necessity to accompany her fear with her need to remain by her son's side, using her heart as a shield to all her fears.

Whatever arguments critics have about Gibson's *The Passion,* the film, the one aspect no one has critiqued thoroughly is the role of Mary, or for that matter, any of the women in the film: Mary Magdalene, Claudia, Pontius Pilate's wife, and Veronica.

His grasp of women in this film is astounding. His ability to show the idea and the woman's depiction of that idea, the abstraction of love and its expression, as each woman is different in her capacity and each represents the complexity of what is possible for each. Mary, as well as the others, is transformed, and her role unstated in the Bible is articulated, as a compassionate witness of the unbearable suffering of the evil mankind is capable of on the guiltless. Her love imitates divine love in its steadfastness, awareness, and acceptance without judgment.

In the film, Mary transforms the blindness of the violence by her unfaltering love, on the one hand, simultaneously transforming the blindness of others into knowledge.

When they take him from the cross and place him in her arms, she holds her son the way she held him at his birth, in her arms, unyielding. She again delivers him. One could argue that Gibson, in fact, depicts her as Christ-as-Woman.

The movie ends with a new order: a cosmic reconciliation of the opposites, woman and man, man and God, God and Man, God and woman—the woman who in the last two thousand years has been the West's only image of a woman acceptable to God and his son—Mother.

SARAH A. ODISHOO's most recent work was published in *Gastronomica, A Journal of Food and Culture* (University of California Berkeley, Fall 2008), *Argestes Literary Journal (*Spring 2009). Her work has also appeared in *New Letters, Confrontations, River Teeth, Laurel Review, Aura Literary Arts Review, Berkeley Fiction Review, Florida Review, Fugue, Georgetown Review, Jeopardy Magazine, Laurel Review, Left Curve, Libido, Limestone, Lynx Eye, Pikeville Review, Portland Review,* and *RiverSedge.* She was nominated for the Pushcart Prize in Short Stories (1997) and has been a finalist in competitions, such as the Nelson Algren Short Fiction Competition, Nimrod Poetry Contest, and the Saint Agnes Eve Poetry Contest. Sarah Odishoo is a professor of English at Columbia College Chicago, teaching classes in mythology and film, as well as in world literature.

LUTHER ALLEN

The Dream of Elk

searching for the blood of a prayer
free-hand shot at cow across canyon, last day.
i glance up, a bull still-framed above me, watching, caught —
or was he phantom, apparition
shape-shifted from the hunger of desire?
yes, he was real.

i waste an instant to check a legal rack
i waste an instant thinking wait for the broadside shot
he turns, runs broadside through oakbrush, i shoot.
knowing I have killed him, seeing him jerk away
i hold the second shot to save meat.
yes, the bullet is in his heart.

i find the tracks, deep gouging
earth dark fresh, bloodless
after bloodless bound
now knowing he will go on forever.
yes, i have missed.

but i am in his heart
as he cleaves the shimmering air
surging back into the phantom wild
carrying my phantom bullet
the sound of the shot ringing, ringing.
yes, he is in my heart

forever.
yes, it will take that long
to understand why
the bullet missed
and we both went on
to other lives, real and imagined.
in deeper ways.
yes.

LUTHER ALLEN has been exploring the nature of nature, hunting and writing for over forty years. The relationship continues to evolve in ever more fascinating ways. When possible, he hunts near his former home in southwestern Colorado. Most of the protein he eats at home is gathered from the wild, a process that is profoundly instructive. He lives in the Northwest and is actively involved with community poetry.

MICHAEL STUTZ

Inside the Mind of God

WHEN BLAKE HENNAMAN DIED he was one of the lucky few given the privilege to see and know the inner workings of a place that no one's ever spoken of intimately—the place that's somewhere out there just beyond the door of death.

It happened in a flash, as if all his long living were a problem and this the final answer. Suddenly there he was, lingering at a white doorstep that apparently opened into a field of clouds. On the threshold, Hennaman—that is, the soul of him—was immediately offered a guided walk-through, a sort of open-access tour of the place he was now very consciously a part of. His guardian angel, whom he was finally meeting after over forty earthly years of partnership, was his guide.

"Would you like to get a rundown of what it's like here, inside the mind of God?" asked the angel, who was all sweetness and light.

"Why, sure!" beamed Hennaman—perhaps, he immediately felt, just a little too loud. He was in that twilight time where he'd been getting adjusted to his new arrangement, while feeling sensations of the old one slip away into odd-fitting memories. "I mean yes, of course—absolutely love to!"

The angel smiled happily, then turned to lead the way. "This way then, over here—I'll show you."

Hennaman, a soul alight, eagerly followed the angel open-eyed through pearly skies and starry nights. They sort of floated along, the angel's birdy, breast-white wings waving stiffly in occasional slow, flapping motions. Hennaman concentrated solely on the task of following his celestial, golden-haloed guide, but moving as he did in an effortless and stepless glide. No longer did the old ways matter—and gone away with the flesh of earth were all carnal worries and concerns.

"What, are we going to observe a great, celestial model of it?" he eventually asked as they rose among the stars.

"No." The angel turned, letting out a golden laugh. "I'm going to show you the actual workings, so you'll know firsthand what they're like—what it looks like right inside the heart of it—how it feels and acts—what it does. You'll get to look right at the thing itself, at what's inside the mind of God."

"Wow," Hennaman's voice finally hushed out, in what to mortals would be called a shaking quiver. "That's. . . ."

The angel smiled another golden, happy smile. "Miraculous? Heavenly? Impossible?"

Three times he nodded gravely.

"And precisely what I'm here to show you!"

AS THEY DRIFTED UPWARD into the solid vision of an expansive room, Hennaman's first thought was that they were far away from the hospital where his body had spent its last living moments, with plastic tubes connected to heavy equipment with digital screens and a vague pall of dirtiness on everything, like public restrooms. This Heaven seemed very clean, but like the hospital it was overly mechanical. They were on a long catwalk, now hovering over a mile-wide expanse, overlooking machinery with a series of large, slow heaving cranks and pulleys. With a gigantic screen before them that was blank in a dim, after-sunset blue and with everything else that he could discern—metal walls in the distance that were fused together with rivets—it seemed to Hennaman like the innards of some kind of gigantic submersible.

The angel turned to him curiously. "The life you lived, you still remember it?"

"Of course!"

Hennaman had left a lover, a family, friends—his life had been full, if financially underwhelming. He'd worked hard, had dreams. But now all of that life, the forty-odd years of it, felt more like the first fading memories of a vivid dream itself, something that gradually broke up and rippled into hazy nothings. Its status had shifted from what he'd once thought was the one sure reality to what was unquestionably a temporary immersion, a brief sojourn he would never return to. He realized now that all those years were nothing.

The angel was talking. "Here's that life—just look, none of it's been lost, it's all here, right in the heart of things."

The angel glided forward along the catwalk toward a golden lever, about belly high with a rounded nub. Following the angel's movement, Hennaman watched in a gasp as the private moments of his life played out upon the giant screen—when it went alight, it covered his whole field of vision, turning him and his angel into two small silhouettes connected at the trunk.

On the screen his former life went on again like a long, languid sleep, with all the old stream of thoughts and passing feelings right there as he'd initially had them, but this time with a distance that allowed him to contemplate that life as it replayed. With a sharp sadness he saw how his countless transgressions had pulled him down, and he saw how each resistance against them was a monumental victory in the battlefield of life. Slowly he grew conscious that the angel was watching there beside him and seemed to know even the most intimate moments as they played upon the screen.

"You, uh, seem quite familiar with all this."

The angel laughed gently. "Are you kidding? I was right there the first time. I was there to watch and guide through all of it!"

To Hennaman's surprise, his meek, meek life had been constantly interloped upon. He'd received the guidance and protection of his angel countless times but hadn't ever recognized it so. For instance, twelve weeks ago on the ride to the doctor's there had been a perilous instant he'd already forgotten, and it was the angel who had tapped the wheel just a hair. Other times, the angel came in glints that he'd thought only had been light, and its push had been felt in sudden urges for action or inaction on his part. As the life on the screen played out, Hennaman learned and saw how countless occasions, from the start to finish of his life, had bore the careful influence of the angel.

"That was me right there. . . ."

"Oh, you're kidding, that was you again?"

"But even with my help, you still made all your own decisions," the angel quickly added. "Every last one of them was yours. Everything you thought, every motion you chose to make, you could have done any number of things. You could have thought about so much, moved so many ways, but you chose this"—a pearl-white hand raised gracefully toward the illumination of the gigantic screen—"and it was only just a single, small conception of an infinite array. Do you realize that? Here, it's better if I show you."

Now with clean blinks Hennaman saw the same scenes he'd just witnessed, but as they replayed, they unfolded in completely different ways: he saw the conscious moments of his waking life take different paths, as his former mind thought different things. He saw how these thoughts modified the future possibilities—literally, they changed everything. Thought, it seemed, had the most profound effect on all the world.

This played out for a while, during which Hennaman watched his whole entire life as it might have been, had he done just one thing differently—the tiniest of motions had wide effects that funneled out upon everything—and here he only had to suggest to the angel, to sort of think of it, and the life as revealed before him would appear with that one thing changing all the reality beyond it. He spent long dreamy epochs watching with a quiet eye, digesting the great array and variety of these variant lives of his, inside their variant worlds, while the angel hovered closely at his side.

"Let me show you some more conceptions," the angel suggested when Hennaman was finally through. The angel pushed quickly through another thousand variations. Hennaman was nearly blinded by the flash. The angel stopped when Hennaman clearly had the understanding that it went on and on to every possible degree.

"You mean there's even more?"

"Going backward and forward in both directions."

"And it doesn't end?"

"Not here."

"Wow."

Again the angel pushed and pulled on the golden lever, and the scenes before them flashed forward in a lightning frenzy.

"See, when you pull on the lever here, we cycle through the infinite conceptions." The angel motioned to Hennaman. "You want to give it a try?"

"What, me pull on the lever?"

The angel's sheet-white palms were upward before it, in an expression to say that the lever was now at his mercy. "You can't break anything here, if that's what you're worried about."

Pushing on the nub, he went far inside the possibilities of the life his soul had left. He saw it played out again a thousand times, in fast blurs, slowing down and stopping at little moments with incredulity and awe—especially when his potential self gazed into a mirror.

"That's me! Look, that's me there! But—I'm so different!" He turned to the angel whose kind, sure nod confirmed these facts. Hennaman smiled, eyes wide, looking over at this view of what he was and could have been: it was the same body he'd been given at some ageless hour long ago, but changed through different choices, different circumstances, different motions through the physical world. At times he had to squint to recognize what became of him. Often it made him shudder, but he was always enthralled by it.

"Now who's that over there, my wife?"

Golden lips of the angel parted dryly: "One of the many possibilities, yes."

Hennaman pulled back slightly on the lever, reversed the scenery a bit, and watched what happened.

"Not many of these variations get you here, so you probably won't be interested in playing them out all the way," the angel warned.

"Why, how do they turn out?"

"Like most of them—riding what you think is very high at first and then finding yourself alone and deep, deep down," the angel answered, making a sad face. "You know, it isn't pretty."

BLAKE HENNAMAN'S SOUL was safely tucked away inside the mind of God, and he knew it. But the lever—the humongous room they seemed to be operating out of, hovering in, and even that wide viewport of a screen they looked at—it all seemed a little odd, a little off. This was Heaven? The mind of God? They came in sure trickling, these few stray smatterings of doubt, and soon Hennaman wondered if he should say something. He eventually decided that he should—after all, this was the final disposition of his soul.

"It all looks so industrial! And kind of dated. . . ."

"That?" the angel motioned kindly out toward the cranks and wide boilers below them and then up along the seam lines with their neat rivets, the long metal ladders fused onto the walls.

Hennaman nodded. He thought of Art Deco, very old cartoons, and the musty visions of the future that lived on the display shelves of antique shops.

"Oh, well that's nothing. That's only just. . . ."

"One single, small conception?"

The angel nodded happily. "Of an infinite array, yes."

They stood looking outward at the gigantic screen before them, where one of his potential lives was frozen still, like at a drive-in movie when the projector sticks mid-feature. "This whole conception can change completely, almost like a skin," the angel added after a silence.

And then to prove his point, the industrial boilers and churning motors and big, riveted tanks all fell away with a moment of the angel's concentrated gaze, and Hennaman blinked to see himself immersed inside a whole new world. Everything brightened with a hidden light, and they were suspended in earthly skies fat with clouds, somehow firmly placed and standing—the catwalk was gone. The angel held a tiny wooden box that Hennaman could peer into.When he did, he saw and felt the full-frame image of his life commence.

He bent back up to the angel. "It's all in there, just like on the giant screen!"

The angel smiled and let him have another look.

"These things can change—they can be anything, really," the angel explained as the thousand clouds around them were sucked neatly away inside the little box, and then the empty sky itself was vacumed up, and they were alone again in space. "They can be whatever you like."

To demonstrate, they lulled dreamily through a chambered city of mossy walls and pleasant fountains. A moment later that too went away. This happened again a dozen times. Nothing seemed to touch them, but the world whisked quickly all around, as if everything of every shape and size and color was being shaken up inside a massive blender, and they were the solid blades. Hennaman found himself stepping among milk-white control rooms, wide mother-of-pearl desks, high celestial perches, tiny game-board forests, and even his favorite childhood bedroom with the quilt and bookshelf but now built into the turret of a tall floating castle and coasting slowly a quarter-mile above a medieval green. The angel showed him a thousand happy worlds and ways. "See, so this changes infinitely, too."

Hennaman considered it.

"And what about us here, this actual meeting?"

"You mean this conversation we're having and the events as they're now unfolding?" the angel asked in a bright happiness, clasping his fingers while his dove-white wings clapped slowly behind his shoulders.

"Yes," Hennaman said, thinking about it now as another depiction of where they stood came into light around them, with sleepy Nebraska fields and a tiny, intimate sky. "All we're doing and saying, what's happening now. Does this—can this change?"

"It can," admitted the angel, who then bent a smile that was goldenrod and matched the endless field in view behind him. "In fact, it does—it occurs in a multiplicity of ways. It's all here, in every way you can imagine."

"Is it really?"

"Why sure."

Hennaman looked down, and back up at the angel, and then all around.

"So even all this we're doing here, it's only . . ."

The angel nodded slowly, with a broad, radiant smile that blessed down upon him. "Just one single, small conception in an infinite array."

Hennaman pondered this revelation in a daze. His soul was held by a power that clasped him tighter than anything he'd ever conceived—and he knew that this small understanding was only the tiniest atom in the universe of mind he'd been set free in. "And then it must be that the whole array of them . . ."

The angel nodded. "Only one conception in an infinity of more."

"And—beyond that?"

"Always more."

"Forever?"

The angel's smile was affectionate and warm. "Heaven doesn't run short!"

"So what should I do? What's next?"

"Just about everything."

"And do I—do I have to start on all this right away, or is there time?"

The angel chuckled with a soft, cherubic face the way clear, sunny waters make you want to pat the surface gently with a giant palm. "Of course there's no hurry, take your time. You can start whenever you like."

Hennaman stood a minute, his mind reeling with the power he'd just been given, one small chance to see and know. When he was ready, he went away to where the angel took him, to those places that to us remain unmapped and tucked away, down in the earthy regions somewhere deep inside the mind of God, where there was just all of this and more.

MICHAEL STUTZ is the author of the technology bestseller, *The Linux Cookbook,* and has contributed to *Rolling Stone, Wired, McSweeney's,* and many other magazines. He grew up in "the wilds of the net," an experience he has recently transformed into a traditional novel.

Lenses 7
The Darkroom

W.E. REINKA

For All I Know

HOSPITALS ON WEEKENDS have an after-hours feel. Walking the quiet halls of the Sacred Heart Hospital (Eugene, Oregon) on Super Bowl Sunday, I feel as if I'm roaming the mall after the Cineplex has let out and all the stores are gated for the night.

I've seen too much of the inside of this hospital over the last few months. Non-Hodgkins lymphoma, a hematologic malignancy similar to leukemia, is running helter-skelter through my body. Usually my wife, Louise, accompanies me here, listening attentively to the doctors and then translating the medic-speak for me on the way home. In waiting rooms, her endearments soothe me as she responds to my nervous prattle. Other times, I wait with my eyes closed; my hand hooked in Louise's elbow, as she thumbs through magazines with the address labels torn off.

Louise herself survived a nasty bout with cervical cancer five years earlier. I know from that experience that, as much as I feel the stress of what has been diagnosed as an ultimately lethal disease, it is easier to be the patient than the hand-wringing loved one. Louise offered to come down with me this Sunday, but I'm only here for a finger stick. I can handle that. She's earned a day off.

The Temporary Care Unit waiting room sits empty when I arrive. The nurse turns on the TV to the Super Bowl for me and then kindly puts on a pot of coffee, since I may have to wait awhile for the mobile lab technician who will administer a blood test to measure the relative clotting level of my blood. They'll keep testing me until they can settle on the proper dosage of Coumadin to help dissolve the blood clot that ballooned my left calf earlier in the week. Clots are common in cancer patients.

Opposite:
Shell Mask.
American Indian,
Mississippian,
conch shell,
7 15/16 x 6 13/16 x 2 3/16 in.,
ca. 1700–1200,
Tennessee.
Cincinnati Art Museum.
Gift of Thomas Cleneay.
(1887.20607)

After a few minutes, two older gentlemen join me in the waiting room. We chirp a cheery "Back again?" to each other. They were here yesterday at the same time I was. Twenty-four hours earlier, the man who is under treatment confirmed that he was born in 1920 before he gave up a few vials of blood for testing. I remembered the year because my father was also born in 1920. Hospitals often ask patients to state their full names or birth dates before chemotherapy, blood draws, or surgery. It's a last-minute double-check to ensure they're about to treat the proper patient.

The man under treatment is diminutive with crew-cut white hair and carries a plastic-handled shopping bag as if it were a briefcase. A tube leading from the bag disappears under his blue sweat suit. I surmise the tube leads to a catheter. His friend seems close to the same age, though he dyes his hair a Ronald Reagan reddish-brown. He wears a turtleneck under a stylish black leather jacket. I presume that the fellow in the leather jacket is the other's caregiver and gay partner—the hand-wringer in the relationship. They may simply be friends or neighbors, brothers-in-law for all I know.

Gay men my age—Baby Boomers—led the mass breakout from the closet. Gay men my father's age—the World War II generation—tended toward closeted public personas that became lifelong second natures, passing themselves off as "confirmed old bachelors."

Fairy tales feature queens and kings, princesses and princes. Books, movies, and music reinforce the heterosexual norm as we grow older. Husband and wife, Louise and I shine in society's mirror. On the other hand, these two men are conditioned to stand before smudges in the mirror. They don't touch hands or whisper in waiting rooms. All the same, the entwined roots of their love run as deep as ours.

I turn my eyes back to the Super Bowl, but my thoughts remain on the worry that deepens the crow's feet around the caregiver's eyes. If the men are gay partners, God blesses and manifests their love as He manifests His presence to me through Louise. There's no distortion in God's message to love one another as he loves us.

Maybe the white-haired fellow isn't really that sick. Maybe they're brothers-in-law. But if they are gay partners and death does slip in their door, I pray it tiptoes into their closet so that they may squeeze hands a final time and whisper: "Don't worry about me, lover" in the presence of God and beyond the range of those who don't bless their devotion.

W.E. Reinka is a frequent contributor to print and electronic media nationwide. This is his fourth contribution to the Chrysalis Reader.

ADAM BURNETT

Nothing New

"I saw a UFO today"
    she told me
    and I looked up from my
    crossword
    adjusted my glasses
    but didn't bother folding
    down
    my newspaper
    she was staring at me
    intently
"That's nothing new" I told her
    "you're always
    seeing something"
She continued to stare at me
    told me
    "No,
    that's not true."

ADAM BURNETT lives in Toronto, Ontario. His stories have been published in *Down in the Dirt, Rhapsoidia, Peeks and Valleys,* and *Midnight Times.*

TURNER SAM

Honeymoon Delayed

THEY'D DATED FOR A GOOD YEAR AND A HALF, but it was a long-distance thing. Nearly seven hundred miles separated the two, and while they'd, once a month, trade off destinations for extended weekend stays, they'd never spent more than eight consecutive days together; hence, a number of those more private-time nuisances, those haunting little idiosyncrasies they'd eventually learn to despise in one another, failed to reach the surface in time. Moreover, she, being of the religious sort who didn't take kindly to a premarital cohabitation, and he, certainly not in any place to push the idea, reached the agreement of waiting until legally bound to one another before moving in together. Ah, but that process, although both could barely see a glimmer of it among their impending futures at the time, approached much more hastily than first thought when she discovered herself as late and he gained that tiny boost to the ego all men take pride in when discovering how, regardless of the circumstances, they are, in fact, quite the fertile male of the species. A ring was then prematurely assembled, the chapel reservation pushed way up, and before anyone could notice that she'd begun to show, the two were situated before a minister and a kiss concluded the ceremony; there was no honeymoon, for there simply wasn't enough time.

The following six months were a blur, with the selecting of a house within their price range, the prepping of the baby's room, and the attending of class after class so to allow the entire pregnancy process to advance without error. While she was downing prenatal vitamins by the bottleful, he was writing checks for bassinets and rattles, and all the while neither seemed to be able to secure enough time to simply enjoy one another's company. All too often, they'd crawl into bed at the end of another day of her excessive nutrition and his wrist cramping from the various signatures inked down, and both would simply drift off to sleep while mixed up among the mutual fret as to whether they were in any way prepared, physically, mentally, emotionally, and practically to take on the responsibilities of caring for a miniature person. Of course, under the circumstances of their relationship thus far, they had yet to reach that elementary level of understanding between each other and, therefore, never so much as voiced their concerns to the one sharing the same set of sheets. They simply dealt with the issues as best they could alone, and alone turned out to be a terribly lonely means of problem-solving.

The child was born as a healthy, slimy, wiggly miracle in and of itself, and before he'd been properly rinsed off, both parents realized that, although the marriage itself was due an assessment from both ends, it would have to be put off until the child was fully taken care of in the meantime, and the meantime ultimately lasted several years—two, to be exact.

Two long years of diapers, ointments, and gaining an appreciation for the accomplishment of the little guy's first step consumed the couple's life. They became devoted to the point of obsession, actually, and although on the surface they believed their interest in the child was for its own good, further down was the deeper-rooted fact that the infant was serving as a suitable enough distraction to occupy them from addressing their own issues.

They might have kept going on like that, and likely been a content enough couple for the remainder of their lives, while smothering the tot; but eventually, regardless of her being told explicitly that she was not welcome, the wife's overruling mother—the only grandparent, in fact, that wasn't either deceased or disinterested completely—felt the continued reception of pictures documenting her grandbaby's growing up simply would no longer suffice. Grandma wanted to feel the critter in her arms, wanted to teach the child to say "Gammie," wanted to let him loose in the park and watch as he explored both tactilely and orally all things he came in contact with. Grandma was flying in, whether they wanted her or not, and assuming they couldn't handle her presence—well, then they best find some way to fulfill their time elsewhere because she was going to be there for a full seven days and not a minute less.

After her arrival, the couple joined in with Grandma's playtime with the child. They watched as she read stories, gave pointers when it came to softening his cries, and even instructed on the child's preferred lullabies when putting him down. Once Grandma seemed to be hitting her stride, they then gave her space, while accomplishing a bit of their own when tending to things so overdue that they might have unknowingly spoiled in the meantime. As it turned out, these personal matters turned out to be few, being that so many of those old memberships and hobbies had actually expired as an interest of theirs; and this they both found disconcerting. What else were they to do with their time if they couldn't get the satisfaction of being with their child or even relishing in the comfort of being by themselves? This left only one option remaining, and Grandma knew it, knew it was even more overdue than any of their other preoccupations, and had actually added it to her "things to do" list when packing for that weeklong trip. While leaving all things else unresolved—whether it was a sting to their egos or not—they needed to begin considering one another as much as the child, and the only way that could be accomplished was when they were alone together.

While Grandma had initially thought a gentle suggestion would be all that was necessary to dispatch the two off on a much-needed evening out, her countless attempts kept being ignored, one after another, eventually frustrating her to the point of making a clear and bold remark when attempting to wipe a line of apple sauce from her grandbaby's lips, all the while being crowded and forced instructions on two entirely different alternatives for correcting the mess. Amid this flooding of teachings, she stood up straight, shifted her shoulders back, perked her eyes wide, and flung the tiny, green, plastic spoon she had in hand across the kitchen so it struck the refrigerator door. The outburst received looks of shock from either parent flanking the high chair, along with obvious questioning within as to whether this woman had gone senile and could even be trusted around such a delicate thing as a two-year-old.

She directed in a steady tone, "Let me first say that there's no denying that you two are great parents. And I know that this little gurgle-monster here appreciates all you do for him. But you two have got to get some air; you have to do something other than leaning over my shoulder every second of the day, or, when you're not doing that, isolating yourselves off in separate parts of the house."

"We don't do that," the wife replied.

"Yes, you do. You both do. Now I need some alone-time with my grandson. On top of that, you two need to go out and enjoy yourselves awhile; it's something I know you've been ignoring since he came into this world and something that's missing. I can practically smell the awkwardness in the air; it's so thick. So it is my wish, and if that's not acceptable then it's my order, that you two go upstairs, dress yourselves for fine dining, and then make use of your best clothes by having just one evening together without the distractions of the next and previous generations. Can you do that for me, please? If not, I'm going to make you."

Somewhat shocked at her assertiveness, the husband and wife, after glancing to one another, in the end did exactly as instructed for fear of arousing any more preaching from the woman and within moments were climbing the stairs, showering up, and putting one leg at a time into pressed pants or shimmying into a pleated skirt. Once his tie was knotted and a spritz of perfume had absorbed into her neck, they proceeded back down the stairs, and, upon making the corner into the living room, beheld on the floor Grandma and the child stacking blocks one after another.

The ruffling of mother's shoes on the carpet brought over the eyes of either playmate, at which point the child remarked, "Pretty."

"You are right, there, kiddo. They are a sharp pair," Grandma confirmed.

"Why, thank you," the wife sweetly directed to the child.

"We'll be back before eleven," the husband informed.

The following twenty minutes of driving were consumed with discourse regarding the well-being of their child, after which they paused the conversation long enough to be seated at a table for two and sips from their respective water glasses were indulged in.

Next, a bottle of wine, selected by the husband, was provided and poured out for both, after which the wife took a sip and remarked, "Oh, it's been such a long time since I've had wine; good wine, that is."

"The wine you have back at the house isn't good?" the husband bantered, while perusing his menu.

"Oh, it's fine, but there's something about having it poured for you and tasting it with a room full of chatter all about that just makes it all the sweeter."

"I never realized you enjoyed dining out so much," he added, his eyes peering over to follow her reply.

"Oh, I do. Don't you remember back when we'd go out all the time; back in the beginning," she added, after securing eye-contact.

"Sure I do. Maybe it's been so long back that I can't claim to be as familiar with it as I should be, though—with how you loved it so."

"I know. It seems like ages, doesn't it?"

After they had placed their orders and continued with their comfortable banter, eventually her plate of lamb was delivered, while his medium-well rib-eye settled ahead bathed beneath a layer of thick amber sauce and mushrooms.

"It's so good. My gracious, how steak gets me at the heart," he moaned amid chews, after slicing forth a wedge and guiding it into his mouth.

"So it's better than the TV-dinner steak?" his wife mentioned through a smile.

"Not even close. In completely different worlds; of totally different times altogether, those two are."

"I always thought you liked the microwavable ones—at least a little bit?" she queried.

"Not even a little. I think they're atrocious, actually."

"Then why do you eat them?"

"Because you buy them."

"I only buy them because I thought you liked them. You know there are other options I could go with, right?" she reminded.

"I know; I just didn't want to trouble you over it."

"It's no trouble, sweetie. It's very easily done, in fact. I'd do it for you in a second; I'd do just about anything for you, if only you'd ask."

"Do you really mean that, or are you just saying it?" he stated plainly, while surrendering his utensils to the edge of the plate.

"Of course I mean it. Why wouldn't I?"

"I don't know why I asked that. I guess, lately, it seems that we're so caught up in other things—in the boy and such—that I'd forgotten how devoted and wonderful you are."

"You still think I'm wonderful?" she replied, her eyes gone glassy from the suggestion.

"Absolutely, although I'd suspect you might have questioned that in the past for the same reason I wasn't sure about you."

"I have felt that way, but, you know what, I don't feel it now. I can't even remember what it felt like, actually. All I feel at this moment is how much I love you; how much I adore you," she followed up as a pair of tears breached her lower eyelids.

"Must be the good dining," he chuckled.

"I think it is; I think it's exactly that. Also, I think it's a must we keep this up; we have to do this every week, if it's all right with you, being that it seems to bring out the best in the both of us."

"I think that's a wonderful idea; so wonderful it's every bit as wonderful as you," he mentioned, and the two went right on through their meals, plus dessert, more crazy over one another than they'd ever been or might ever hope to be. The luckiest couple in the world they considered themselves through the cleaning of their plates, the paying of the check, and the settling of the tip.

Upon exiting the restaurant, they were overcome by a sense of cheer and pleasing anticipation of the life they'd newly committed to. She felt more in love with him than ever before, while he'd rediscovered all the particulars about her which first made him fall so easily. Arm-in-arm they strolled along the sidewalk toward the parking lot, so very much re-infatuated with the other, so bleary-eyed and consumed with romance, in fact, that the lone crossing signal they had to obey in order reach their awaiting vehicle was all but ignored when conveying a halt of their stride. Sure enough, their ignorance of the warning proved fatal as they stepped into the thirty-eight-mile-an-hour path of an oncoming bread truck and were taken down instantly upon meeting its unyielding front bumper.

The last-second attempt to swerve sent the truck into a skid transitioning the vehicle onto its side, the back doors slinging open, and several hundred loaves of bread being hurled from within throughout the intersection. Most of the bread was salvageable, the driver received a minor case of whiplash, and the husband and wife died instantly upon impact, while still caught up in the merriment of their moment and without even the faintest awareness of their approaching fate.

TURNER SAM resides in the western United States. He greatly admires the short stories of Larry Brown and Dylan Thomas

Lenses 8
Mirror, Mirror on the Wall

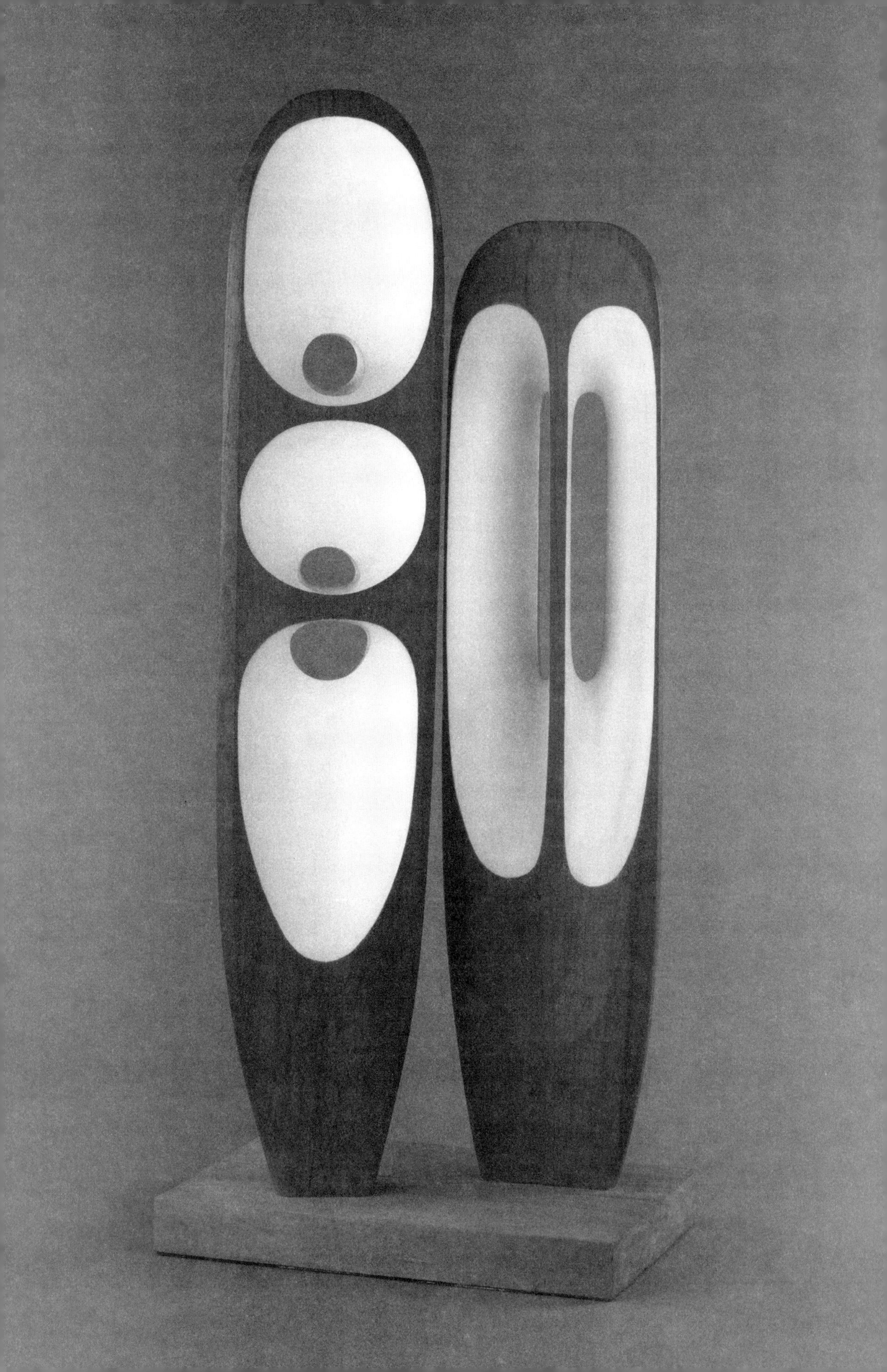

MARGARET KARMAZIN

An Awakening

CLAIRE DUBOIS TOLD HER SISTER, "When I was young, even into my late thirties, I still believed humankind was basically good." She and Tara were lunching at Brie's, a self-important little cafe in a newly renovated part of town. The waiters, snooty college students, rattled off lists of the offerings, all painfully healthy and organic.

Claire said, "See the pretension around us?" She circled a hand in the air. "All of them, customers and staff alike, believe they are superior due to education, dress style, and real or potential salary."

The waiter set down their drinks and disappeared. "At least," Tara said, "these people are clean. They create pleasant surroundings and promote culture. And no moronic bar fights."

"I just haven't gotten to that crowd yet," said Claire. "Give me time." She sprinkled sweetener into her ice tea and stirred. "Don't forget the rednecks riding around in their flag-strewn, America-stickered gas guzzlers—unthinking, insatiable consumers of anything wrapped in plastic, nary a thought to the earth's well-being or future. Yeah, they're wonderful too." She took a long slug of tea.

Opposite:
Barbara Hepworth (English, 1903–1975).
Two Figures (Menhirs).
Teak and paint, 57 x 24 x 17½ in., primary view, ca. 1954–1955.
The Art Institute of Chicago. Bequest of Solomon B. Smith. Photography, © The Art Institute of Chicago. (1986.1278)

Tara eyed the tofu/veggie, non-gluten pizza set before her and picked up her fork and knife. "Leave out anyone?" she said.

"I don't know," said Claire, "pick a spot on the globe. Go ahead."

Tara shrugged. "Oka-a-a-ay, how about Africa."

Claire dug into her sprout-and-soybean salad. "Let's see—how about let's keep messing around, cheating on our wives, and then wonder why we're all dying of AIDS? Or let's ride to the villages in army vehicles, shoot all the men and rape the women instead of building schools and roads and then wonder why we're so poor and helpless.

"Everyone thinks they're innocent," she continued. "Our country, for instance. It would say, since we only help people and bring freedom to the world, why do people burn effigies of us! All we're doing is just cramming our faces with donuts and wearing our tenth pair of sneakers that some starved-to-a-stick kid sweated in some factory to make for us!"

"But you and I don't do evil things," protested Tara.

"I am the same as all of them," said Claire. "Every person on Earth believes they're sweet. If they held a mirror up to their own actions, they'd see a different story. Everyone in India, China, Nigeria, France, New Zealand, the U.S., everywhere on the planet—every last one of them thinks he's innocent as new-fallen snow and everyone else is bad."

Claire waved her fork. "I am just as bad as everyone else! I am a self-absorbed, conniving, manipulating weasel that would step on my grandmother's head if I had to in order to supply my earthly needs. And, like everyone else in this sorry world, I'd lie to protect my 'innocent' persona and viciously attack anyone who pointed out the opposite. Let's face it, Tara, we're all slime."

"KID, I LOVE YOU TO PIECES — BUT YOU'RE SLIME TOO"

"You think I'm slime?" Tara asked, eyes wide.

"I love you, kid, but yeah, you're slime too."

Tara said, "I feel sorry for you, Claire."

Claire was pensive. "I feel sorry for me, too. The thing is, in my spiritual readings, they state that underneath we're all One, that if you could see the world with Christ-like eyes, you'd be overjoyed at the beauty of us all. Well, honey, I would love to see like that. But try as I might—meditation, prayer, you name it—all I have to do is turn on the news, and all that stuff flies right out the window."

Claire had indeed given up hope that she would ever see things differently, and had settled for being a hedonist of sorts. *I'll watch movies. I'll be glad I have a good husband, a cozy house, and friends who put up with me.*

A week later, Tara telephoned. "There's this guru guy coming to speak at the Holistic Center. He's going to 'speak on the Oneness of humankind and the Universe' and he will 'lead his listeners into a vision of the Oneness.' How do you like that? Is that not *amazing?* I mean, considering that you were just talking about that very thing!"

Claire was silent.

"Are you still there?"

"Yeah. That is interesting. A crock, but interesting."

"Maybe he's one of those gurus who poke you in the third eye and you keel over in ecstasy," Tara said.

"Like those evangelical healers who smack you on the forehead and suddenly you can ditch your wheelchair?"

Tara didn't say anything.

"Do you want to go?" asked Claire, trying not to laugh. "You know how I hate gurus. Oily egomaniacs, every one of them."

"Okay," Tara said, "but I'd like to go."

"Al-l-l-l-l right, we'll go. But you owe me one."

During Claire's New Age exploration phase, she'd run into various types who considered themselves gurus. At first fascinated, her interest palled after watching them using mind games to control people. Then there were the followers who took Indian names for themselves as if a moniker could bestow holiness upon them.

If, she had always wanted to ask, you profess to exist outside of your bodies and to reincarnate through the ages, what difference does it make what you call yourself now?

"All of it is hogwash," she muttered as she dressed for this new guru and set out to pick up her sister. "Total bull," she muttered once Tara was in the car.

"It's something to do," said Tara.

There was a small crowd of hippie types, and the guru was relatively handsome. Not young, although he looked supple, and had large Indian eyes that seemed to drill into you. Or, Claire supposed, he *imagined* they drilled into you. The meeting began with a low-key lecture on the meaning of love, and the speech wasn't actually bad.

"He's not a complete ass," she whispered to Tara. "Although while I don't really doubt this all—encompassing love's existence, I do doubt one's ability to access it. Certainly my own."

"He's rather hot looking," said Tara, apparently missing the point.

Claire persisted, "I suppose soon people will be spouting about their own heavenly experiences of 'seeing the unearthly beauty of other people's souls,' blah blah blah."

"Bad as a prayer meeting!" chuckled Tara.

"Worse," said Claire.

The guru directed his gaze at them and asked, "Do you two have comments you would like to share with the rest of us?"

"Just like junior high," whispered Claire. She raised her voice: "All that is well and good, but the fact is, swami, for all our reaching, neither I nor anyone I *know* has crossed the barrier into seeing others with Vision. If they did, would the world be as it is?"

"Come see me at the break," said the guru. "And by the way, I am not a swami. I'm just a regular person." He smiled.

Claire made her way toward the man as everyone else was milling toward a refreshment table.

"Ah," he said as she approached. "The cynical one." He motioned for her to follow him into a small side room. There was an odd moment of silence while they regarded each other, before he said, "Would you prefer if it were different, that you actually could drop the veil and see with holy eyes?"

She didn't feel like playing games—Sunday school games when she was little, patriotic and church propaganda when she was older, the peer pressure of "spiritual" groups, the empty promise of religion everywhere, sick to death of it all. "Don't joke with me," she almost growled.

"I'm not," he said. "If you wish to see, then you will see." He reached into his rather voluminous robe and pulled out a small object. "Hold out your hand," he said. "I don't do this for everyone."

"Do what?" she retorted, examining the object he placed on her palm—something hard and flat in a small, soft leather pouch.

"What is it?" she said.

The not-a-swami nodded. "It is very old," he said. "When you're finished with it, I'd appreciate your returning it. I'll give you the address where you can mail it."

"You trust me?" she said. Not that she figured this apparent piece of junk would be worth anything.

He laughed. "Oh, once you use that, you'll be entirely trustworthy, believe me."

"*Use* it?" she said. "What do you mean?"

He gave her a long, speculative look. "In spite of your nasty attitude, I sense that you really mean what you said."

"What I said?" she repeated stupidly.

"You are indeed a person who is, no matter how you may act to cover it, suffering deeply over this issue of not being able to see."

She was silent, biting her lip while she studied his face.

"There is a metal mirror in that pouch. Choose a time when you are alone. Look into that mirror and look for as long as it takes, which may not be long. Your suffering will end."

"But . . ." said Claire.

The man dismissed her response with a wave of his hand. "Do as I direct, and your problem will be over."

"Have you done this, whatever it is, yourself?" she asked.

"No," he said.

"Why not?"

"I'm not ready."

"And you think I would be ready for something that you, the guru guy, would not be?"

He looked disgusted. "You are ready simply because of your misery with what you see now. You've reached the point where there are only two directions to go—despair and possible suicide or addiction, or true understanding. I have not reached that point. Now go."

She understood that he meant right then. She supposed he didn't want her contaminating his lecture any further.

As she turned her back, he said, "Be careful."

She wondered what he meant.

Although she considered the whole thing silly, she approached the moment of dealing with the mirror with some respect or apprehension. She had privacy—her husband was on the road, the phone was off the hook, and the blinds pulled shut.

The mirror was less than four inches across. So how much could it do? She sat on the carpet, lifted the thing, and looked into it.

She stared at it fully. Then, something occurred she could not have described, a sort of inkling deep inside of her, as if a bell rang, some ancient yet very familiar sound. Suddenly she saw *through her face* to what lay behind—not muscle, blood, and bone, but far beyond. The radiance! The unearthly colors! The utter *beauty!* It could never be described, not in any language! So this was what a human was! Not at all what she had imagined!

Astonished, she jumped to her feet, dropped the mirror, and danced backwards, banging into the wall. "Tom!" she yelled, wanting to tell her husband about it. Then she remembered he was away.

She darted about like a crazy person, finally stumbling out the back door. There, across the fence, was the neighbor, Mr. Pavone, watering his flowers. She squinted at him. He was radiating luminous color and so were the flowers! She saw that *everything* was phenomenal—the ant crossing the driveway, the cat stalking by the hedge, the fly that buzzed, the gravel on the ground. The *grass* was fantastic, the picnic table, the fallen twig, the loosely wound garden hose! Everything was a fantastic temporary construct, a very complicated reality running inside a vast, magnificent, wonderful, glorious Mind!

Bursting with delight, she danced in front of the fence. "Mr. Pavone! Mr. Pavone!" she called.

The elderly man turned to look at her with alarm, accidentally spraying her with the hose. "Oh!" he cried.

She lurched to a stop in front of him, hardly noticing that she was wet. "You're such a wonderful man!" she said. Did he know that he was radiating light like a spinning universe, that he was made of God Himself?

He backed away, terrified. "Mrs. Dubois!" he exclaimed. "Are you all right? Do you need some help?"

But Claire only saw his magnificence and replied, "Why, Mr. Pavone, I never told you before how incredible you are."

Tom returned the next day to find the house empty, chocolate wrappers strewn across the kitchen table, and photo albums scattered

"SOMETHING'S DIFFERENT... WAIT, DON'T TELL ME."

about the living room. The back door stood wide open, the declawed cat gone, and the dog was whining in the yard, hungry. Claire's car and purse were gone. There was a stamped and sealed envelope on the kitchen counter, addressed to someone with an Indian name and containing something hard and flat.

"I LIKED HER MUCH BETTER WHEN SHE HATED EVERYONE."

After several attempts to reach her by cell phone, Tom finally heard his wife answer. "Where are you?" he demanded.

"Oh, honey! I'm down here with the street people behind the old shoe factory? You wouldn't believe how wonderful they all are! Hey, let's all have dinner together tonight! You can come here, or we'll come there. Chinese or pizza?"

He tried to remember if there was a history of mental illness in his wife's family. There was that cousin who claimed her father shot her in the face although the father was loving, and the girl had no scar or hospital history. Clearly nuts. And the great-grandmother who'd hung herself upstairs over the dining room while her family was eating dinner. Not hopeful.

He picked up his wallet and car keys and hurried out the door to save her.

Word spread about the woman who saw good in everyone, spinning her happy tales to neighborhood children, leading lively discussions with street people, and holding forth in cafés and bars with college students.

"She's wildly popular," bemoaned Tara to her brother-in-law. "Of course, how can anyone resist a person who loves everyone and tells them they're divine?" She sniffed unhappily. "I miss her. We don't do anything together anymore."

"Tell me about it," said Tom. "I don't think she and I have eaten a meal together for over two months."

Tara sighed. "I liked her much better when she hated everyone."

It was dim in the Anarchy Café, but Claire was a light unto herself. She laughed because the others still did not know they also were Light. "You want me to explain how it happened again?"

She pulled out a chair for the most cynical student. He was thin and dark with spiky black hair and a beard.

"This is how it went, David," she said, looking at the crowd around the table. She paused, enjoying their bright young faces.

"When I looked in that mirror, I saw my real self. From there it morphed into the Whole. I saw I was really the Whole. And reasonably, although reason had little to do with it, I understood that all of you were that too. There ended my hatred and disgust with humans, with anything, for that matter."

"Everything was equal?"

"Yes, everything. We're the same as a chair leg. Beautiful."

"I don't get it," said David.

The students lit cigarettes and nodded.

"Imagine that each of you is a drop of water that lives on a leaf on a tree branch. A few other drops, your family and friends, are on the same leaf. You can see other drops glistening on nearby leaves. You even see other trees, close and far, and you figure there are probably drops on those other trees. That's your view of your world, see?"

"One day the wind blows and your leaf tilts. You slide off and fall into a puddle below the tree, and the instant you land in the puddle, you join with it; you *become* the puddle. Now, you have the consciousness of the puddle; you know everything the puddle knows, all about its edge, the ground under it, anything floating in it, the air above it. You *are* the puddle, see?"

The students, even David, nodded and blew smoke.

"Now, this puddle begins to trickle along a little groove until it empties into a stream. The instant it enters the stream, it becomes the stream; it has the consciousness of the stream. The stream meets the river, and when it enters the river, what does it know?"

"Everything the river knows," said the students.

"And the river," said Claire, her eyes sparkling happily, "flows into the ocean, and that once-finite drop now knows everything all the oceans know. That is what collective or cosmic consciousness is. We only *think* we are separate drops of knowledge."

DON'T WORRY, MOMMA—
YOUR LITTLE DRIP
WILL BE AN OCEAN SOMEDAY

"What does that mean in practical terms?" asked Melissa, a stern-faced black girl.

"Well . . . " said Claire, "it means that if you try to make someone's life miserable in any way, you're just criticizing yourself."

"It doesn't seem that way!" said David, pulling at his beard.

"No, and that's because we're playing in this huge, vast virtual reality program. We imagine we have bodies and our bodies are separate from each other. It's an illusion, get it?"

"Well, if we're in this virtual reality, why not play the game instead of opting out? Maybe we signed up to play, and that's the deal."

"Good point, David. But let me ask you all this: are you happy?"

They were silent. "Melissa?"

"No," the girl said, somewhat shyly.

"And you?" she asked each of them in turn.

The consensus was generally no.

"Okay then," she said. "I'm happy, all of the time. Sleeping and waking, no matter what I'm doing, no matter if I am alone or who I am with, I'm happy. Get it now?"

Oprah called; it had only been a matter of time. Tom sighed as he handed Claire the message. "Oprah, if it was really Oprah."

Oprah answered immediately. The date was set. Claire was to be on the show three times, beginning two weeks from the phone call.

"Do you want to come with me?" Claire asked Tom.

He didn't.

"I know you think I don't love you anymore, Tom," she said. "I do so very much, but I also love *everyone*."

She had not missed that her marriage was crumbling. Tara had pointed it out more than once.

"It doesn't matter," Claire told her sister. "I am married to Creation."

The first Oprah show ran smoothly, and afterwards Claire joined the cast to celebrate. A limo took her to the airport for her return flight home, but she got sidetracked by some interesting tourists from Czechoslovakia and went off with them for a few days in L.A. When she got home, it was nearly time for the second Oprah appearance.

"Oh, you can't imagine the sights I've seen," she told Tom on the phone. He was now in St. Louis.

"Like what?" he said coldly.

"There are so many people in the world," she said, "and everyone is perfect. Everyone is a light like a sun."

"Listen, I gotta get to bed," said Tom.

"You do that, honey," Claire said, "and know that you are loved more than you can imagine."

It was the last thing she said to him before leaving for the second Oprah show.

Outside the studio, a crowd had gathered. They waved signs on sticks that read, "Daughter of the Devil! Promoter of Evil and Heresy!"

A woman shouted, "You're an abomination to God, Claire Dubois!"

Claire turned to face them all and could not speak, so overcome was she with the rainbow rays of light that shone from them all. She did not hear their words.

A man stepped out of the crowd and fired at her. She fell to the ground, while her frantic escorts fumbled for their cell phones to dial 911.

As she lay on the sidewalk, she expanded into galaxies and creations beyond the imaginings of any human. No one watching had an inkling of what she saw.

MARGARET KARMAZIN's stories have been published in numerous literary and national magazines, including *Rosebud, North Atlantic Review, Potomac Review, Confrontation, Virginia Adversaria, Mobius, Chiron Review,* and *Aim Magazine.* Her fiction in *The MacGuffin, Eureka Literary Magazine, Licking River Review,* and *Words of Wisdom* were nominated for the Pushcart Prize. She co-authored the introduction and authored a story in *Still Going Strong* (Routledge, 2005) and was published in *Ten Twisted Tales* (San Francisco Bay Press, 2008). Piper's Ash, Ltd. published a chapbook of her science-fiction stories, *Cosmic Women* (2003). Her novel, *Replacing Fiona* (2007), was published by etreasurespublishing.com and is available at online bookstores.

For this satire by Margaret, the illustrations were drawn by MIKE TAYLOR, who works for the U.S. Army Corps of Engineers in San Francisco. His cartoons have appeared in numerous publications, including *Tricycle, The Writer, Writer's Chronicle,* and in the books *Buddhist Guide to New York* and *Buddha Laughing.* He is also a published haiku poet and songwriter.

THOMAS R. SMITH

The Return

Unto Him all things return.
—THE KORAN

Walking on the lower park road
early morning, summer solstice,
we came to a place in the still-
shaded cool where, looking
up a grassy hillside,
we could see, through a gap
in the trees, the rising sun.

Burning clear with all
heat and strength befitting
the day of its longest dominion,
the sun, boiling out of its
high nest of foliage,
lit a silver swath
of sparkling, dew-bent

grasses all the way down
the drenched slope to our feet.
So brilliant was that aisle
or lane the sun unrolled
down the hill to us, we had
to stop where we were
and sit awhile in pure adoration.

And I remembered the old
secret promise, perhaps unwise
to speak, though who could
believe otherwise seeing
the grass-people, humble yet
adorned, nodding together
on their way back to the sun?

And soon enough we got up
again and wandered on into
whatever we had to do
in the light, though not unblessed,
having followed for a little distance
on the morning road of their return
those illuminated pilgrims.

THOMAS R. SMITH is a poet and teacher living in River Falls, Wisconsin. His poems have appeared in hundreds of periodicals in the U.S. and abroad. His most recent poetry collections are *Waking before Dawn* (Red Dragonfly Press, 2007) and *Kinnickinnic* (Parallel Press, 2008). He teaches at the Loft Literary Center in Minneapolis. Poetry has been his spiritual practice for thirty years.

ANDERS HALLENGREN

An Angle of Vision

The Seer in Contemporary Perspective

HOW FAST CAN INFORMATION BE TRANSMITTED? PEOPLE WONDERED. Can you in some sense be present at two places at the same time? It is still there, the Sahlgren House at Norra Hamngatan in Sweden's harbor city, Gothenburg, where Emanuel Swedenborg was having dinner on Thursday, 19 July 1759, when suddenly he had a vivid vision of a conflagration in Stockholm—405 kilometers away as the birds and airplanes fly—the flames drawing nearer and nearer his home in the Maria parish at Södermalm. The host William Castel and the fifteen guests were alarmed, reports say, and the news spread rapidly in the city producing deep concern, because in those days fire brigades were almost helpless and emergency meant catastrophe. At about 8 PM Swedenborg with relief reported that the fire had halted at the third door from his house. The next day he was summoned to the Masonic provincial governor Johan Fredrik von Kaulbars, who was worried by the rumors, to give a detailed account of the course of events, a statement that was shortly corroborated point by point by a Stockholm news dispatch that arrived by the regular stagecoach, the fastest means of communication at the time. All this is evidenced in contemporary documents. The huge city fire is well known in historical records, being one of the worst in eighteenth-century Stockholm, where it destroyed Maria Magdalena Church and three hundred wooden houses.

There are two elements that are particularly noteworthy in this singular communication—the difference in speed, and even more, the widespread consternation immediately produced. There seems to have been no lack of confidence and credence. Swedenborg was taken at his word.

The event was apparently very notable, too. It was not only the talk of the harbor city but would be reported all over Europe. In Gothenburg, Swedenborg was to get his first followers, later creating a great stir and a religious lawsuit that would upset everyone, including the visionary. Antoine-Joseph Pernety, librarian of Frederick the Great, collected testimonies, as did the theologian and oculist Johann Heinrich Jung-Stilling, a friend of Goethe and Herder, and a councilor of Charles Frederick, Grand Duke of Baden. The Prussian philosopher Immanuel Kant, who never left his Königsberg, commissioned an English merchant named Green to visit Swedenborg, to order his exegetic work *Arcana Coelestia* (eight volumes purchased for seven pounds sterling), and to collect all available witness reports. In the years to come, much was to be told about Swedenborg's strange faculties. There were many extraordinary incidences, particularly in the 1760s. Like diviners and mediums still today, he was asked to tell the whereabouts of lost things. An old neighbor of his, the disheartened widow Madame de Marteville in the Van der Nootska Palace at Södermalm, who had wrongly received an urgent reminder to pay a debt and could not find the verification among the belongings of her late husband, was such a client in straits. Swedenborg did not disappoint her, or anyone, although he always played down such doings, all done by courtesy and not worth mentioning, he thought.

At times, when there was imminent danger, he acted on his own initiative, however. At another dinner in Gothenburg, he abruptly and insistently urges the manufacturer Bolander to leave for his cloth mills, where a piece of cloth had commenced to burn near the furnace, which threatened the whole factory. But even in small, everyday matters he gave a helping hand to friends. An evening at his follower Johan Rosén's in the same city, the party begins to argue about a certain book, and Dr. Rosén then regrets that he has no copy, whereupon Swedenborg feels obliged to put in—"not here, but in the attic," which settles everything. In most cases, Swedenborg preferred to keep things to himself. Jung-Stilling, in a 1762 conversation with Swedenborg in Amsterdam, suddenly finds the man he is talking to deeply distracted and unreachable, and after continual asking the latter very reluctantly announces: "At this hour Tsar Peter III died in jail"! Heir to the thrones in both Sweden and Russia, Peter died in custody at the castle of Ropsha on 17 July.

Swedenborg inspired curiosity as well as fear, since he seemed to know more than he possibly could—and definitely more than he should! In his presence, it was difficult to keep secrets. He left most of these things out of accounts because he considered them unimportant and also somewhat embarrassing. He had an important message from a higher source and wanted no focus on his own assumed and much-talked-about ability to make out various things and pick up certain data; or trace lost receipts and such trifles. . . . Was there no gratitude in this world?

Did he have a sixth sense? people asked. Closely examined, many of the reported cases of extrasensory perception or clairvoyance could be viewed as instances of telepathy or, to put it differently, thought-reading or mind-reading. If we study his early works carefully, we can appreciate thought-transference as the lengthened shadow of sympathy or the extended range of empathy. He obviously observed early this strange gift, with such astonishment witnessed by so many people around him, and as always he sought for an explanation. After all he was the man who wanted to know! In his paper *On Tremulation* (1717) he had observed how easily we can enter into the thoughts of other people and know what they are up to, since all life consists of vibrations, and accordingly minds can resonate in harmony as one string can vibrate in resonance with another if they are tuned in the same key. For this reason people can be in rapport at long distances. The spirits of life can travel through space-time. His friend and colleague Christopher Polhem happily agreed and had developed the same idea in his thoughts on the nature and habitat of spirits, *Tankar om andarnas varelse.*

But there is something else we ought to consider to understand what was happening. Emanuel Swedenborg was lucky to be a male, a bishop's son, and a metropolitan nobleman. Gifted countryside women with such alleged supernatural skills and undertakings were still charged and put on trial for witchery. Cases of second sight, such as seeing what was happening in a distant place, had brought people up before the court. At the solemn churches, sovereign clergy spouted fire-and-brimstone caveats. His relative and academy colleague Carolus Linnaeus, who fought against superstition in his own mind and indeed believed in divine retaliation and severe punishments, was keenly aware of the fate of his great-grandfather's mother, who had been burned at the stake. Carolus and Emanuel lived in an age where fabulous animals and ogres were still realities and the Earth largely unknown. When Swedish prisoners of war in Siberia discovered a mammoth tusk, it was taken to be either the Biblical monster Behemoth, mentioned in the Book of Enoch, or the horn of a unicorn. At their old-fashioned university at Uppsala, founded in 1477 by the Pope's consent, the fantastic Rudbeckian worldview was still lingering, and the annals of archaic times and Old Testament history merged with Swedish antiquity, the Scandinavian Peninsula being connected with Eden and Atlantis. That was part of their background and the mindset of the time.

The circumstance that the seventeenth-century-born Emanuel in the course of his life gradually advanced into the Age of Reason and the Era of Enlightenment may have contributed to dispel some contextual illusions, but the change did not make life much easier for spiritually-minded people, mavericks, occultists, or the esoteric. On the contrary, a new kind of witch-hunt replaced the old one, and in his native country Swedenborg was one of the many preys. He was grouped with alchemists, mesmerists, magnetizers, tricksters, treasure-seekers, exorcists, and somnambulists. Scoffing Royal Academy member Mr. Kellgren deplorably set the mark with lasting consequences and had the laugh on his side for hundreds of years, in coquettish rococo lampoons—*Madness Does Not Make You a Genius*—dismissing the man as a loony nitwit and a conceited fool. The guffaw was so loud that it can still be caught in the quiet alleys of his old hometown, where the Swedish Academy resides. Is it surprising that laughter has been connected with evil?

Hell was near, but Swedenborg knew his way about and was never in fear. Sometimes the ground was getting too hot around him, but he kept cool. There were places to go and printers of anonymous books, no questions asked. Secret friends, too, men and women of influence, including royalty, and all the loyal craftsmen that lodged him. His needs were humble, and he remained amiable and confident, usually expressing himself in moderate terms. Indeed he had strange stories to tell, but his reputation as a clairvoyant attracted more attention for the simple reason that this peculiar power could be seen in action. It could be tested, and there was an answer-book available on this side of the grave! To others, as to him, *seeing is believing*. The stories of the beyond were accounts of what *he* had "heard and seen," not *they*. That was the major difference.

He convinced the senator, Royal Chancellor Anders von Höpken, that death is as trouble-free as drinking "a glass of water" and consequently nothing to be anxious about, but Höpken advised Swedenborg to omit the "memorable relations" from his works, since they made them less believable, that is, verifiable. After all, they lived in our time, the age of empiricist reasoning. However, Count Höpken advised the king to introduce the Swedenborgian faith in Swedish colonies—if there were to be any—since its rational creed made people unafraid of the end and new beginning. On one occasion, but just once, he also testified to his countryman's strange feat as a go-between of the dead, an achievement that had shocked the queen and the court, perhaps the whole government. Did Swedenborg, the citizen of arcane knowledge, have access to state secrets, too?

In the secret proceedings of the so-called Exegetic-Philanthropic Society, the first Swedenborgian association ever, circulated in a country where there would be no religious freedom until 1860, the former premier Anders von Höpken later observed:

> Swedenborg was one day at a court reception. Her Majesty asked him about different things in the other life and finally whether he had seen or had talked to her brother, the Crown Prince of Prussia. He answered no. Her Majesty then requested Swedenborg to inquire about him and to remember her to him, which Swedenborg promised to do. I doubt whether the Queen meant anything serious by it. At the next reception, Swedenborg again appeared at court; and as the Queen was in the so-called white room, surrounded by her Ladies of Honor, he entered gently and slowly approached Her Majesty, who no longer remembered the commission she had given him eight days ago. Swedenborg not only greeted her from her brother but also gave her his apologies for not having answered her last letter; he also wished to do so now through Swedenborg, which he accordingly did. The Queen was taken aback and said: "No one, except God, would know this secret!" The reason why she never adverted to this before was that she did not wish anyone in Sweden to consider that during the war with Prussia she had carried on a correspondence within a hostile country. Her Majesty exercised the same caution during her last visit to Berlin. When she was asked about this episode, which had been made public in a German publication, she dodged the question. (Memorandum of 9 Feb. 1784, trans. A.H.)

Still, his contemporaries found it easier to accept the psychic than the theosophist. That is true also of the philosopher Immanuel Kant, who in his enquiry into the mysteries reported from Sweden took pains to collect and ascertain all facts available in the Swedenborg case. When I read his disrespectful treatise *Träume eines Geistersehers [Dreams of a Spirit-Seer]* and even more the earnest truth-seeking account of Swedenborg in his private letter to Ms. Charlotte von Knobloch, I am struck by the similarities between his assiduous and acidulous approach and that of the detective invented by the spiritualist Conan Doyle: only facts speak! Kant concludes that data are insufficient to prove the veracity of Swedenborg's so-called *memorabilia,* his eyewitness reports from the other side. It is easy to feel Kant's disappointment when he finds it necessary to refuse the claims of the mystic, since he does want to know: *sapere aude,* "dare to know" was to become his motto. However, he perceived that all observation passes through human lenses, for which reason he looked upon knowledge as relative and subjective. Consequently, Kant becomes a skeptic in the sense that he does not deny the possibility of supernatural things, but he asks for objective evidence. He concentrates his researches on this world, focuses on Swedenborg's remarkable extrasensory perception, and scrutinizes every source to find out the truth behind all the stories about the man's strange feats. In doing so, he assembles such a collection of double-checked witness reports that Kant has supplied posterity with the most compelling and persuasive collection of examples ever put together in the history of psychical research and parapsychology. If the existence of clairvoyance or telepathy were ever proved, Kant did it!

Likewise, the Swedish contemporaries were amazed by the oracle. Swedenborg's theology, for long published anonymously abroad, known only by the secret spirits in his garden and the angels of heaven to whom he talked in his chamber, in the street, or in his stateroom at sea, were more delicate matters. His major research project, outlined in *De Infinito* and the aim of the unfinished series of volumes entitled *Regnum Animale (The Kingdom of the Soul),* empirically and sensibly to demonstrate the immortality of the soul—*ut ipsis sensibus animae immortalitas demonstretur*—was precisely the proof that the surrounding world in bewilderment was looking for when his deep-sounding approach by means of scientific investigation came to a close and was succeeded by the revelations that answered all his questions. The readers had access to his accounts, not to his experiences. The skeptic Kant concluded his treatise by encouraging some patience regarding the eternal life: just wait a little and you will see for yourself when you get there! Why all this haste? Death is a beaten track and the inevitable destiny of all. In the meantime, cultivate your garden and make the best of your talents, since your virtue probably determines your fate in the future world *(in der künftigen Welt)!* That is Kant's final advice, affirming the hereafter and suddenly expressing himself in tune with Swedenborg's doctrine of life.

This last sentence touches the core of all Swedenborg's concepts: it is what you do, not what you believe, that counts! In a sense, this was the most world-shattering idea in his theology—downgrading the importance of faith, the focal point always being works, a decent life. "The Lord's church is with all in the whole world who live in goodness" irrespective of what religious creed (*The New Jerusalem and Its Heavenly Doctrine,* paragraph 246). As things turned out, Kant's refutation of metaphysics was to serve as a basis for a new metaphysics, the very foundation of the Romanticism of the next century, when the Swedenborgian movement flourished and its thoughts spread worldwide, but that is another story.

Again, this makes us understand even more clearly why Swedenborg did not want any focus on his own person, on his own powers, or psychic phenomena, which tended to overshadow everything else, and which he didn't want to talk about and never mentioned in his writings. Contrary to this, eyewitness reports abound, as we have seen. The sad result, from his point of view as well as *sub specie aeternitatis*, was that people tended to believe in what he could show rather than what he could report. They asked for miracles, as people asked Jesus and (in vain) Mohammed, whereas Swedenborg maintained that miracles are invisible and continuous. Add to this the fact that the supernatural was penalized and banned, and the depth of the conflict becomes obvious and broadens into an abyss.

He never became a doubting Thomas, but all the misunderstanding surrounding him was enough to drive him or anyone into despair. This can sometimes be read between the lines. In late letters to Ludwig IX, the Landgrave of Hesse-Darmstadt, and to his minister, who gave him a hearing, he highlighted that he did not perform *miracles* but propounded *memorabilia*, things worth remembering (pleading letters written in Amsterdam in July 1771). Mostly he turned the other cheek. He always refused to get into polemics and disputes or even defending himself, although he was often publicly attacked and ridiculed, but to his correspondents, the tone could be importunate. And, in a way, he in these letters adduced the proof that Kant was everywhere looking for and which was the reason for Kant's many inquiries: he confirmed that the affair with the queen of Sweden, etc., was based on contact with the world of spirits, and thus the former confirmed the latter.

The Reverend Samuel Noble remarked that the stories did indeed prove that Swedenborg had the privilege of conversing with spirits and angels. The politician Christopher Springer, who had escaped life imprisonment and moved abroad, was shocked at Swedenborg's insight into the secret peace talks between Sweden and Prussia, his intimate knowledge of Springer's connections with the Russians, and of his unwieldy private dealings with Prime Minister Claes Ekeblad, all these things reported to Swedenborg by the dead. So, this civilian did indeed have access to state secrets. They belonged to heavenly secrets heard and seen, *ex auditis et visis*.

In Gothenburg, the most substantial outcome of his theological work was the small circle of adherents that gradually formed in the seaport. This eventually brought a crisis where the doctrines as well as the visionary were in the balance. His close neighbor at Södermalm, Carl Robsahm, whose family helped to rebuild the Mary

Magdalene Church after the fire, recalled in his memoir: "During the Diet of 1769 a cunning stratagem was planned by some members of the Clergy, by which Swedenborg was to be summoned before a court of justice and after the first examination to be declared a man who had lost his reason by religious fads and fancies, whom it was at any rate dangerous to leave in freedom and who therefore ought to be confined in an asylum. As soon as a certain Senator, Swedenborg's friend, heard about this, he wrote him a letter in which he disclosed the scheme and advised him to leave the country. This made Swedenborg very sorrowful, and going straight away into his garden he fell upon his knees and in tears prayed to the Lord and asked what he should do; whereupon he received the comforting assurance that nothing evil should befall him—as was the case." At that crucial moment the ending of his mission and his life was very near. There was to be a continuation, however, and a clandestine following too.

PERSPECTIVES SHIFT CONTINUOUSLY, and our altering mirrors distort the picture. All these stories, all these people, and all these occurrences should be viewed and judged in historical and social context, but we are all as shackled, bound hand and foot, as ever Loki, Prometheus—or even Clio, the Muse of history, since we are children of an era and cannot free ourselves from the times. My own words are of such mythical and fleeting stuff. Considering the most basic bias, my inescapable viewpoint in the passage of time, I am thinking of the perceptive historian Geoffrey Barraclough, who in his *History in a Changing World* concluded that all historical writing is contemporary history. On the other hand, if future readers will smile at our misapprehensions, they should be compassionately reminded that they will share our fate. But when I am finishing this essay, I receive a call of distress from an unknown young Swedenborg reader who, under suspicion of religious whim, has been locked up for compulsory institutional care. *The times they are a-changin'*, the itinerant refrain reads, but I wonder.

ANDERS HALLENGREN is a Swedish author, a Harvard alumnus, and a Fellow of the Linnean Society of London. He received his doctorate for a dissertation on Emerson's philosophy (*The Code of Concord*, 1994) and is an associate professor at Stockholm University. The author of many books, including *Gallery of Mirrors: Reflections of Swedenborgian Thought,* he is also the English translator of *Swedenborg's Dream Diary* and other works. An essayist and also a poet, Hallengren was awarded a prize by the Swedish Academy in 2008. In 2009 he has lectured at the Swedenborg Association of Australia, the Hurstville Society, and the Linnean Society of New South Wales.

Lenses 9
Camaraderie

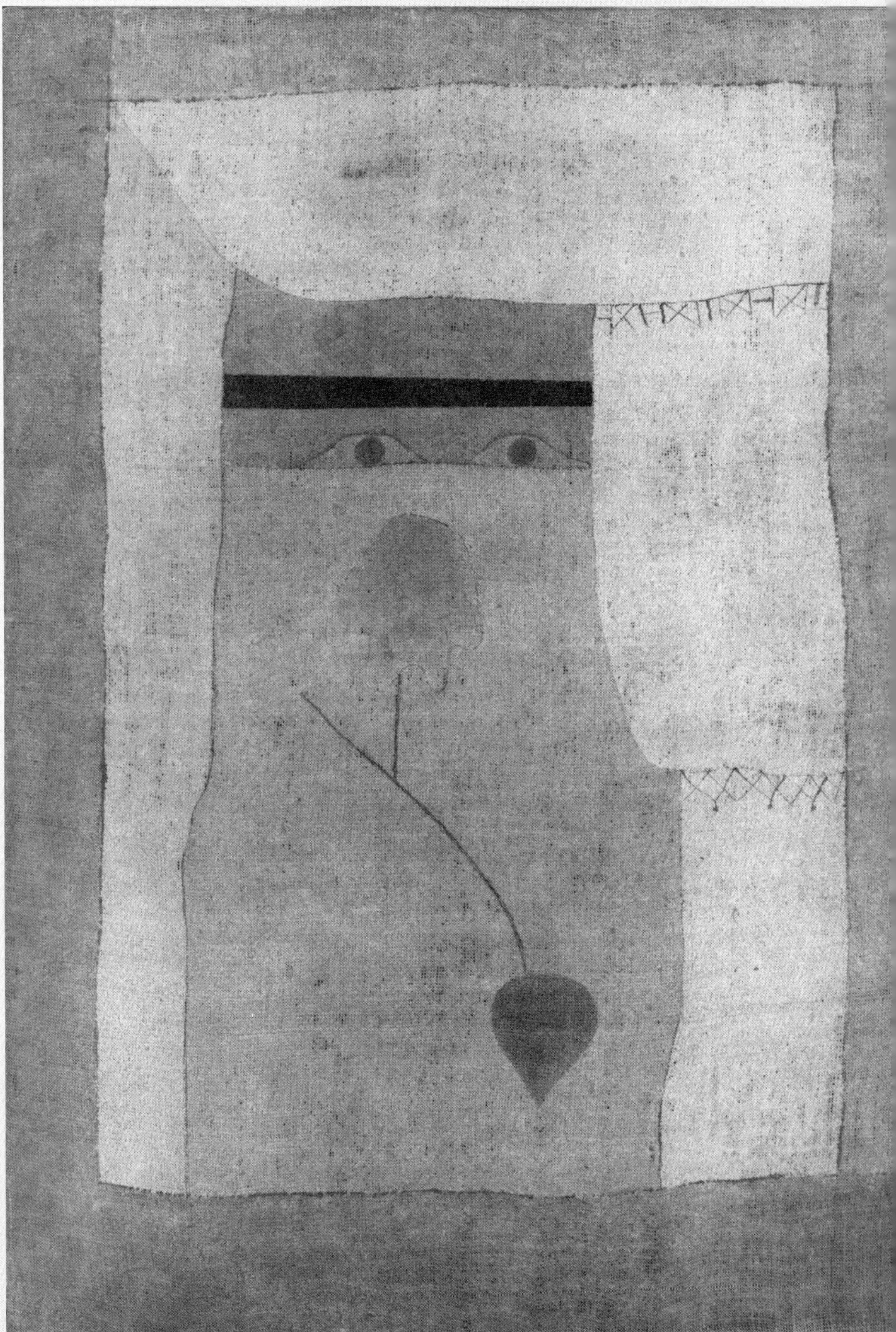

TOM LOMBARDO

Cindy's Falls

GRIEF IS IN THE EYE OF THE BEHOLDER, sometimes. When I opened myself up to my grief and allowed myself to accept help from family and friends, I discovered that magical things happened.

Thirteen days after Lana's funeral, my friends invited me to go on a hike in the Smoky Mountains. I was grateful for the invitation. Lana and I enjoyed these mountains—the highest points along the Appalachian Trail—mostly in the winter, when the leaves were down, the views better, the air cooler, maybe a layer of snow or rime, and few hikers. We loved hiking to frozen waterfalls and, when the mood struck, left the trail for a quickie in the hidden hollows, thick with rhododendron bushes.

My friend Ron called me on a Friday night, with plans for a hike with Claire, Suzanne, and Cindy. My mother said, "You should go. Take a break. I'll just read and relax." I realized that Mom needed a break, too, from our crying together, from the paperwork of death that she had been handling for me, from opening doors to visitors and feeding them her spaghetti and meatballs and chocolate-chip cookies. My father had already returned to their home in Vegas a week before, back to his senior softball team, to shed his tears over Lana in private. I realized that Mom could use the time alone, and I could use the time with my friends. Saturday, April 27, 1985, turned out to be a beautiful sunny day—six days after my thirty-fifth birthday and fourteen days after the death of my wife.

My friends pick me up. Claire is driving her Honda Civic. She pops the trunk, and I stash my hunter-orange, teardrop Columbia daypack and toss in my heavy, Vasque backpacking boots with all the others' gear. Ron, with the longest legs of us all, sits in the front seat. I squeeze into the back with Cindy and Suzanne.

On the drive along Alcoa Highway, we scan the so-called "Blue Bible," *The Hiker's Guide to the Smokies,* and select the Ramsey

Opposite:
Paul Klee.
Arabian Song.
Oil on burlap,
35⅞ x 25⅜ in., 1932.
The Phillips Collection,
Washington, D.C.
Acquired 1940.

Cascade trail, which is one of Lana and my favorite winter hikes—falls that would sometimes freeze to a trickle over four-story-tall ice-stalagmites. The altitude of the falls is at about four thousand feet, which makes them the highest falls in the Smokies.

We park along the side of the road near the trailhead, which is blocked by a Park Service brown metal gate and locked with a heavy-duty chain and padlock. Deep ruts from fat, knobby tires of pickup trucks have dug trenches right up to the gate. We pile out of Claire's car and get our packs and boots from the trunk. Ron and I have both hiked this trail. As we lace up our boots, we give Claire, Suzanne, and Cindy our perspective. It's about a three-mile hike one way, up to the falls, and along the way some of the largest tulip poplars and sweet birch trees in the U.S. The trail meanders back and forth across a small stream that feeds the North Fork of the Little River. Suzanne and Cindy are rookie hikers and express a bit of reluctance about the length of the hike. Suzanne and Cindy are city girls, from L.A. and Chicago, and don't exercise much. They both wear cotton T-shirts, are packing only light cotton sweatshirts, but I don't tell them how useless cotton becomes in wet weather, when the temperature out here drops precipitously. Thin and wiry Claire, fit New England Yankee, has hiked in New Hampshire's White Mountains and down here in the Smokies since moving to Knoxville, Tennessee, to join the fast-growth media company where we all work. Claire, also in a T-shirt, has packed a lightweight, poly-pro overshirt. Ron, the true athlete of the group, always seems to have the latest in gear, left over from his ski trips to the Rockies or his triathlon training. He's packing an ultralight, wicking T-shirt, and an even more ultralightweight rain parka. I like wool a lot, so I'm wearing my heavy wool shirt over top of a Thinsulate, poly-pro T-shirt, and I plan to strip the wool shirt off when I start hiking uphill and sweating under April's cool, clear skies. I tie my rain parka around my waist.

Ron reassures Cindy and Suzanne that we'll start out slowly, and then hike at their pace. I feel that we have enough daylight to make it to the falls and back, no problem. As I remember, it's not that steep a hike at first, with some sharp climbs near the falls.

We step over the gate and start up the old logging road. The trail goes for a mile or so along the abandoned road, which has not been used since President Franklin Roosevelt designated the Great Smoky Mountains National Park in 1934. The trail is overgrown, but still wide enough for the five of us to hike abreast. Then, we enter deeper, older-growth woods as the trail abruptly narrows down to a footpath, which becomes steeper and clotted with what Lana would have called stumble-roots. It's warm enough for all of us to wear shorts, though once we get under the old-growth canopy, it's cooler than we expect. I am glad that I have extra clothes. I tell my hiking friends that Lana and I always hike with extra clothes. No matter what season. No matter how warm it is. "You never know when the weather will turn," I say. I tell them that Lana and I live by "the ten essentials" of all backpacking guides, of which extra clothing seems always number ten on the list of such things as first-aid kit, repair kit, extra food and water, dry socks, etc. All four of my friends listen politely as I continue, "I always keep this old, blue, wool, ski sweater strapped to the bottom of my pack, so I don't have to go looking for it. Its purpose in life is to live on this pack."

I stop talking when they don't respond. They change the subject to what's been going on at work, and I catch up on all the office gossip. I haven't been to work since Lana's death, and I enjoy hearing the news. Cindy reveals that she has broken up with her lover, another coworker at our office, with whom she'd been living. But I don't feel like listening to someone else's stories while I'm still living in my own. I change the subject. I tell them I always pack a bottle of wine, and I tell my friends that Lana and I always enjoy a bottle of wine with the view at the top of our hikes.

My hiking friends seem to tolerate my babbling, but they seem to avoid all talk of Lana, of her auto wreck, of my grief, of the funeral. So, I stop saying her name and realize I don't want to talk about any of that stuff anyway because it's all I've been thinking and talking about for two weeks. I decide to just enjoy a day off. It will be a nice break for me, and I see that the trees just now starting to bud, smell the fresh spring air, and let the friendship of my friends touch me, wash over me. As usual, they are clever, witty, and self-assured. Soon, we are chatting and laughing our way up the trail.

After a couple of hours, Ron says, "We're about two miles along." Cindy asks how he knows that. There are no mile markers on these trails. "My uphill hiking speed is generally two miles per hour," he says. I agree, but I don't mention that Lana and I have timed ours at two-and-a-half miles per hour. Ron could hike faster than that, I'm certain. What has slowed us down, and I know that Ron has taken this into his estimate, is that Claire insists on stopping and identifying each and every early spring wildflower in her *North American Guide to Wildflowers.* Even at this slow pace, Cindy and Suzanne start to wear out.

Ron suggests a lunch stop. We find a cluster of flat rocks near a small brook. A steep cliff overlooks our rock-seats from about thirty yards away. The cliff is almost as tall as the tallest hemlocks in this section of the forest. The brook cascades over the cliff, creating a sprinkle of a waterfall that reforms at the bottom and flows through some low rhododendron bushes and some lower hollies, down to the rocks we're sitting on and across the hiking path, then down into a shallow col between the ridge we're on and the next one to our right, and enters the downward flow of the watershed to the North Fork of the Little River. Where it crosses our trail, the brook is narrow enough to big-step over and shallow enough to step right into its middle without flooding over boot tops.

Suzanne cuts up some Jarlsberg Swiss to make pita sandwiches. Claire shares some bananas and apples. A bag of Ron's special home-made gorp gets passed around. I'm rooting through my pack for my Swiss army knife so that I can use its can opener to pop the can of smoked oysters for the pita sandwiches. We chatter about the hike, the Smokies, spring, wildflowers, and work. But no one mentions Lana, and no one notices that Cindy wanders away.

After a few minutes of chewing my pita sandwich, crunching my gorp, I hear a rustle of leaves, a crash through branches, and a splash, and a scream.

"It's Cindy!" I yell.

"Where is she?" Suzanne screams. "I don't see her!"

Claire starts down into the col, following the downstream course of the brook. "We're coming, Cindy! We're coming!"

Cindy screams again and again.

Ron says, "There!" He points at the cliff upstream. Cindy looks like she's suspended about halfway down the cliff side. Ron calls to Claire, who's halfway into the col, "Claire! This way. Cindy's up there!" Claire swings around, puzzled look on her face.

Cindy screams. She sounds like an animal in a leg-trap.

Ron and I run alongside the brook toward the cliff, followed by Suzanne, then Claire, coming up from the col. I have a mouthful of gorp that I'm trying to spit out as I run. Ron looks at me, "Are you alright?" I can't answer. I can hardly breathe from adrenaline and spitting out pieces of nuts and oats. At the foot of the cliff, I look up to see Cindy lying on a narrow ledge halfway up the side of this cliff. "Please! Help me! I'm here!" Cindy screams, and her drawn-out, high-tension vowels screech down at us.

I circle to the right of the cliff to find a way up to the ledge. I start scrambling up, and the others follow. When I get to the ledge, I see Cindy lying right in the middle of the brook, its spray of falls splashes against the rocks on one side of her, and then flows under her, and over the ledge. The brook is not deep, barely a trickle really, but deep enough to cover her back, and she is soaked in the cold, spring runoff. Cindy lies lengthwise along the ledge, with space on either side of her for us to walk over to her. Her leg is twisted under her.

Cindy screams. "My leg is broken!"

I can see that it is. I can see the sharp turn in her thigh, about halfway between her knee and her hip. Her thigh swells as I watch. *She's in bad shape,* I think.

"We have to move her out of the water!" Ron says.

Our first effort is awkward and brings more of Cindy's screams.

"We gotta do this! She'll get hypothermia!" Ron says.

"Noooo!" Cindy screams.

"Let's do this right," Ron says. "Put your parka there."

I lay my rain parka on the ledge, a few yards away from the water. Ron holds Cindy's shoulders. He tells me to grab her around her waist. Suzanne quickly grabs Cindy's good leg. "Claire, you got the bad one," Ron says, and Cindy screams as Claire inserts both of her forearms behind Cindy's knee, supporting the broken thigh.

"OK, ready," Ron says. "One, two, three. Lift." And we lift in unison.

Cindy screams to God as we carry her and lay her back down quickly, on top of my spread-out parka, a couple of yards from where she had fallen. She's out of the running brook and its falls, but on this ledge, there's no truly dry spot. Just cold, wet rock and moss. Claire's arms are stuck behind Cindy's knee. Claire tries to move them out, but Cindy screams when Claire moves them.

Ron, a triathlete, a skier, a marathoner, doesn't wait for us to nominate him. "I'm running back for help," he says.

"We'll keep Cindy warm," I say. "Before you go, bring all the packs and the food up here."

Ron scrambles back down over the rocks and scrambles back up to the ledge with our gear.

"Ron, leave a layer," I say. "Everyone, get out your layers."

"I'm outta here," says Ron as he hands me his ultralight parka.

"Break a land-speed record, buddy."

As Ron starts back down the cliff side, Suzanne pats Cindy's arm. "Ron will be back any minute," she says. I look at Suzanne and shake my head.

We won't see Ron again for three hours.

I get my blue, wool sweater from its home on the bottom of my pack. I sit Cindy up, and we pull off her wet sweater and shirt. She's not wearing a bra. I'm surprised by the size and shapeliness of her breasts. Lana's breasts were small. I haven't seen breasts this large since Mary Beth, the dark-haired migraineur whom I broke up with just before I met Lana—ten years ago, and I get lost in my thoughts of all those years. Gone in a split-second.

"Tom, stop looking at my tits," Cindy says, almost in a normal tone. I take her admonition as a good sign.

"I can't help it, Cindy. You have great breasts."

Claire shoots me a witheringly disapproving look, all black eyes and tight eyebrows. Suzanne smiles, bright blue eyes. I look from one to the other. "This is the difference between New England and L.A.," I say.

We dress Cindy, first in Claire's poly-pro pullover, then my old, blue wool ski sweater, then Ron's ultralight parka. I also have a heavy wool ski cap in my pack that I put on Cindy's head, covering her blond hair.

Suzanne wraps her sweatshirt around Cindy's good leg.

Claire once again tries to free her forearms, still tightly wedged behind Cindy's knee, between Cindy's calf and the back of her broken thigh. Cindy screams. Claire's forearms are somehow helping take pressure off the break, and when she moves them, it causes greater pain. But Claire's hands are turning red.

"My hands are going numb," Claire says.

Cindy's cries of pain alternate with periods of lucidity, tinged with anger. Her thigh has swollen so much that it looks like a softball is strapped to it. It's starting to bruise, which I take to mean it's bleeding internally.

I have aspirin in my first-aid kit. We debate whether to give Cindy some. For the pain, I say. No, says Claire, it will make the bleeding worse. "The worst thing right now is shock," Claire says. We can't agree.

Cindy decides. "No aspirin! Gimme the damn wine!"

Suzanne locates my Swiss army knife in my pack and pops the cork on the wine. She pulls a red plastic cup from her pack but fumbles it over the cliff. I hear it rattle into the rhododendron bushes below. Suzanne gives Cindy sips directly from the wine bottle.

Despite the dry clothing, Cindy starts to shiver, so I kneel down beside her and lie on top of her to keep her warm. I wrap my arms around her. Cindy starts to cry softly into my ear, then sob, heaving uncontrollably. I squeeze her tightly, as if to suffocate her sobs.

"I'm so stupid," Cindy says as her sobbing eases. "I thought I could step over the stream. I knew as soon as I stepped that I should not be doing it."

"Poor Cindy," Suzanne says.

But Cindy growls, "The rock was covered with moss." She wails, "I never even got a grip. . . . *Where the hell is Ron!*" she yells. I pull back from her a bit and put my hands on her cheeks. Her eyes show panic in their quick darting movements. I shout, "Cindy! Look at me!" And her eyes slow down and focus right into mine. Blue eyes. Unlike Lana's green eyes. It's a shock to look into another woman's eyes like this, so close, and see a different color than what I've been accustomed to seeing. "Ron is on his way. He'll be back. The main thing is that you try to relax. Can you relax?"

"No!"

Suzanne pats Cindy's good leg reassuringly, like a mother pats her colicky baby's bottom.

"Okay," I say, "then just let me hold you."

I am whispering into Cindy's ear, stupid words, like "must stay calm," and "calm down" and "dream of the ocean." I try to find words with Ms and Ns. When I see that's not calming her down, I shift gears. I ask her if she's ever had sex with a man. My question must startle her because she stops shaking, and she inhales slowly, fully, then exhales. I can feel her body start to relax as she talks. She tells me that she dated guys in high school and had sex with one. She says that she knew as far back as she could remember that she was a lesbian, but that she didn't know the word or what it meant until she reached college. I ask her how many lovers she had in college, and she tells me, "not a lot."

"But I felt free and I liked it," she says.

My back starts to cramp from bending over Cindy, so I have to rest my back by sitting up straight, sitting back on my haunches, knees on the mossy ledge. When I do this, I see that Claire, the human splint, is in distress. Her hands are turning purpler by the minute. "I can't do this," she says, "My shoulders are cramping." Every time Claire's arms start to droop or spasm, Cindy screams in agony. Suzanne grabs Claire's arms and holds them in place and tells her to relax her shoulders. "I'll hold your arms," Suzanne says.

"Like Aaron and Hur," I say.

"What the hell are you talking about?" asks Cindy.

So, I lean back down over top of her and breathe into her ear the story of Moses and the battle of the Israelites against the Amalekites at Rephidim. When Moses held his arms up, the Israelites' army under Joshua would gain, but when Moses' arms tired and drooped down, the Amalekites would surge. So, Aaron and Hur each held one of Moses' arms up, and the Israelites won the day.

"What a great story," Cindy says. "Where'd you hear it?"

"It's in the Bible," I say. "Somewhere in the Old Testament. When I was a kid, I loved reading the parts about the battles. Read them over and over again. It's the last remnant of my Catholicism."

I sit up again to rest my back. Claire's purpling hands cause me concern. Claire starts to softly cry and tries to hide her tears from Cindy, who is nearly oblivious to anything beyond her own pain. I suggest the aspirin for Claire, and Suzanne finds it in my first-aid kit and gives her three, helping her to wash them down with sips of wine. Suzanne then goes back to propping up Claire's arms.

Cindy doesn't want to eat, but she asks for more of the wine. "It's a good Rhine," I tell her. "It's nice and sweet and goes down easy."

Cindy starts to relax a bit more. She stops shivering and stays warm as long as I stay on top of her. I whisper into Cindy's ear, "It's not going to be long." This is a mistake because Cindy gets pissed off. "*Where the hell is Ron?*" she screams right into my ear.

"Ow. Cindy, not so loud," I whisper. "I'm right here. Ron is going as fast as he can. He's a triathlete. He can run and swim, and if he had to ride his bike to get the ranger, he'd do that, too. He trains six days a week. He'll get there. The rangers will be here soon. Let's talk about something else." I ask Cindy about her recent breakup with Maria. Cindy says she was devastated. "That butch bitch," as Cindy refers to Maria, fell in love with another femme, and one day, "cold as ice," then corrects herself, "cold as this darn rock right here," simply moved out, leaving her two cats behind and a note on the dining-room table saying that her new lover was allergic to cats. Maria was Cindy's first long-term lover. Cindy thought it would go on forever. She thought she had a life-partner. She'd gone to see a therapist this past week.

I sit back up for a few minutes to rest my back. Suzanne puts her hand behind Cindy's neck and lifts her head up, tilts the wine bottle into Cindy's lips. My knees start to hurt, so I stand up just to get the blood flowing in my legs, which have been bent for too long. I walk behind Claire and massage her shoulders. "How much longer is this going to go on?" she says to no one, and no one answers her. I go back to my spot beside Cindy, kneel back down, and bend over and put my arms around her, and press my chest against hers and exhale my warm breath onto her neck and down her back.

She asks me about Lana. I take a deep breath, and I tell her everything, all the details, the call from the nurse, my drive to the hospital, the suffocating conversations with the doctors, the visit from the policeman who was kind enough to tell me "she didn't need the ambulance's siren," my interactions with Nurse McGinnis, seeing Lana's lifeless body on the gurney, staring into her gaping black pupils where green irises used to be. It's the first time I put the whole story together. It's the first time I tell it to anyone. It's the first time I hear it in my own voice. I tell Cindy that Lana and I had made love that morning, and how that is an abiding memory for me. I stretch out the story of the death of my wife—give away my own personal treasure—as long as I can, an hour it seems. I tell Cindy she's the first woman I've held since Lana died, and that I've been missing that part of Lana more than I believed possible. Just holding a woman in my arms, the physical closeness, feeling feminine warmth against my chest. Cindy understands what I mean. I whisper into Cindy's ear what great breasts she has and that if she were straight, I would feel them right now, and I wouldn't care what Claire thought. That makes Cindy laugh.

"What are you two doing?" Suzanne says.

I'm breathing as much heat onto Cindy's neck and back as I can. I tell Cindy how much she would have liked Lana. I tell her intimate details about Lana's body, which only a lover would know. I'm trying to kill as much time as I can; I'm giving away all my memories; I'm distracting Cindy from her pain, substituting something, anything else for what's happening on this wet, cold ledge.

Cindy says, "This is the most I've ever enjoyed a man's body—*ever.* It's enough to make me go straight."

I feel as close to Cindy right now as I've ever felt to anyone in my life.

When I run out of things to talk about, Suzanne fills in with discussions of favorite movies, books, TV shows. The three of us descend into the cultural detritus of our lives. I tell them about the book I am reading currently, which I selected precisely because of its thickness and its slow, turgid prose: the memoirs of General Horace Porter, the staff chief to General Ulysses S. Grant during the Vicksburg and Wilderness campaigns, 1863 though Appomattox. The book puts me to sleep each night in my bed that has no more Lana.

Claire begins to weep quietly.

RON TOLD ME HIS STORY LATER. This is what happened during our trial on the ledge. He ran down the trail as if one of the Smokies' wild boars were chasing him. He claimed he set a personal best for the distance, stumbling over roots, skinning a knee, a half-hour down the trail that took us two hours to hike up. He ran all the way to the end of the gravel road to find a public phone. The phone didn't work. He flagged down a motorist who drove him to a house, where he knocked on the door and made the call. The ranger on duty was all the way around on the North Carolina side of the Smokies, and on this April Saturday, he was the closest one. It took the ranger almost an hour to drive all the way around to the Tennessee side of the Smokies, to meet Ron at the trailhead, to unlock the gate, and to drive as far as he could up the old logging road that Ron had just run down. At the end of the logging road, where it narrows to a footpath, they jogged and walked up the hiking trail. The ranger had called ahead for another ranger, emergency equipment, and an ambulance.

With a ranger in tow, Ron hails us from the trail. Suzanne shrieks, "They're here! The ranger's here!" Cindy gasps, "Thank God!" Claire's shoulders and arms slump down, and Cindy screams, and Claire straightens back up. Ron and the ranger climb up to the ledge where

I am lying on top of Cindy, Claire still is a human splint, and Suzanne holds Claire's arms. Three hours have passed since Ron left us.

"Hi, Cindy. I'm George," the ranger says.

"George, I hope you have some drugs," Cindy says.

"No, I'm sorry. We're not allowed. Only the EMT guys can administer drugs." Cindy curses.

"My job is to get you there as fast as your condition allows," he says.

George looks at Cindy's leg and says, "It looks like you've broken your femur. You're lucky it's not compound."

"How did this happen?" he asks.

Cindy says, "I really screwed up." Cindy starts to cry. She points up to the top of the cliff. "I didn't realize I was so close to the edge."

"From up there?" he points up to the cliff top.

"Yeah," Cindy says.

"It's amazing that people aren't eaten by wolves," he says.

"There aren't any wolves in the Smokies," I say.

George smiles at me. "I used to work Glacier."

He bends down and gently touches Cindy's thigh, where it's swollen and says, "We're going to put you in a stretcher, but first I'm going to have to straighten out your leg. This may hurt a bit. But not for long."

"No!" Cindy is begging.

I bend back down to hold Cindy. She grabs my ears, and I firmly remove her hands. I don't want my ears ripped off. I hold one of her hands in mine tightly, and Suzanne grabs the other. Claire's arms are still locked in place.

George grabs Cindy's ankle with one hand, and places the other hand on her knee, and while pulling on Cindy's ankle, pushes down on her knee and straightens her leg. Cindy's scream is long and loud and echoes through my head and beyond for miles, we learn later from other hikers.

Claire's arms fall limply, and her hands hit the mossy rocks. She turns away, and Suzanne rubs her trembling shoulders.

George pulls an inflatable splint from his pack, positions it around Cindy's leg. It reaches from her hip all the way to her ankle. He inflates it with a small, handheld canister of compressed air, and in seconds, Cindy's leg is locked in a straight position, protected by a taut cushion of air and plastic.

By now, another ranger has arrived with a basket-like stretcher. The two rangers lift Cindy carefully into the stretcher. It takes them about a half hour to drop the stretcher down the cliff side, using ropes. They take great care and seem to enjoy this task that calls upon their training and that uses their emergency gear. I help them carry

Cindy's stretcher down to the hiking trail. Then I go back up to the base of the cliff and pick up the red plastic cup that had fallen into the rhododendron bushes.

By the rocks we had sat on some three hours ago, I see a device I've never seen before. It's like a wheelbarrow, but without the barrow. It's got two wooden handles on each side. The stretcher snaps exactly into clips atop the single fat wheel. I take one side, George takes the other, and we wheel Cindy down the trail. We make good time. Cindy yells at us to slow down over the bumps. She seems to be feeling better now that she's off the ledge and headed for medical help.

On the way down the path, the other ranger asks Suzanne for Cindy's address to put on some paperwork. Suzanne lives in an apartment across the street from Cindy's. Suzanne thinks for a second, then cries because she can't remember the address. Claire says, "173 Clinch Ave. Apt. 2B." Those are the first words Claire has spoken since her forearms' liberation.

A bit farther down the path, we run into a group of hikers who tell us they heard Cindy's scream. One of them tells us he's a physician, and tells Cindy that she would feel better if she could evacuate her bladder.

"You mean piss my pants?" Cindy asks.

"Well, yes," the hiker-doc says. "If you could just let go, it would help."

Suzanne and Claire try to relax Cindy by singing nursery rhymes, but Cindy can't let go.

At the end of the narrow footpath, where the old logging road begins, an ambulance waits, and two EMTs stand by its open doors. The rangers and EMTs lift Cindy into the ambulance. We watch one EMT pin a line into Cindy's forearm, and as the door closes, I can see that he is preparing to catheterize her bladder. The four of us pile into George's Jeep. We lead the ambulance down the logging road as it takes Cindy to the open field beyond the trailhead. A Lifestar helicopter is parked there. As the EMTs pull Cindy on a stretcher out of the ambulance, I tell her, "You're goin' in style, honey." The rangers must restrain Claire, who insists on riding in the chopper with Cindy. "They're not allowed to take anyone but the patient," Ranger George says.

"Someone has to go with Cindy!" Claire says, as if her arms were still attached to Cindy's broken femur. "I need to go with Cindy!"

I say, "Claire, let it go. Cindy's with the experts now." Ron puts an arm around Claire, "She'll be in the hospital in five minutes." The chopper revs up and takes off, headed straight across the Tennessee River to Knoxville. The hospital is barely ten miles by direct flight, although it will take us an hour-and-a-half to drive back on winding mountain roads to the Alcoa Highway bridge. Ron steers Claire toward her car, in which we had driven to the Smokies this morning, now more than eight hours ago.

Claire asks Ron to drive. "My arms are killing me," she says.

I sit in the backseat with Suzanne. I can see Ron's eyes in the rearview mirror, and they show a crinkly smile as Claire and Suzanne talk about the "what ifs . . . what if Cindy had fallen on her head, what if the fracture had been compound . . . what if she had bled? . . ."

Ron says, "George told me that Cindy's situation was not too bad. They've had hikers who've fallen a lot further and were injured a lot worse. EMTs have had to hike in with gear, set up camp, cook dinner, and stay all night with patients before they could be moved."

As I fall asleep, Suzanne puts her arm around me. My head rests on her shoulder, and she says, "I just didn't know. You can die because of a misstep. Nature is indifferent . . . "

I dream about Lana. She is massaging my back. I can smell her. I am holding her again. I wake up as we pull in the parking lot of the same hospital Lana was pronounced dead in two weeks ago. Ron looks at me in the rearview mirror. "Tom, can you go in here? I mean, so soon?"

Claire gasps, "It was here?!" Suzanne squeezes my hand.

I'm just too tired to care. I say, "Well, I'm not staying in the car alone."

We get out and go into the ER, ask about Cindy, are told to wait. Nurse McGinnis walks by, and I call her by name. She stops to look at me. "Thank you," is all I can say. I don't know whether she recognizes me. I'm wet and covered with mud and moss stains and probably smell from the sweat of hiking and stress. Nurse McGinnis nods and hurries away.

Cindy's doctor arrives. He's quite nice to us and asks a few questions about Cindy and her accident. He says he is a hiker, too, and that he loves the Smokies. He takes us into a room where Cindy's X-rays are hanging on a light box. He explains that Cindy's femur had snapped in two places, and the fractures were spiraled. He points to the X-ray and the breaks are very clear, with some pieces of bone sticking out here and there.

"This is a very bad break," he says, pointing at the image. "She's very lucky she didn't cut her femoral artery. She could have bled to death, very quickly. All things considered, she came here in great shape—no shock, no hypothermia."

"Where is she now? Can we see her?"

"Prepping for surgery. We must go in right away and clean up this mess. Call the hospital tomorrow. She'll be a bit groggy, but she should be okay to visit."

"Will she be able to walk again?" Ron asks, pointing at those shattered shadows on the light box.

"Oh, she'll be fine," he says. "But she'll have a long road ahead."

He starts to leave, then turns and says, as he backs through the swinging doors, "From what I heard, you guys did everything right. She's in good shape, all things considered."

When I get home, I tell my mom the story, leaving out most of the details because it's something that's so far from her personal experience. All she can say is "that poor girl." It's difficult to bring something like that to life when you're not right there in the middle of it, thinking you're saving someone's life. To my mom, it's just a broken leg, it's okay now, the doctors have her, "let's have dinner."

That night, I fall to sleep without General Horace Porter's help.

Cindy ended up with eight screws, six weeks of traction, followed by several weeks in a cast. During traction, her leg was suspended by wires from a structure above the bed, with pulleys and ropes. Her exposed thigh was surrounded by two traction rings, each of which had four metal pins that passed through the ring and penetrated Cindy's flesh, into the two halves of her broken femur. The rings were on either side of a grease pen mark on Cindy's thigh, which I assumed to be the point of the worst break. "They have to let the femur heal slowly back together," Cindy informed me when I visited her the following day, "so they pull it apart at first, then they will reduce the pressure on the traction device a little bit each week so that the bone mends straight and true." The device looked like something out of an old Frankenstein movie, but I noticed other such devices, some far more complex, through open doors on the orthopedic floor.

I visited her often during her weeks in the hospital. Cindy believed that I helped save her life, and that made me feel good. On one of my visits, I saw a pickle jar filled with water on the nightstand next to Cindy's hospital bed. Cindy told me it was from the mountain stream she tried to step over at the top of that cliff. Claire had hiked back up there during the ensuing weeks to fill the jar and had presented it to Cindy with a card that read "Cindy's Falls." We laughed at this personal addition to the local hiking nomenclature. After all, this was a tiny stream, and we may have been the first humans to give its cascade over that ledge a name. It had come at a great cost for Cindy.

But for me—I'd been walking in a haze of shock over Lana's sudden death, and the cathartic release of telling Cindy everything, revealing my own lost treasure in Lana, giving away my secrets to help take Cindy's mind off her own predicament—these events shocked my own grieving process to life, like a defibrillator would for a silent heart. While Cindy's tractioned femur knitted itself back together over those weeks and months, I began my own recovery.

I opened Cindy's bedside copy of Emily Dickinson, flipped to #254, and started reading aloud to her. . . . "Hope is the thing with feathers—."

TOM LOMBARDO is the editor of *After Shocks: The Poetry of Recovery for Life-Shattering Events,* an anthology featuring 152 poems by 115 poets from 15 nations. He is poetry editor of Press 53, a literary publisher in Winston-Salem, North Carolina. His poems have appeared in many journals in the U.S., U.K., Canada, and India, including *Southern Poetry Review, Subtropics, Ambit, Hampden-Sydney Poetry Review, New York Quarterly, Kritya: A Journal for Our Time, Orbis, Salamander, Ars Medica, Pearl, Asheville Poetry Review,* and others. His criticism has been published in *New Letters, North Carolina Literary Review,* and *South Carolina Review.* His essays and other nonfiction have appeared in *IEEE Spectrum, Leisure* magazine, and other publications. His nonfiction has been nominated for a Pushcart Prize, Best of the Small Press (2009). He has taught courses in aesthetics and in creative writing at the Atlanta College of Art. Tom was the founding editor-in-chief of WebMD, the world's most widely used health website. He lives in Midtown Atlanta, where he works as a freelance medical editor. He earned a B.S. from Carnegie-Mellon University, an M.S. from Ohio University, and an M.F.A. from Queens University of Charlotte.

BLAYNEY COLMORE

Chalk and Cheese

GRETA, MY STEPMOTHER WHO DIED LAST WEEK, and Bish, my father, who died eighteen years ago, were, to use that Limey expression, chalk and cheese.

They were each sixty years old when they married, both well beyond the age at which anyone finds anyone else fascinating enough to make the futile effort younger couples do, to change.

Greta owned a cabin on a point of land on an island on Penobscot Bay many miles off the Maine coast. It had been in her family since the earliest days of the twentieth century. Although she was as sophisticated and urban a woman as I have known, she loved the quiet, rustic old place and the clunker car she kept there. The shingled cabin grew moss and lichen and suffered the wounds of a century of Maine winters.

Bish loved it equally. But he was a no-nonsense businessman and decided the neglected place needed tighter management. Greta liked it the way it was, but she wasn't into control, so when he began drawing up plans to improve the place, she stayed on the sidelines, bemused.

Having spent summers on the island her whole life, she could smell what was ahead.

Before they returned to Baltimore for the winter one year, Bish drew up an elaborate set of instructions for work to be done over the winter, a schedule to be followed, and had a meeting with the one guy on the island who did this sort of work. The other seventy or so people who spent winter there braved treacherous water trapping lobster.

Buster (I gave him that name) listened to Bish's directives impassively and took the work schedule Bish handed him, which Bish took to be an implied contract.

There was no contact between the island's winter and summer residents until Memorial Day, when a few hearty Baltimoreans braved the lingering Maine winter to check on their places. Bish asked one of them to see how Buster was coming with the work on Greta's place.

They returned a week later to tell him nothing had been done. Greta seemed to enjoy his noisy exasperation, likely anticipating the next chapter.

When Bish and Greta moved to the island the first week in July, the cabin was just as it had been when they left on Labor Day, perhaps a little the worse for an unusually snowy winter.

Bish sought out Buster, finally found him hanging out in the quasi grocery store, trading stories with the lobstermen. Bish—usually polite to a fault—lost it. Interrupting, not bothering with a greeting, lit into Buster.

"I gave you a list before Labor Day of the work you were supposed to do and a schedule. I am appalled that you haven't even started."

He went on like that for perhaps a couple of minutes, while Buster and the others regarded him silently, expressionless, as they might an old dog. When Bish finally paused for a breath, Buster spoke for the first time:

"Guess you haven't heard."

"Heard? Heard what?"

"I don't work for you anymore."

Bish was even more exasperated that Greta enjoyed the story. She waited—not long—for Bish to repent, crawling back to Buster—the lone islander who did that work.

"Whenever you think you can get to us, Buster, we'd be most grateful."

The work was done over the following winter.

Greta smoked, loved gourmet food, good wine, museums, the symphony, all mere pretensions in Bish's life before her. My affection for her was kindled when I discovered she was addicted to chocolate. Not any old chocolates. There was a chocolatier near her in Baltimore who not only made chocolates like no other, but began concocting special candies just for Greta. Of course, they were as precious as Tiffany jewels.

Despite Bish's scolding and shaming, Greta continued her near-daily stops for whatever they had cooked up for her, bringing home a box—and a bill—that would raise Bish's blood pressure forty points.

They fought. Well, Bish fought, while Greta looked bemused at his efforts to reform her.

A few years after they married I was visiting. Bish was in his big leather chair, watching football on TV. He reached over to the table next to him, picking up a small, white cardboard box. He opened it and reached across to me.

"Have one of these chocolates. They're like nothing you've ever tasted. They make them especially for us."

I suppose it would be specious to try to make anything of Bish—disciplined, abstemious, tight-ass—dying at seventy-eight, while free-spirited, high-living, unrepentant Greta lived another eighteen years, dying at ninety-six.

A few days before he died, I asked Bish how it had been being married to Greta—how the chalk had liked the cheese. By then he was weak, mostly uncommunicative, the cancer sapping his remaining energy. He smiled:

"Most exciting chapter of my life."

Must have been the chocolate.

BLAYNEY COLMORE, retired Episcopal parish priest, using arcane and numinous theological education, explores reality that recognizes no boundaries nor is confined to human consciousness. Only, he discovers, by seeing the human place in our universe alongside rocks and quarks can we transcend our dread of extinction and embrace this season between birth and death. His two books, *In The Zone* and *God Knows,* take a stab at it.

JOHN KELLY

Grief's Best Music

"There's no other R&R station quite like Serenity Point," I said to Marianne, my ever-cheerful nurse. She smiled down at me while changing the fluid that dripped into my veins.

"You going to dazzle me with tales of debauchery?"

I chuckled, wheezing out precious air. "No, dearest. Not quite. The only debauchery I ever indulged in was with my beloved Sara, and even at our most adventurous we were well down the rung of the debauched ladder."

Marianne's eyes shined at the mention of my wife's name. My nurse loved Sara. She took care of her when Ranar's Dementia pulled her away from us.

"As I was about to regale you, Serenity Point is on Jordan II, stretching out from the arms of an emerald inlet on the Sea of Catherine. Oh, that is a fair spot, Mare. The complex stretches upward, piercing the sky with its grand needled dome. These marvelous little shuttles leave every hour to take you the mile out to the Point. And the sea . . . oh, she's this copper color that lulls you into tranquility. Serenity Point's welcome carpet."

I sighed, thinking of the way that place made me melt into bliss. The place became a favorite watering hole of mine in insurance days in the Treltan sector. Jordan II has many a fine stellar saloon, but only Serenity Point has Liguarion Root and the view to sip it by.

"No, I always made Jordan II my last stop on claim days so I could spend an extra day at The Point. By the end of the week I usually needed it. I'd sit at the dome, watching the Treltan serpents acrobat out of the sea and drink my Root. That, my dear Mare, is life at its finest."

Marianne capped off the line, scrutinized the oxide level, then covered my feet with a favorite afghan for good measure.

"I hear the beginnings of an old wives' tale, Sims."

I laughed. She knew me well. When the pain grew I found the only thing that would numb it would be a story. Travels, closed sales, narrow escapes—not that there were many—and of people met.

"You've found me out," I smiled.

"Found you out twenty-five years ago, old man."

"Old I am and not taking to it very kindly, thank you."

Marianne nodded, pulling up a chair next to my flow platform, studying the myriad of diagnostic readings it kept spitting out about me.

"Well, then I expect you should tell me a tale. Ideally one I haven't heard."

"There aren't any new tales, my good woman," I said, then closed my mouth thinking of something faraway. Sadness pinged a distant memory.

Marianne must have seen something in my face. "What?"

"I remember . . . something."

"Sara?"

"No," I said, the memory slowly focusing from the depths of my mind. I was seeing . . . an outline of someone. Of course. It was him. Flowing amber hair streaked with gray, a fine-formed musculature silhouetted by the setting Jordan II sun . . .

"The bounty hunter?" she said, inputting numbers on the diagnostic bed.

I looked at Marianne, surprised.

"You've told me a few tales of him. You do remember, don't you?"

I was drawing a complete blank. Vagueness seemed to take over.

Marianne studied me closely, brushing hair away from my forehead. "Oh, come now, you've spent a fair amount of time telling me of this fellow's exploits and how you two met. I think I've been privileged with three or four adventures."

I'd raised my head from the support foam, staring at her. "Gaelen. We're talking about Gaelen of Kaarileen?"

"The hunter with the long hair. Good-looking chap, all the rage in this solar for—"

"Honored warrior."

"Excuse me?"

"Honored warrior," I said, faintly remembering now of telling her of meeting Gaelen at Serenity Point upon my first visit there. "Not the bounty hunter; much more than that. And yes, I do remember introducing you to Gaelen in some of our past conversations. And if you'll remember correctly, I told you he was a regent warrior, not a run-of-the-mill hired gun simply tracking down bounties."

Marianne smiled broadly. "Yes, you did."

I chuckled. "So tell me, so that I may not repeat myself. What have I told you about him so far?"

She drew in a breath, looking up at the transparent ceiling. "Well, you told me how you two met at Serenity Point, when you first got the Kaarileen Solar account, fifteen or so years ago, right?"

I nodded, wondering if I could borrow her recall for awhile.

"And let's see . . . some about this Son of Zeus's exploits defending Kaarileen from the Allorians . . . some about the green world of Kaarileen . . . how the foliage is so thick that much of the transportation is underground . . . and that some of the most beautiful homes on that world rise above the hundred foot tree line . . . how am I doing?"

"Perhaps I'll listen and you should talk."

"No, Sims, that would only confuse our roles. You're the sick, old man who likes to eloquently jabber, and I'm the good but short-tempered nurse."

"Yes you are, ma'am; good, I mean, not necessarily short-tempered."

She held my eyes. "Then why the look of sadness a moment ago when thinking of him? I don't recall any of your tales to be particularly depressing. In fact, they all seemed to have a bit of high adventure to them. Kind of reminds me of those ape-man tales from Old Earth that Nana used to tell me about."

"I told you of his home world, a bit about him and some of his reputation as a skilled fighter and diplomat?"

"Yep."

"Did I ever mention Lorayna?"

She thought a moment. "No, I don't think so."

I sighed. "Oh. Well, it is . . . sad. It was the last time I saw Gaelen, I think."

"Several years ago, then?"

"Yes, easily five or six years now." I tried to take a deep breath, but there was little relief. I wheezed, then coughed hard. Marianne brought down the dialator from above and made me suck on it. Air filled what little lung space was left.

"Why don't you try to sleep?"

I shook my head. "Sleep doesn't come much anymore. Besides, talking about Gaelen makes me feel better. I want to." I reached over, taking her hand. "Please stay?"

Her eyes crinkled in compassion. "Of course."

"All right, then. I suppose I should take us back to Serenity Point."

"Don't you always?"

"Hush woman, I'm about to be eloquent."

Marianne laughed and I let my mind drift back to the last time I saw Gaelen Sorenth.

"ANOTHER ROOT, MR. TRAVIS, and I'll have to send you to your room on a hover plank." The waitress was a waif-of-a-thing but pleasant enough.

"A final Root, please, and I'll be off in good stead," I said.

"Okay." She keyed in the code, handed me a receipt and my glass of golden nectar rose out from the center of the table.

I stared outside at the Copper Sea, leaning over the sofa and looked at the water twenty stories below. The bronze waves curled in spirals, cresting, while Treltan serpents broke through the surface, their silver scales shimmering until they disappeared back into the surf.

I loved this place. It was certainly a congretory for many of the high-end business folks in the Kaarileen system, but I was fortunate to take advantage of it when commissions were good. And this month had been one of my best. Good thing, too. Sara and I were retiring in three weeks. Anxious wasn't the word I was feeling. Darn near splitting in two with anticipation was more like it. As far as we were concerned, Jordan II fit the bill.

I lifted the Root to my lips when I spotted him. He moved slowly through the dark side entrance, his large frame sliding gracefully through the archway. He stood on the great balcony near the front of the lounge, staring outside. Eyes glanced to him then looked away again. No one bothered him, not even a waitress. He simply stared outside looking for something and nothing. His repose was dramatic on the wind-blown deck, furs flowing from his waist. His eyes, hooded by a large brow, were piercing in the light of the setting sun. He scanned the sea below, his eyes like a predator bird's, searching, unwavering. Strength rose off him, musty and powerful.

He must have sensed me staring, because he slowly turned his head, setting his dusky eyes on me. I couldn't help but smile. It had been two years since I'd seen him last, and we always tried to meet when I came to The Point. I raised my glass to him. He nodded, almost imperceptibly, then looked back to the sky, which was now turning a flaming orange. As I watched him, I knew something was different. Despite the fur linings, he was cloaked in something else—heaviness, a lostness, even.

He turned toward my table and approached, head down. His walk was weighted by slightly drooping shoulders. His long hair was not its usual neatly ribboned dark fall but laid about his shoulders in a gray and brown mass, like a winter fox.

"Gaelen. How wonderful to see you."

His eyes were framed by wrinkles, and a small smile creased his whiskered face. He simply looked at me, hiding nothing.

My heart broke. Something was deeply wrong. Everything his body was projecting was magnified a hundredfold in his face. His mouth hung from his face, although he tried to fool me by smiling with his eyes when he could not with his lips. I saw before me a man nearly broken in two.

I set my drink down, leaning toward him. "What is it, my friend? What has happened?"

His eyes shone with moisture as he looked away, leaning back. His chest heaved in a deep sigh.

"It's good to see you, Simon," he said in a husky whisper. "It's been too long."

"Yes, it has."

He looked back at me. "It has been a grievous two years."

I pressed the light for the waitress. "Hollow Brew for my friend here. Is it still to your liking?"

"Yes. Thank you."

The waitress plugged in the order, and a few moments later the bark beer rose from the table. Gaelen fingered the glass.

I let silence play between us because I knew he would speak in his own time. I sipped my Root, taking in the salty musk of the sea. It was hard to watch such a palpable ache in another being. Especially one of which I was so fond.

Gaelen finally lifted the mug to his mouth and drank deeply. He combed a large, callused hand through his mane and sighed again.

"When did we last meet?" he said, trying to engage in conversation.

"Two years, as you say, or thereabouts. I had just sealed an insurance deal with the White Forest Colony, and you were helping me celebrate."

He smiled. "I remember. You were generous in buying meats and sipping wine."

"And you were gracious in helping me back to the hotel pod."

He chuckled, but it was quickly vanquished by an invisible sigh.

"I think of you often wondering how the chief regent business is," I said, trying to keep the talk light.

"Political," he said. "When is it not? I sometimes yearn for the days when kaari sticks would do the talking instead of schemes and lips that can only spew lies."

Gaelen was one of Kaarileen's foremost experts in his native world's weapon. Two knobby pieces of diamond hardwood, blunt on one end and hooked into piercing talons on the other. When Kaarileen was defending itself against the Da'Oreon race, it was said that Gaelen led a force of ninety to vanquish a thousand intruders. He alone laid siege to nearly two hundred Da'Oreon Fury Fighters. It was always hard for me to reconcile the gentle soul who shared drinks and friendship with the brutal warrior of his reputation.

"Perhaps," I said, finally, "but remember veracity and perseverance can puncture the hot air of spouting blowhards in the Senate."

"Spoken like an armchair politician who does not have to endure marathon voting sessions and intolerable maneuvering."

"And you'd be right," I said, straight-faced.

And he laughed, and the Gaelen Sorenth that accompanied me on treks through the Jordan system was once again before me. He seemed to relax some, savoring his drink. He swept the hair from the side of his face, nodding.

"Thank you, my friend."

"For what?"

"For treading lightly with a broken-down fool."

"I see no fool. I see a man encased in some sort of sadness. I am here to listen."

He considered for a long moment. Sitting forward, his immense shoulders throwing a shadow over our table.

"I've told you of Lorayna, have I not?"

"Yes," I said. "In fact, if memory serves—and that's no longer a guarantee—you were about to wed a month or so after we last met."

He nodded. "Wed we did. Quite the affair, that."

"Pomp and circumstance to please the families?"

"Yes," he said, his head tilting at the memory, "but it was very special."

"How so?"

His eyes locked mine. "I was now joined to the one I was meant to be with."

The combination of conviction and sorrow nearly made my throat hitch.

"Oh," was all I could manage. There are times when words diminish things.

Gaelen took a slow sip from his beer, staring into his glass.

"Forgive me, Gaelen, but has something happened to her?"

"Yes."

"What can I do to help, my friend?"

He shook his head slowly, his eyes intent on the glass in his hand. "There is nothing." He took a healthy swallow, finishing the beer, and set the glass down gently. He looked at me.

"The last time I saw Lorayna she had left to collect saplings from the Twilight Forest. She had in mind to make a special sup for us as it was our one-year anniversary. I had brought home some Cloudberry wine to mark the occasion. I remember setting the table and waiting outside for her on the front steps. The breeze was blowing in pine husk and lavender. Strange the things you remember."

He looked out toward the Copper Sea again.

"When it was obvious she was past due, I went into the forest looking for her. I found . . ." his lips pressed together.

". . . she was gone."

Gaelen had came upon her sash and a scattering of saplings. There was some blood, and Lorayna was indeed gone. He tracked through the night and into the next morning, when he came upon a messenger. Da'Oreon messengers could speak in hundreds of languages and often willingly sacrificed their lives at the hands of those to whom they delivered their messages. It was a high honor to be a messenger. This particular messenger articulated in a calm voice that Lorayna had been shipped out on an early morning transport, heading for an unknown system.

"I was told that she was to be joined to an ambassador and that I would have no say in the matter. This ambassador and his family have been fond of Kaarileen women for centuries, and Lorayna is from a prominent family."

Gaelen's face drew taut, and he did not try to hide the moisture dappling his cheeks.

"You're saying she was kidnapped, taken against her will?"

"Yes."

"Well, there are laws and means –"

"—that rarely reach into the boundaries of interplanetary politics."

"This is outrageous!" I nearly yelled, drawing attention from the tables around me. "My God, man, there must be some recourse!"

The look Gaelen gave me told me all I needed to know. I downed the rest of my drink in frustration, seething.

"There's been no word?" I asked, finally.

"No. Not as such."

I hated to ask, but I knew he was waiting for me to. "How long has she been gone?"

Gaelen wiped his face and sat back. "One year, seven months, ten days, a few hours."

"Ah, Gaelen."

"I have not given up. There was a small trail when I discovered a trader on an interstellar carrier that came across a royal family. The ambassador of this family was accompanied by a most beautiful wife, who followed him several yards behind in a silk cage surrounded by ten Hesla creatures, their fangs dripping with toxin. That was several months ago. The trader seemed to take pity on me but had no idea where the royal party was headed. He guessed to the Jordan System but couldn't be sure. I wanted to inquire further, but the man and his menagerie of felines took their leave."

"So I have returned to Jordan II, but I do not seem able to muster my hope as well as I used to," he said solemnly. "I fear I am losing the battle."

"I cannot imagine, Gaelen, to have encountered or even experienced an iota of what you have gone through. I am profoundly sorry. I wish there were something I could do to help or even say, for that matter. But I know there isn't."

He managed a small smile. "Your company and this firewater does its share."

"Do you have quarters to reside in while you're here? You're more than welcome to share my room at the Exquisiter."

"No, but thank you. You're generous, as always, Simon. I need to stay mobile while here on the Jordan world. And what about you? Are you going home?"

"Yes," I said, thinking of Sara and an upcoming holiday. I felt selfish for having the thought. "In the morning."

"Well then you must give your wife my greetings—"

The sun seemed to burst in front of my eyes, and I was catapulted over my table and into the next party's table. I landed on my back, seeing stars and then some. There were screams. I tried to raise myself but bolts of pain shot through me. I was disoriented and patrons began moving furiously through the bar. I managed to roll over and grab the seat of a chair, raising myself to my knees. Light tubes winked on and off, and an eerie mantle of fog seemed to play through the room. I could barely make out figures, casting shadows, what was real and what wasn't.

As I peered over a table panel, I saw what appeared to be energy blasts. From behind the bar a wisp of a fur shawl floated for a second then disappeared. A dozen or so Heslas fired again, their black tongues rolling over their bulbous lips. Suddenly one went down, his energy cannon flying across the room. Another launched back into the adjacent wall. It shrieked in agony, clawing at the implement that impaled it, a kaari stick.

Gaelen leapt from behind the bar, plunging another stick through the throats of two other Heslas. The others turned their weapons upon him. I had never seen anything like it, nor shall I think I shall see its like again.

The weary warrior came to life in front of me. Fury embodied, he slashed and spun so quickly that I could not see distinct movement. Screams of pain erupted from the Heslas. Bones cracked, tissue tore, and bodies were launched across the room. Gaelen never stopped moving. There was a moment when a shaft of dying sunlight caught the action, stilling it almost. Gaelen was covered in blood, only his eyes visible.

I think I fell backwards at that point, still weak from the initial blast concussion. I don't know how much time passed, but I recall seeing Gaelen's mane of hair and soft eyes over me. He asked if I could walk, and I said I thought so. We moved out of the bar and onto the terrace. We seemed to have missed the Protocol Units because we were never tracked or question.

Leaning against the railing, the evening breeze cooling us, I found Gaelen looking at me with concern.

"I'm fine. Really."

"I'm sorry you had to see that," he said, removing his blood-stained cape and folding it over the rail.

"Are you all right?"

"Yes. No harm."

"I've never seen a Hesla up close like that. Vicious creatures."

"Bred to be," he said.

As I looked at him I saw something I hadn't seen all evening. "You know something, don't you?"

He nodded, ever-so-slightly. "They were sent to kill me. Someone knows I'm looking." He turned to me, his eyes wide with possibility. "Which means I'm closer than I thought."

I smiled, putting a hand on his shoulder. "Grief's best music."

He cocked his head a bit.

Tears came to my own eyes as I gripped his arm. "Hope, my friend. Hope is grief's best music. You must never let go of it."

He drew in a deep breath, as if resurrecting himself.

"I must go."

"I know."

He took my hand, clasped in his. "Thank you for your friendship, Simon. I cherish it."

"As do I. I will pray for the two of you."

He nodded, slung his cape over his shoulder and moved down the terrace. He turned once more, that great mane of hair blowing across his face, and disappeared into the darkness.

"THAT WAS THE LAST TIME YOU SAW HIM?" Marianne said, rising and tapping on the fluid dispenser.

"Yes," I said, coughing in a painful spasm.

"We need to sit you up." She raised the diagnostic comforter so that I was more upright.

"Thank you. I guess . . . I guess it's your turn to give me a story."

"I think you need your rest," she said. Her eyebrows scrutinizing me.

"One would assume I'm about to have plenty of rest, eh?"

"One might assume that, but I wouldn't. Don't go talking like that in front of me. I'll give you a proper whupping."

I started laughing and couldn't stop. The wheezes turned into coughs, and the coughs racked my body in a shuddering grip. But it was worth it.

A bleep sounded, followed by a small red beacon over the door.

"Thank the Risen One," she said. "Now don't go anywhere. I'll just be gone for a few minutes."

"I'll try to contain myself."

"You do that," she said and went out the door.

I turned toward the portal that let the only daylight in and guessed it was mid-morning. Breathing was getting more difficult. I tried to even it with slow, long breaths. Not a whole lot of air was getting in. I waited for the panic to set in, but curiously, it didn't. I felt calm. Indeed, a restful peace settled over me. Thoughts of Sara came to me, and for the first time in the years since her death, the hollow longing was replaced by anticipation. I drifted in and out, sleep not quite able to hold me. And then Marianne returned.

"Sims?"

My eyes tried to focus on her.

"Sims, there's someone here to see you."

"Oh," I managed, not really wanting any visitors.

"Look at me, dear."

I strained to remove the fogginess from my brain, staring at my wonderful nurse. She smiled broadly, her hand coming down to rest on my cheek.

"A friend is here. He would like to talk to you."

"Well, all right."

Marianne stepped away from my field of vision. And then the chest of a large man came forth, blocking out the light. I tried to raise my head but couldn't. Slowly, a great mane of hair bent down. It was streaked with strands of thick gray. The face that followed was lined but still chiseled, and the steel blue eyes met mine.

"Oh my," I managed.

His large hand reached across, resting on mine. "It's good to see you, Simon."

"Gaelen. Is it really you?"

"Yes. I'm here."

"I have thought so often of you, wondering how you are. Please tell me you're well."

"I am." His fingers slowly caressed the back of my hand. "I had hoped you were doing well, too."

"Oh I will be, shortly."

He smiled, his eyes holding mine. "There is someone I'd like you to meet."

"Yes?'

From behind him a woman of radiance stepped out, moving around the bed and taking my other hand.

"Hello, Mr. Travis."

"Oh. . . . Hello."

"Simon, this is my wife. Lorayna."

There were no words.

"It's wonderful to finally meet you, Simon. My husband has told me about you and your travels together. He's very fond of you."

Her emerald eyes were accented by auburn brows, and shimmering platinum hair framed her exquisite face—a face that held you in its honesty and warmth.

"I . . . am so very pleased to meet you. Lorayna." My tears came—tears of wonder, relief, and of treasures lost and found.

My friend and his bride hovered over me, soothing kindness to me, bringing tenderness to my ever-decreasing world.

And when sleep came, I dreamed at length—of whiteness, of love, and of the familiar hand that had cradled mine for so many years and now led me home.

For fifteen years, JOHN KELLY has written over a wide spectrum. Dozens of his short stories and articles have been published in national publications, such as *American Airlines Magazine, Horizon Air, Grit, Southern Ohio Magazine, Inside Kung-Fu, Stage & Screen, Lake Country Journal, Prairie Business Journal,* and many others. He is the co-founder and creative director of Adams.Kelly.Austin, a brand development company specializing in high-end corporate writing, directing, and producing.

Lenses 10
On the Run

Lester Johnson. *Main Street.*
Oil on canvas, 60 x 50 in., 1976.
Albright-Knox Art Gallery, Buffalo, New York.
Gift of Mr. and Mrs. David K. Anderson, 1984.

MARY W. MATHIAS

Crossroads

WHEN LITTLE DAVY AND I LEFT HOME, it was to travel a few hundred miles to Downhill Farm in Pennsylvania, get our heads straight for a couple of weeks, and then go home. But in those days, 1973, the road had its own rules. There were turning points, as clear as road maps of the heart and instantaneous decisions that changed the direction, the distance, the destination, and hence all else.

After leaving the Scientology commune, Silent Steam, in New York, where we had stayed for two weeks, we were dropped off in a small town with a wide, wet main street. It was a rainy morning, not ideal for hitchhiking, though somewhat protected by the overarching shade trees. I had my thumb out. A black car pulled over and stopped, and a well-dressed, heavyset woman got out and came walking toward us. My first thought was *Uh oh.*

Her expression was at once wary and saccharine. "Do you need a place to stay?" she asked, approaching slowly, as one might approach a horse that was ready to bolt.

"No, thanks," I said, "We're traveling."

She stopped a few feet away. "We have a place here you can go to, with food and shelter, and we can help you and your child."

All the red flags in my mind were waving. She came closer. I looked around for any escape. "No, thanks, we're doing fine," I said, backing away.

"And where are you going?" It occurred to me that she was planning to call the police or child protection.

"Chicago!" The word tumbled out. Where had it come from? I had been heading directly to Hancock, Maryland, on the Pennsylvania border.

My would-be Samaritan, or social worker, or warden dropped her jaw in horror: "Chicago?!" she echoed, making it sound like the ends of the earth.

My heart began to sing *Yes, we are going to Chicago. Where Debbie had gone. We'd find Debbie, and after that? Well, after that . . . to the ends of the earth.*

Chicago. It must have been a magic word. Once uttered, it sent a message out to the universe, and the message was heard. A beat-up, black pickup truck pulled over. I grabbed Davy's hand, shouldered our pack, and we ran for it. I threw our pack in the back, hopped in the cab, and never looked back at the lady beside the road, her mouth still open. I had the sweetest sense of a close call and narrow escape. Only then did I turn to the driver and say, "Hi. Thanks for stopping."

"Looked like it might've been a bad scene back there," was all he said. He was heading west, and that's where we were bound to go.

After adventures at Lake Pomatuming, Cleveland, and Chicago, we found ourselves in Minneapolis. My college friend Sally lived there. We called her from the road, and she said, "Sure, come along," and so we did. Sally and her husband, Chuck, were both associated with the University of Minnesota.

Here was the template of the perfect suburban life. Sally and Chuck, two children, big house, decent values, housekeeper, and au pair. I was so different. I wanted a life close to the soil, whereby I could be self-sufficient, where money wouldn't matter. It's not that we even talked much about it; I was on the road to visit communes, looking for a place to live. While we were at Sally's house, we lived their life, and I pondered what my life was all about.

When we started out, on July fourth, from northern Vermont, I had ten twenty-dollar bills rolled up tightly together in a tiny cylinder hidden in the bottom of my backpack. By the time we got to Minneapolis, four weeks later, we'd spent about $25. Our main expenses were snacks—crackers, cheese, fruit, and Davy's favorite canned food, which he called "poked oysters." This was before bottled water, so we always carried a jar of juice: cranberry, apple, or V8. Laundromats back then cost twenty-five cents, and the drier was a couple of dimes.

On the last morning in Minneapolis, Sally and her kids drove us to the edge of town. We hugged, and Sally slipped an envelope into my hand. "Bye, Cuz," we said to each other, because it's what we've always called each other. There were tears in her eyes, which brought tears to mine.

After they drove off, I stood at the edge of the road feeling a vast emptiness—what were we doing? Debbie hadn't been in Chicago, not in any of her old haunts. Instead of turning back east, we would keep going west. Why? Now I wondered, on the outskirts of Minneapolis, the highway stretching both east and west, where were we going and why?

I opened the envelope—a note wishing us luck and a twenty-dollar bill. Now I wondered about the tears in Sally's eyes. Was it because she was sad to see us go or was she appalled at the depths her old friend had fallen to? Davy lifted up his hand, "Look, Eric gave me one of his new cars!" No empty road for Dave that day—he was ready to travel. We put out our thumbs and were off to the west.

On that whole trip, we were given as much money as we spent. It seemed at the time to be a karmic thing.

Weeks later, a waitress named Terry picked us up at the edge of the Andrea Borrego desert in California, just as the border patrol had stopped to question us. She knew the border patrol guy and waved him off. She took us to a Denny's where a friend of hers worked, and they treated us to a whole meal.

Heading east again one August night through a long line of thunder squalls, we were riding with a very intense hippy couple, their two children, and another hitchhiker. We stopped for gas in western Kansas, and instead of paying, the guy driving took off, speeding east along the straight interstate. We'd gone sixty miles when a Kansas state trooper came whooping up behind. It was pitch dark and 11 PM. Everyone was asleep except the driver.

"Say, you folks forgot to pay for your gas about sixty miles back." He was smiling and affable. "They're still waiting for you. Make a U-turn right here, follow me; I'll escort you back." The driver set his jaw, crossed the median behind the trooper's car, and cussed everything out for the whole hour it took to get back to the gas station. They took up a collection, and I put in a couple of bucks. The vibes got so bad, we pulled over for the night in a rest area. In the very early morning, a couple of guys who'd also been sleeping there under the picnic tables invited me and Davy and the other hitchhiker to join them, and we did.

A day later, Davy and I met some people from Versailles, Missouri, who shared their Kentucky Fried Chicken with us—as a vegetarian at the time, I ate only the mashed potatoes. When we got out of their car, the driver slipped me a ten-dollar bill as we shook hands goodbye. Amazingly, later that day, riding in another car, we passed the scofflaw hippies, still heading east, the guy with his jaw set and still cussing, while we'd had meals and money and good times.

That's what I mean about karmic. It seemed that the guy with the clenched jaw was scaring good things away. He never saw us go by; we were just another car. But I thought about that too, about noticing the world around you, seeing what was right there all along.

Maybe that's just how the world looks when you're happy and free, heading where you think you want to be. We'd been on our adventure west. It was early September, and we were going, finally, to

Downhill Farm, and then home to the hills of Vermont. I knew now where home was, as I hadn't known when setting out, thinking about finding a new place to live. Sometimes you have to go away to find out where your true home is. Home looked good from I-70, with the West at our backs. There were a few more adventures ahead before we topped Bly Hill in East Charleston and started down into our valley. But I knew better than to second-guess the future by that time.

MARY W. MATHIAS is a writer and social worker. Life took a turn when she and her family moved to the Northeast Kingdom of Vermont and took up a farming life with a group of like-minded people for fifteen years. She has written several memoir essays about those days, and the mystery, always, of how it came about, what it was like, and why it ended. She holds a bachelor's degree from Wellesley College and a master of social work from Boston University.

LAURENCE HOLDEN

Driving West

I saw the body immediately
crumpled beside the highway.
Road kill.

Like a book thrown away
flayed open,
its fur-like pages fluttering
to the wind of passing traffic.

A desolate country here
cut over, pines timbered out thirty years ago
and nothing but scrub will grow back.

A bobcat for sure
far from its home range,
its wildness of want and fear
wagered against a country of crows.

And my own cat comes back to me
thirty years ago pushed down hard
against the vet's steel table.

even now her want and fear
pumping against our hands
unyielding, alive, unforgiving.

He injected first
a sedative, then a killing dose
to stop her heart.

She trembled in my hands
and I hoped for peace,
hoped for anything but this,

then, now, even here.

So she shivered away
into the silence of things stilled.

But things move so
from light and breath, sensate,
to insensible dark and rock

and then back again.

A blood feud
never ends between us,
hoping, wanting, fearing,
not knowing.

LAURENCE HOLDEN draws from his daily experience in living along Warwoman Creek in the North Georgia mountains to paint and to write poetry.

CHARLENE WAKEFIELD

Crossing the Line

ON SUNDAY IT SNOWED—a wet, icy, sleety, and slippery snow. It was the kind of snow anyone with a brain would know not to go out in, and if they did venture past their front door, they would certainly not drive anywhere. It started in the morning and got worse as the day wore on.

My daughter, Clover, was running in the Boston Marathon the next day. She dropped her son, Colin, off at the New England karate extravaganza and headed to Boston with her husband, Scott. My part was to pick up Colin at 4:30 at the Keene Sheraton, take him home to change, and then drive us both to my sister Zoe's house just outside Boston so we could all watch Clover run by us the next day.

Clover had been frantic about what to wear—how many layers and what layers she could throw away along the course. With a pulled hip muscle and the terrible weather, I worried about her running at all. But she insisted that this was her only chance: she qualified, she spent all winter training, and she was going to do it no matter what, even though it was the last time. Her goal was to finish in less than four hours.

Clover's Story

THE MORNING OF THE MARATHON I get up, put on my layers, and arrive in the hotel lobby by 8:00. My hotel is near the starting line—only one town away—but there are no hotel buses taking runners over to the starting line, unlike the downtown Boston hotels. I had lined up a limo service to pick me up at 8:30. In the lobby, I recognize another runner by his orange, numbered bag. Each of us had been given an orange bag for warm-up gear to be delivered at the finish line. I wonder how he is getting to the start, so I go over and introduce myself and ask.

"The hotel has a service," he tells me.

"They told me they didn't," I say.

We go to check with the desk clerk. "Yes, we have a service, but we only started it two days ago."

Rather than paying thirty dollars for a limo, I decide I might as well take the hotel shuttle with Doug, the other runner. I call the limo to cancel, but he is already on the way. When he arrives, I offer to pay him some money, but he won't take anything. He is so nice and understanding that I feel like riding with him anyway—and I should have.

The shuttle arrives, and Doug and I get in. The driver looks Pakistani and doesn't speak English. He doesn't know the way to Hopkinton, the very next town over. When we tell him to get on the interstate, he refuses in terror, saying, "No interstate!" Over and over we respond, "Yes, interstate!" Finally, he is convinced, but when we reach the Hopkinton exit, it is closed. He pulls over and won't drive.

We see the buses arriving from Boston hotels just below us parking by the underpass. We should have gotten out then and walked down. Instead we convince him to drive one more exit to Hopkinton State Park. The exit sign says "Hopkinton State Park and Boston," and the driver freaks, "No Boston!" He stops the shuttle right in the middle of the highway—he doesn't pull over or anything; he just stops and refuses to move!

"No Boston," we assure him. "Hopkinton State Park," as we point to the sign. Cars are zooming by, blowing their horns. Finally, he takes his foot off the brake and drives down the exit. At the exit toll I reach across him and throw a dollar of coins out the window into the basket. Buses suddenly appear, driving by us. We decide we don't care anymore where we are—we will just walk. I hand the confused driver another dollar for the return toll, wish him luck, and we get out. Half a mile or so later, we are at the starting line.

The start is a giant mob scene with a magnet at one end, pulling everyone in the same direction. I am in the second wave, which starts at 10:30, the first wave having started at 10:00 and the wheelchairs at 9:30. It takes me five to ten minutes to get to the starting line, but it doesn't matter because we have little electronic chips in our shoes which register our start times. There are also scanners along the course to keep track of our progress. Once underway, I look at my wrist to start timing myself, but I'd forgotten to put my watch on. What a nightmare. Now I don't know my pace or how to estimate my finish time.

Along the route are big signs telling how much time has elapsed. I try to do mathematical calculations—counting the mile markers and dividing up the time as I subtract the estimated distance and time it has taken me to get where I am. I am distracted from the cold, rain, and wind, and the stress of getting to Hopkinton weighing on my mind. If my calculations are right, I am doing terribly! I am running over nine-minute miles.

At the five-mile mark, I see Scott cheering me on. I take off my warm-up jacket as the rain had let up and throw it to him. I also throw him my hat. I'd been prepared to lose those things by dropping them along the way, but his placement is perfect. I'd cleared it with Mom that it wouldn't hurt her feelings if I abandoned the hat she'd knitted for me when I was in college, but I'm glad I'll see it again.

At the slow rate I am going, I can't figure out why I feel so bad, why it is so hard, and why my energy is so off. Maybe I need to pee. I run over to a port-o-pottie but see the lines are long. Instead I veer into the woods and squat. That's one advantage of being a runner from the sticks!

A few miles later I figure out that the times on the digital signs are based on the start of the first wave, not on my wave at all. I'm not doing as awfully as I'd imagined, but my brain is getting foggier and foggier; any figuring is useless. I keep at it, trying to ignore the pain building in my feet. I'd bought that expensive lotion to reduce the friction of rubbing—I'd put it all over my whole body, especially along the seam lines of my clothes—but I'd forgotten to put it on my feet! I can feel blisters starting to form in my new Brooks running shoes. I'll never make it all the way if I don't do something. I stop at the next first-aid station, where they take off my shoes and socks and cover my feet with good old Vaseline. Then back with the socks and back with the shoes, which they even tie for me. It feels good to be pampered. I don't stop to loosen the laces until I am out of their sight.

Around the ten-mile mark I start to feel better. From somewhere strength fills me, and my spirits lift.

While running up a hill in Newton, I feel strong, running past people who had decided this was the place to start walking. Then I see Colin, then Mom, and then Zoe! Colin runs alongside me, and I hand him my gloves—the hill has warmed me up so that I don't need them anymore. Then Colin is gone as I begin down the other side of Heartbreak Hill. I hadn't been much worried about Heartbreak Hill—unlike most runners, who hit their walls at mile twenty-one, the exact beginning of that infamous hill. My wall usually comes a little later, and in this particular race, it doesn't come at all. Other than the severe pain in my feet, the rest of me is numb enough to feel great right up to—and across—the finish line. It is after that when things take a huge downturn.

At the end of a race there's a fenced-off area called the chute where runners slow down and line up in their finish order. We have to keep moving so that the finish line doesn't get crowded with people. All along the chute at maybe twenty-five-yard intervals are tables with Gatorade, water, and space blankets. People are handing out bags of food, which is the last thing on my mind. I feel nauseous. I head to the benches where the race officials will unlace our shoes, remove the electronic chips, and give out medals.

For some reason, the chute in Boston is really long—and slow—and cold. I've just run over twenty-six miles, am exhausted and covered with sweat. I can't stand up anymore. My sweat feels freezing against my skin, and as the wind evaporates it from my wet clothes, I feel as though I'm standing naked at the North Pole. Someone on the other side of the fence helps to hold me up as I shiver uncontrollably, inching forward in the line. It takes a half hour of inching along. The space blankets help cut the wind but give no warmth. Eventually the shivering subsides. When they hand me the medal, I realize that I am suddenly on my own—no more help from anywhere or anyone.

Tons of buses line up to take people back to their hotels, but my hotel has no marathon bus, and I doubt that Pakistani shuttle driver ever found his way back to Milton. I want Scott, but I don't see him anywhere. I want first aid for my feet, my free massage—but where are those things? Faces everywhere blend into the haze of my exhausted brain as I try to find my bearings. I know I can't stand up much longer. Where would they put a recovery area, a place for twenty-two thousand lumps of flesh to turn into humans again? I catch sight of the Prudential Building and for some reason make my way toward it. It is about two blocks away. Somehow I make it to the front door, but the security guard outside won't let me in.

"I just need to warm up. I need to sit down," I tell him.

"Sorry, but you can't go in," he said.

"Then where? Where's the place for recovery?" I ask.

"Well, first you go two blocks over that way," he points. "Then take a left and . . ."

I don't hear the rest. I begin to cry. Every ounce of strength is gone and tears are the only thing left. The security guard calls Scott for me. He is only about twenty-five yards away. The next thing I know, Scott is bundling me up in hat, coat, and gloves. I start shivering again—uncontrollable shaking. Scott tells me it's hypothermia when you stop shivering and then start again when you get warmer. No wonder I've been wandering around like a zombie.

At the first-aid tent I take off my shoes, and there is a huge blood blister on my big toe under the nail—they lance the nail and blood is everywhere. Even the lancer himself is impressed, but I am just glad to have the pressure relieved. Finally, I get my massage, but I still can't warm up. We take the T subway to the car, and the car back to Keene.

It's a good thing we had decided to make the trip in one car—there's no way I could have driven home. Even bundled up with the heater on full blast, I feel no sense of warmth until we get to Gardner. The cell phone rings. It is Mom. She is already home but needs to know if I am okay. I tell her I am.

CLOVER DID WHAT SHE SET OUT TO DO. *She had finished the Boston Marathon in three hours, fifty-six minutes, and nine seconds. She met her under-four-hour goal. She was done!*

CHARLENE WAKEFIELD is a visual artist and writer. She has been published in *The Best of Write Action, The Cracker Barrel,* and *Winter* (a publication of Write Action short stores). Her artwork, a piece created from broken dishes, appeared on the cover of the Chrysalis Reader, *Chances Are. . . . .*

Lenses 11
Finding Home

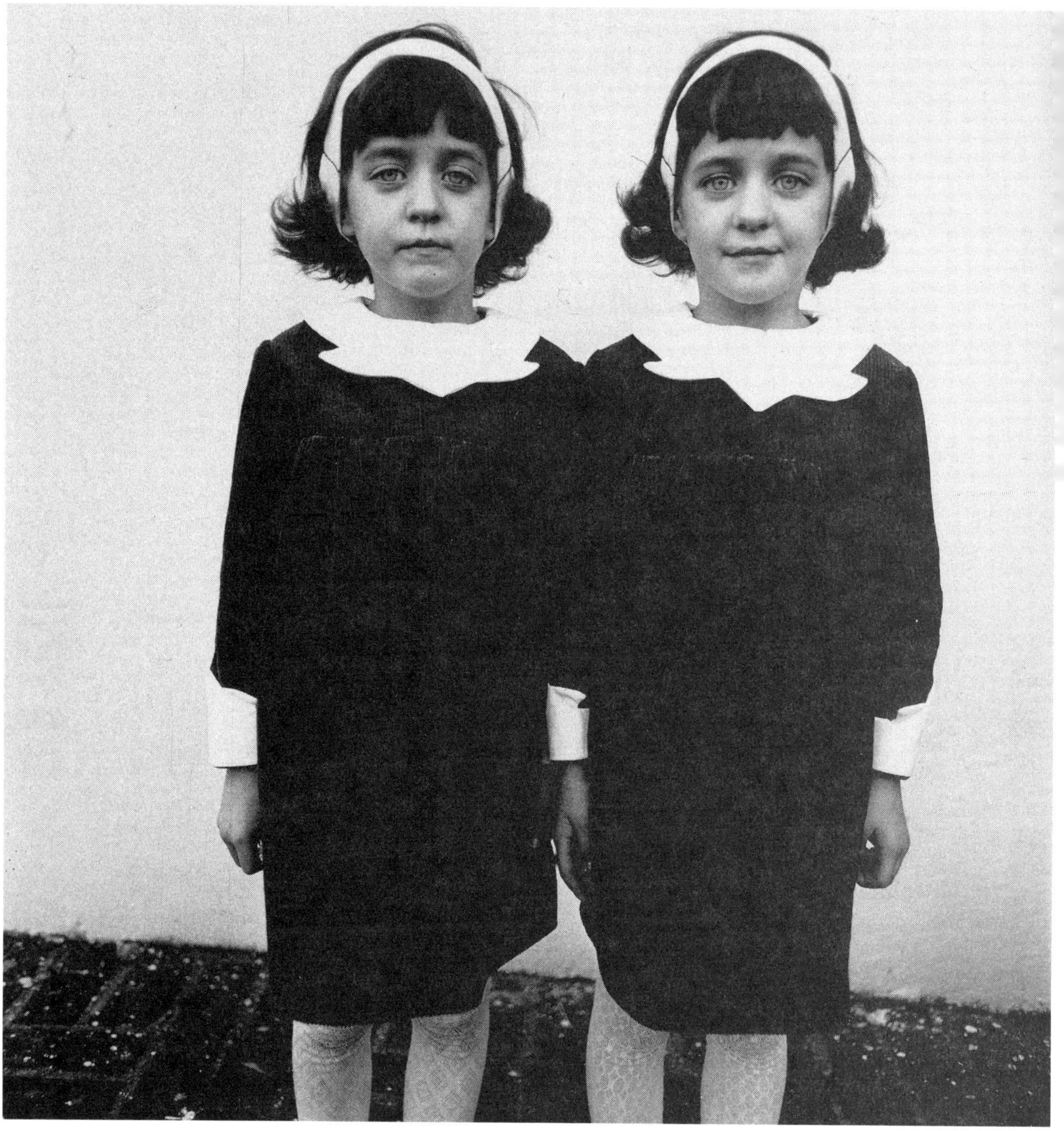

Diane Arbus
(American, 1923–1971).
Identical Twins,
Roselle, New Jersey.
Gelatin silver print,
14.9 x 14.6 in., 1967.
The Art Institute of
Chicago. Gift of Richard
Avedon. Photography
© The Art Institute of
Chicago. (1986.2976)

AHARON LEVY

Adam in the New World

ADAM PINCHNIK WAS NOT A SCHOLAR, so he was sent to America. When he was in Zvina, his classmates bent over scrolls, studying as their bodies grew thinner, paler, and more paper-like each day. This was proper work. But when the rabbi dipped Adam's finger into the honey to spell Adam's first Hebrew letter, the Alef, the rabbi instructed Adam to lick his finger, to make learning sweet. Adam faltered. It was summer; the yeshiva's windows were open, and flies had settled into the letter's sticky tangle. Seeing them, Adam shut his jaw and rippled his tongue.

Now, after sixteen more years of similar failure, Adam wrapped his tongue around years of poisoned words and thought of how he should have just eaten the insects. It hadn't been such a great challenge. In the Talmud, men had to wrestle lions, angels, monsters. What were bugs to a four-year-old?

AROUND HIM, others made their way back to boarding houses, more people on every corner than in all of Zvina. Exhaustion was a puppeteer who had made their bodies slack, and, if they looked up at all, their focus led them over the horizon back to the villages they had come from, willingly or not.

In the American settlement society's onion-scented classroom, the English lessons passed through Adam as if he were a pane of glass. The teacher held up objects, asked the class to name them, and all except for Adam sang out the words. A lefl? It was not a lefl. It was a spoon. A vane was not a vane; it was a tub.

Commanded to go out into a foreign world and know its words, Adam felt saddled with a task both impossible and pointless. The holy gossip contained such stories: men sent on missions by a God who forgot them as soon as they left His sight. At least, Adam thought such stories existed. He was not a scholar himself, so he could not be sure.

Outside the classroom, the city birthed goods in torrents, announced on every street the thrilling possibility of more, more, more. But for Adam, there was little means to buy these things. What foreman would want someone who's too good to eat bugs?

The last of Zvina's grudging coins were spent to help Adam succeed in America and send money back to Zvina. Adam imagined the students huddling at the yeshiva's single stove, wondering when the first remission from him would arrive. When nothing came, rumors would abound: he was a thief, he was an apostate, he had perished at sea. If he had had parents, they would have argued on his behalf. But he was an orphan, dispensable to the New World so that Zvina could continue its hard work of understanding the ancient letters.

They had warned him, those who had never strayed a day's walk from the houses in which they were born. America was apple and serpent all at once, so delicious in its possibilities that a man would think it more divine than it really was. Still, here was success, even for one who had failed at everything else. But how could he succeed if he did not even know what a spoon was?

This and other impossibilities had gnawed at him since his seasick emergence from the ship's hold. In a shop window he saw his first globe, amazed to discover that the Jews' forty years of wandering had covered no more than a thumb-smudge of the planet. How likely was it that he had come across half a world in just a few fevered days?

Thinking these thoughts, Adam jumped over a slushy puddle, dodged a stooped man yoked to a rag-cart, and looked around. Where Zvina had had sky, there were now rickety teeth of masonry and the arms of chimneys, splinted with clotheslines and covered in fire escapes and bearing a constant, swelling cargo of people, working, yelling, watching, pushed to the edge of air. Where there had been dirt streets, there were cobblestones; where there had been simply Jews and the familiar unknown of Poles, there was now a bewilderment of species. Hairy laborers emerged from excavations in the ground, so dusty that they might themselves have been carved from rock. Yellow men, black men. Impossible smells, wires strung up and torn down, nocturnal illuminations and rumbling trains and billboards thick with advertisements for the theater, the baths, for medications and delicacies and things whose purpose Adam could not discern. Men and women sold wares from carts and from coat pockets, mustachioed police tapped away with their sticks, glancing about with a bored violence. The unfamiliar grew as he walked and walked.

At a corner, watched over by black-windowed factories, he stopped and saw someone familiar. The hooded figure hurrying down the opposite sidewalk, self-importantly polishing a watch, could be no one but Grosz.

"Hey!" Adam yelled, forgetting all the city had taught him about hiding himself. The man looked up, slipped the watch back into his pocket, and quickened his pace.

"Hey!" yelled Adam again, not surprised by the denial. Grosz the peddler, Zvina's sole seller of crackers and flour, was a man of great importance. "Grosz!"

"What are you yelling for?" asked the man, his accent slurred but unmistakable. He had paused at the far side of the intersection, one foot arched in front of the other, prepared to flee.

"Grosz!" Adam yelled, "Grosz! You know me! From Zvina!" Adam threw up his arms, the improbability of it all evaporating in this gesture.

The man snorted, pivoted, and was gone, his fat bottom swaying as he disappeared into the sidewalk crowd.

Adam set after Grosz, excitement exploding in him as he shoved through the massed walkers. But before he had gone twenty paces, another recognition came upon him. It was Yassky the cobbler, standing before a barrel of apples and unconvincingly calling out their merits.

"Yassky!" Adam yelled, rushing to embrace the man, burying his face in the tobbacoey scratch of his whiskers. Adam sobbed in joy, unmindful of the pedestrians' stares.

Yassky's first knock dropped Adam to the edge of the street, and the second threw him into it. The third and fourth blows were not for Adam but for those watching, to discourage them from repeating the mad stranger's mistake.

When Adam awoke a few moments later, he began to laugh. Of course it would not be so easy. These apparitions possessed a meaning he had yet to grasp. Something of Zvina was hiding in the city. Would they have shut him away in the dark hold of an imaginary ship as they remade the bright world around him; would they have summoned the city's swirl of thousands and gone to such fantastic lengths only to give themselves up so readily?

He was being tested. He thought of Jonah, Abraham, Solomon; that much he remembered. Somewhere in the shoulder-thrown anonymity of the narrow streets, there was an answer.

So Adam walked. The city, which he had imagined as monolithic, revealed tiny tears in its surface. Among a thousand birds on a sooty ledge, one would for a moment twitter a song last heard in

Zvina. Two bright eyes on a receding wagon surely belonged to Zalmann and Mandel, half-blinded yeshiva classmates. It was day, then night, then day again. He stopped a man, Kepler for certain, and felt a chunk of bread pressed quickly into his palms. But Kepler himself ran away. Adam tore into the bread and then bent to drink from a cold puddle, his reflection interrupted by an oak-leaf which could only have come from Cohen's tree. The village was everywhere, and everywhere it ran from him.

When he came upon something of Zvina's, he would make a declaration. At a nonsensical corner where six roads knotted themselves like the stranded poke of a tallis, he found Ripkin. "You," Adam exclaimed, "Your cows give sour milk." He glimpsed a figure at the end of an alley, climbing over a wall, and yelled after him, "You are Dubin! You once fasted nineteen days to make a point!"

Days passed, unnoticed, and he learned from his mistakes. His yells became murmurs as he began to guard his recognitions. Work was forgotten; the boarding house vanished from his mind. He saw Kissler and Krenz, Schumacher and Green, Blatt and Blatt and Blatt, members of an obstinate family that refused to recognize all its own branches. He itched to grab them and sometimes was unable to resist, but they always ran. He once grasped Krimsky from behind and pulled urgently at his sleeves. But the man turned, and Adam saw that he was not Krimsky at all, just a black-coated stranger who muttered, "What do you want?"

"Nothing," replied Adam.

"No," said the stranger softly, "You must want something. Tell me what it is and maybe I can help." His companion, a low-slung woman in a red hat, said something to him in a stream of English, which the man waved off. Adam felt his tongue go numb with embarrassment, and he dropped the man's coat and hastened away.

Again and again, he felt himself stepping on Zvina's threshold; the next instant, he found himself wandering through a wasteland. The city's shell was as thin as a fingernail's line of dirt and as hard to remove. Almost, always almost.

He lived on air and water. His recognitions took on the power of revelation, but always he doubted his ability to tear open the world and step through. He imagined them waiting for his money in Zvina, then laughed at the absurdity of this vision. They waited not on the other side of the world but on the other side of the street, and clearly for something beyond money. His thoughts repeated themselves like ancient wisdom, twisting and forming new versions in his mind.

In the neighborhood, many came to recognize the madman and either abused, fed, or ignored him. They became used to his fervid embrace, the explosion in his eyes. He had such insistence, that this one was Heinbaum and that one Nimoff, that they would find themselves nearly convinced. Shaking off his dream, they would hurry on their way. But later, minds returned to Adam. A wife would look at her husband and imagine another face, untold stories.

When he strayed too close to their wares or their children, the people of the neighborhood would beat Adam. Robbers set upon him, and when they discovered he had no money, they knocked him over and pummeled him. Adam merely pretended to fight back, waving his bread-loaf hands, smacking his chapped lips, and offering such a sadly resigned face that they lost the heart to finish the job.

After this beating, Adam woke to the wet exploration of a pig's tongue on his face. He lifted himself to one elbow and shooed the animal away once, twice, and a third time, but after its final return he relented and allowed himself to be licked. From then on, man and animal roamed together. Adam felt in the bristly bulk of his pig a message from Zvina, one more obscure allusion to be unraveled.

Soon the city turned hot. When Adam awoke each morning, he stumbled on, his shoes gone, his clothes tattered. The pig followed, waiting for him to sleep again so that it could lap up his sweat and nip at the shreds of his pockets in search of an apple core or crumbs.

One day, when Adam opened his eyes from exhausted sleep, he found the weak sunlight blocked by a female form. He lay a moment, savoring the rarity. Women were the first to flee, often before he could be sure they were Zvina's. Stepping daintily forward over Adam's feet, the pig looked up and narrowed its eyes.

She was gray-skinned and bent, with a firm trunk wrapped in a loose black dress and shawl. She squinted down and grimaced, showing a sharp, cunning nose and a mouth of vanished teeth. "So where have you been?" she asked, and kicked him.

"It's quite bold," he replied, finding a tone he had thought vanished from his voice, "for a lady to speak to a strange man like this." He rubbed his leg where the kick had landed and attempted a smile.

She kicked him again, and the pig squealed. She raised her hand and let it crash across his cheek. "A strange man?" she shrieked. "You call yourself that to me?"

Adam nodded, head spinning, frightened at this display of passion. The pig snuffled his ear, and he put a reassuring hand on its neck without taking his eyes off the woman.

"Maybe if you pretend not to recognize me, I shouldn't recognize you, either. I've done long enough without you."

"But who do you recognize?" Adam sucked in the reassuring street through his nose and eyes, uncertain whether he should hope for revelation or just escape.

She crossed her arms and breathed out a sudden puff. She turned her gaze away and blinked, her near eyelid like a black bird diving across a furious sun. "You know who you are."

He shook his head slowly. *How could she say this, this of all things?*

"My husband. You are my husband."

"Impossible," Adam whispered, "I've never seen you before."

At this she turned back at him and began to scream and rain blows, but Adam had already scrambled up, the pig at his heels.

Away from her fists, he turned the woman's face over in his mind. In his ceaseless world-building, she was a blind spot. He had no name, no place for her in his creation. He had no wife. But even as he declared this to himself, the certainty vanished. There were so many faces that he had sought and found, again and again. Hers could be the final face, the village's last riddle. A stranger, a woman. He had failed to understand so much already.

He saw her again and was able to flee as her mouth opened, ready to scold. The street corners seemed to push them together, but he resisted. The pig grew tired of running and did not follow as readily. On a day of merciless sun, Adam merely leaned against a building as she appeared in an angry ripple of sidewalk heat.

"Why are you hiding from me?" she asked, eyes popping with anger. "Is this any way to treat a wife?"

"I don't know," he replied. "I have too many questions."

"Wasting your time!" she exclaimed, "I wonder why I came after you."

Adam started off, but paused as she called after him, "Maybe I should just leave you to your questions if this is how you treat me, Adam." There was the street's crashing commotion, his own attenuated senses, the distance from which she called. But still he was certain, almost certain, that she had spoken his name.

Her face was everywhere, crowding out Mandel and Bresloff and Tambow, all those he had so eagerly sought. She appeared a dozen, two dozen, a hundred times a day, stepping from behind junk wagons, navigating the curb in high-laced boots, chatting with merchants, or dragging sullen children by their grimy hands. He always ran before he was sure.

He imagined a return to his shattered routine. The woman was old; her skin was ash, color-leached like the city's buildings. Married? The age difference would be a scandal. How could he forget his wife?

But as he asked himself this, he remembered the blank faces of those he had approached, their frightened lack of recognition. Perhaps there was no secret task from Zvina. Perhaps a balm of forgetting had cast itself over the entire village, settling only lightly on his mind, removing this single fragment. It was possible. It was as if his memory were a coin he had worn the face from, something of worth debased by simple longing. Could there be space in these cracks for this old woman to slip through? In truth, she was not so old, merely worn, herself.

Thinking this, he did not notice her approach until she was upon him. Her expectant breath pulled Adam from his reverie as her arm snaked forward to grasp his. He looked up, then down at himself. "Please tell me your name," he mumbled.

"You know it already!" she shrieked. "Or have you forgotten?"

"I'm sorry," Adam said, "I did. I forgot everything. I had to leave, to look for work, for money. To send to the village," he finished, hopelessly, the words an echo of impossibility as he spoke them.

Her face softened. He saw that she was perhaps a madwoman but not unkind. How could he deny kindness? Still, he pulled himself away and ran, the woman's silent glare and the pig's squealing heaves dual reproaches.

The next day he did not run and, after approaching him cautiously, she did not touch him. She chewed her lip, spoke softly. "You need money," she said. "Not for the village, but for us."

Adam shrugged, uncertain.

"Get a job. You can send a little money, not right away. We'll find a place to live." She sniffed at the street. "We can't live here anymore."

"There are no jobs."

"You walk the streets with a pig. Of course there are no jobs for you."

He nodded at this. Already, he felt the world recreating itself. Around him, the swirl of the city seemed to pause. For a flickered moment, Adam saw all Zvina arrayed on the sidewalks. The villagers nodded at him, in approval, as confirmation of their suspicions, or simply in agreement at some cosmic wisdom their learning had imparted. Seeing them bid this inscrutable farewell, Adam felt in himself the loneliness of exile—first from his village, now from his madness—and wondered what compensation he would find for it. His bride, whose name he still did not know, stood before him. Behind her the pig meandered away, distracted by the overflowing richness of a capsized garbage pail. And then, tentative but decided, he stepped forward and reached for her hand.

AHARON LEVY lives in Brooklyn. His fiction has appeared in *The Sun*, *Opium*, *Ecotone*, and many other publications. Two films featuring Aharon's screenwriting may or may not be coming soon to a theater near you.

RICK KEMPA

Don't Go Back to Sleep

The door is round and open.

—RUMI

In the perfect silence of night
I open my eyes
to the clock's red digits
and I lie there,
breathing the sure, slow breath of sleep
for a minute, two, five,
until I arise, at 4:59,
to turn off the alarm
before it cleaves the calm.

Descending to my study,
coffee in hand, I pause
at the front door.
Yesterday a friend said,
"You're too busy.
You miss too much."
I denied it then, but now
I think, *So I am. So I do.*
So I go outside instead.

There's not a tremor in the trees,
no violence to disturb the stars.
The air's a cocoon
that coddles me, cool silk
against my ears.
I sit cross-legged in a chair.
The blanket I have brought
to wrap around myself
I drape across my knees.

Out of the canyon to the east
rises the pulse of steel on steel,
the slow growth of a wave of sound
advancing like a flood
upon the neighborhood:
first the trickle, then the swell,
then the tide that overwhelms
as the diesels surge through town
and then the slow recessional.

To be conscious of my life too
as a pulse progressing
along a string,
a vibration felt by every molecule,
coaxing from each
a measure of dew
to moisten the lips
and widen the eyes
in case there were something to say or do . . .

A sound never ceases
as long as someone's listening.
It becomes, finally,
the aftereffect of an echo,
the subtext out of which
the next vibration rings:
an owl's cry thrilling the air.
Don't go back
to sleep.

RICK KEMPA lives in Rock Springs, Wyoming, where he directs the honors program at Western Wyoming College. His work has recently appeared in *Puerto del Sol* (New Mexico State University, Las Cruces), *South Loop Review* (Columbia College, Chicago), *Redivider* (Emerson College, Boston), and in the anthologies *Out of Line: Writings on Peace and Justice* (Garden House Press, Trenton) and *Beyond Forgetting: Poetry and Prose about Alzheimer's Disease* (Kent State University). His first book of poems, *Keeping the Quiet*, in which an earlier version of "Don't Go Back to Sleep" appears, is available from Bellowing Ark Press.

TIM CHAMPLIN

Trifocal

"WHEW! IF THIS KEEPS UP, I might have to take up robbing banks again," Kevin Kirlin groaned as he collapsed onto his bunk.

"What's the problem?" John Hiller asked, sliding a pot of stew off the cookstove and mopping his face with a shirtsleeve. His former partner had always been prone to hyperbole.

"Eighty hours a week is the problem," Kirlin replied. "That old skinflint is killing me."

"Quit grumbling."

Kirlin snorted his contempt. "I don't mind hard work. But ten dollars a week for that kind of labor? Hardly enough to keep an alley cat fed."

"I admit you could earn more by mucking in the mines," Hiller said, backing toward the open doorway of the adobe kitchen. He failed to find relief in the heated air outside as the blazing orb set. "Loading freight in the open is healthier than mining," he continued.

"Yeah, I'll be in the best condition of my life—if I'm still alive at the end of the month. It's a hundred twelve degrees out there . . . hotter in the sun. That darn foreman knows he's got me for starvation wages 'cause I made one mistake and paid for it with six years in Yuma prison. And I'm still paying for it. They won't let a man forget."

"Well, Kev, this is 1899. The new century's only a few months away. Times are changing. With more men settling up the Territory all the time, there's no shortage of able-bodied workers. They didn't want to hire you at all because you've been in Yuma." Hiller could have bitten his tongue as soon as he'd spoken. He turned away and busied himself dishing up their supper.

Kirlin was silent while they carried their plates out the back door to a shaded enclosure formed by an oleander hedge. They often ate outside as a concession to Kirlin's aversion to walls.

Across the valley, the rocky cone of Squaw Peak glowed a soft rose in the sunset. Hiller admired it for a few seconds, reflecting that nature, unlike men, could compensate for its worst extremes.

"Sorry, John," Kirlin said as they sat down at the wooden plank table. His voice sounded tired, resigned. "Don't mean to sound ungrateful. If you hadn't gotten me that job and let me live here free, I'd a been in a pickle for sure." He still wore the cheap cotton pants and shirt the Territorial government had given him when he was released.

"The least I could do for an old partner." Hiller let it drop at that, still feeling some guilt for having succeeded where Kirlin failed. It was all a matter of timing. If Kirlin had stuck it out only a few more weeks, instead of despairing of prospecting and taking to the outlaw trail, he would've shared in the strike. Hiller took a tentative bite of the steaming stew. His strike was small, and he later sold out for $40,000. Impatience and a streak of wildness had driven Kirlin to rob a bank.

Cornered by a pursuing posse, Kirlin was caught and jailed, and later sentenced to a term in the Yuma Territorial Prison. But he'd weathered it better than most men. He wore his forty-four years lightly. The only indicators of passing time were some flecks of gray in the thick, dark hair, and a few faint creases beginning to seam his lean, tanned face. Hiller noted the calloused hands and muscles bulging under Kirlin's faded shirt—a body hardened by two months of toil following his release from that desert hell on the Colorado River. Neither health nor spirit had been broken by the ordeal, yet he was a middle-aged man without skills or prospects. Hiller suspected that in the long months of dreaming and planning behind bars, Kirlin had never envisioned himself in his present situation.

Silently chewing, Hiller realized he had no room for comparisons. His own course had not gone smoothly. Several unwise mining ventures, a few years of easy living, and he now found himself owning a small feed store and little else. "You wouldn't consider a loan from an old friend, would you? I can take a mortgage on the store."

"Never!" Kirlin said. "I already owe more than I can ever repay."

"Why don't you try getting on with the Southern Pacific Railroad?"

"Already tried. Won't hire me, even as a laborer. Guess they're afraid I'll steal something." He paused. "Been thinking of striking out for the Klondike."

Hiller shook his head. "No good. That rush is starting to die already. Besides, winter is coming on up there. With the thousands of stampeders who've headed north, every creek's probably been staked, top to bottom, by now." He reached for a soft, fried tortilla and folded it. "You always had a pretty good head for figures. Ever think of applying for a job with the Phoenix Union Bank? That's a new and growing concern. Maybe get in on the ground floor."

"I know it's a bit of irony—me, working for a bank. But our minds are running on the same track because I already applied." Kirlin paused to shovel in a spoonful of meat and gravy.

"And . . . ?"

"You know Orrin Weatherby, the bank president?"

Hiller nodded "Everybody knows him. Big, jowly man. Arrogant."

"He not only turned me down, he laughed in my face for even considering such a crazy notion. I could've choked him with my bare hands!" he snorted. "Told me I had no experience. He's looking for younger men to train in the banking business." He paused, apparently recalling the humiliating interview. "I went to see him on my lunch hour in my work clothes, and he just drew himself up in that fine, broadcloth suit and looked at me like I was something the last dust storm blew in. I felt like crawling out of his office."

"He has that effect on people. Don't worry about it."

"I'm not worrying about it. I have plans for that bank."

Hiller glanced up sharply, but Kirlin didn't elaborate. "Weatherby hires whoever he wants, regardless," Hiller said. "He's even got a woman working there, I hear."

"I know the woman you mean," Kirlin said. "The widow, Clara Simpson." He sighed. "A rose to grace the green of Galway."

"She's Irish?"

"No, but she should be."

"You know her?"

Kirlin nodded. "We met at one of those hotel dances. Husband was killed in a railroading accident a few months ago. Left her darn near destitute. That's why she applied for a job at the bank." He smiled. "Old Weatherby's sweet on her," he added.

"How do you know that?"

"She told me. We laughed about it. A man his age, and married too, acting like some love-struck lad around her."

"Well, well . . . it appears it hasn't been all work for you while I was away checking the mining prospects at Prescott. Anything serious with this Simpson woman?"

Kirlin grinned, self-consciously. For the first time that evening, Hiller saw a flash of the old Celtic charm that had once been famous at all the fandangos between Phoenix and the Mexican border.

"It's serious on my part. She's fourteen years younger, but that doesn't seem to concern her. After a proper period of mourning for her late husband, maybe she'll come around to having me for good and all—if I can convince her. But right now, the main thing is to get my hands on some money. Can't hope for any kind of future without it. And that's where she comes in."

"Oh . . . ?"

"She works at the bank. The bank is where the money is. The man in charge of all that cash is a soft-headed fool who's sweet on her. *Comprende?*"

Hiller nearly choked on a mouthful of potatoes at this cryptic comment. He took a swig of coffee, but his stomach felt as if he'd swallowed a rock. He had to leave the rest of his supper.

Kirlin was at it again—this time with an inside accomplice. Hiller had seen this desperation before. But how could he counsel patience to a man who'd been through what he'd been through? Honest toil for low wages was evidently not the path Kirlin intended to follow for very long.

Kirlin was up and rinsing his plate and cup in a bucket of water, apparently oblivious to the impact of his words.

Hiller left a few minutes later on the pretext that he had to ride into town. As he swung into the saddle a few minutes later, he glanced back to see Kirlin, chair tilted back against the whitewashed adobe wall, reading a copy of the *Police Gazette.*

Hiller had to get away and think—think of some way to stop this plot to rob the Phoenix Union Bank. This widow Simpson was apparently going to use her charm to gain access to the safe's combination, or to some secret information about a shipment of gold coins, or maybe the key to Weatherby's files or desk where he kept the combination. It had to be something like that.

By the time he turned his horse onto the broad, dusty thoroughfare of Washington Street in downtown Phoenix, Hiller knew what he had to do.

THE NEXT MORNING Hiller paid a visit to Simon Purdy, an old friend from his prospecting days who was now vice-president of the National Bank of Arizona at the corner of Washington Street and Central Avenue. He was shown into Purdy's office, where they shook hands warmly.

"By God, John, where you been keepin' yourself?" He motioned toward an armchair.

"This isn't a social call, Simon. Got some business." He bluntly put forward his request. When he finished, there was silence for several seconds.

"You sure you want to do this, John?" Purdy finally asked, heaving his bulk out of the swivel chair and sitting on a corner of his desk. Except for his quick, practical mind, Purdy bore little resemblance to the square, muscular man Hiller had known twenty years before in the diggings.

"Simon, don't make me feel any worse about it."

"Your store has been free and clear for some time. Why encumber it with a mortgage now?"

"Personal reasons," Hiller said, avoiding his eyes. He couldn't bring himself to admit what he was up to.

"Well, if you don't want to tell me, that's your business. On the other hand, if something happened . . ." He shrugged. "Four thousand dollars is a lot of money to pay back at interest. I'd hate to see this bank wind up owning a feed business. Your store is small and, with the competition from that big Ferguson's Feed & Seed that just opened over on Indian School Road . . ."

Hiller's collar felt tight. Even though he was talking to an old friend, he felt like a beggar. Maybe bankers normally affected people that way.

"Has business been good?" Purdy was asking.

"Passable." Hiller's throat was dry. What if he had to default on the loan and lost his store? How would he live? He'd have to start over and work for wages. It hadn't taken him long to figure this was the only way to raise the money quickly. Maybe if one or two of his claims proved up . . . but that was a long chance, and he couldn't wait. He took a deep breath and looked up to see Purdy staring at him, arms folded across his chest, waiting for him to continue, to make a convincing argument.

But, of all things in life that had value, surely rescuing a friend and former partner ranked high on the list—certainly higher than any amount of money. He thrust all misgivings aside and stood up. "Simon, I need that money. Just give me a 'yes' or 'no.'"

A half-hour later, he strode into the lobby of the big, brick Phoenix Union Bank building.

OVER THE CACOPHONY OF SOUNDS in the high-ceilinged room, Clara Simpson suddenly heard her own name. She looked up curiously to see Maxwell Duke, the young teller, beckoning to her from his cage. A customer she couldn't see clearly, stood on the other side of the barred window. With a sinking fear it was Kevin Kirlin, she glanced around for Orrin Weatherby. The word "President" was lettered in gold paint on his office door at the back of the room. The door was ajar, but Weatherby was not in sight. Good. If Kevin was here, she'd have to get rid of him quickly. It wouldn't do for Weatherby to see them talking.

"This gentleman asked to see you," Duke said as she approached the teller's cage. Then he moved discreetly away.

Clara looked through the bars at a clean-shaven, middle-aged man who, in defiance of the heat, wore a silk-vested black suit with a high collar and cravat. He was a complete stranger to her.

"You're Clara Simpson?" he asked.

"Yes," she nodded, wonderingly.

Hiller paused, and she was aware of his appraising look. It was a look she knew all too well; many men were initially struck by her beauty. Self-consciously, her hand went to the cameo brooch at the neck of her starched shirtwaist. She felt herself redden slightly.

"I'll get right to the point," he said, obviously collecting himself. "I have four thousand dollars in greenbacks in my pocket. It's yours if you resign your job this afternoon, leave Phoenix, and never come back."

Her eyes widened, and her knuckles tightened convulsively on the varnished countertop. She glanced toward Weatherby's office door and then back at the man in front of her.

"I don't know you, sir." She was having trouble controlling her breathing and her voice.

"My name is Hiller, but that's not important. I have good reasons for my offer, and, I assure you, I'm very serious. You are to tell no one about this. If you accept my offer, you will not contact anyone in Phoenix either before or after you leave town. Understood?"

She nodded, dumbly.

He slipped an envelope from his inside coat pocket and placed it on the counter, opening it a slit so she could see the corners of the $100 bills.

She stared at him, and then at the envelope. From his gold watch chain to his obvious maturity, she gleaned the distinct impression this was no silly prank, but could it be some kind of confidence game? If so, she couldn't fathom what sort of trick was being played on her. It was a very strange offer, but certainly not one involving any criminality on her part, as far as she could see. Perhaps it was stolen currency that could be traced, and he was trying to get her to transport it out of Phoenix for him, and then would later take it from her.

To throw him off, just in case, she said aloud, "Why yes, sir, I believe we can change that into gold for you." She reached for the cash drawer just below her.

He looked startled but allowed her to make the exchange, placing several small stacks of double eagles on the counter. Then, taking his envelope, she expertly shuffled out the crisp bills, counting and slipping them out of sight in the cash drawer.

"Now, then, what else can I do for you?" she asked.

His eyes narrowed, but he retained his composure. "I'm not sure why you did that, but my offer still stands," he said, softly. "It might just look a little more obvious if you take all these gold coins from me in front of everyone."

So it seemed to be a legitimate offer, after all, although she could not imagine the reason behind it. What now? She could always take the money, leave town for a while, then secretly set up a rendezvous with Kevin later, she thought. Whatever this was about, maybe she could have both the money and her big Irishman.

"If you take the money and then cross me, you'll live to regret it," he said in a deadly earnest tone.

She bit her lip, hoping her face hadn't betrayed her thoughts. She felt constrained, as if she needed space to breathe, time to think. "Why don't we meet and talk about this?" she suggested. "Maybe this evening. I'm off work at six."

"No," he replied brusquely, glancing around. "I've told you all you need to know. Just give me your decision. Either way, I'll walk out of here, and you'll never see me again."

Although there were no customers waiting, she couldn't continue to stand here, staring at him. The hum of voices died as the last two customers left the bank. Dust motes drifted silently through the shafts of sunlight falling on the polished oak and brass of the teller's window. If she reached for the gold he was now carefully scooping into a long, narrow leather coin purse, would she ever see Kevin Kirlin again? His laughter, his promises, the thrill of his strong arms, and perhaps her best hope for lasting happiness, would be lost to her forever. She loved Kevin, and the plan they had devised together held great promise. And yet . . . and yet . . . she'd been married before and known love and security, as well as the frustrations of living with another person's foibles. Here was something new—financial independence—a no-risk bird-in-the-hand that totaled more than three years of her current salary. She was still a beautiful and relatively young woman, and time was on her side. But time could not be replaced, and she could hear the wall clock behind her steadily ticking away the seconds of her life. The muscles of her throat constricted as she swallowed hard, unable to speak.

She reached out a trembling hand and covered the heavy, leather coin purse.

"Thank you, Mrs. Simpson."

HILLER TURNED AND LEFT THE BANK without another word, his heart pounding. Clara Simpson was a looker, all right. He had to force himself to reconcile that fresh, youthful face with the fact that she was not nearly as innocent and guileless as she appeared.

The next day he entrained for Tucson. In an attempt to recoup some of the $4,000 he'd just borrowed and spent, he sold the dozen

Herefords he owned there. He took the money to buck the gaming tables, but he lost it all except for enough to settle his hotel bill.

He was gone for four days. When he returned on Saturday evening, he found Kirlin, as expected, in a blue funk.

"Sumpin' the matter, Kev?" Hiller asked, trying to keep his manner casual.

"I drew my time today."

"You quit your job?"

"Yeah."

"Great. Then you found something better. I knew you would."

"Not exactly. The darnedest thing happened while you were gone. Remember that widow, Clara Simpson, who worked at the Phoenix Union Bank?"

Hiller nodded.

"She disappeared. Just quit her job and left town. From what I can find out, she didn't even tell any of her friends good-bye. Nobody seems to know where she went . . . or why." He looked forlorn. "That sure kills my plans."

"Oh, really?" Hiller basked in the inner satisfaction of having saved an old friend from himself.

"Yeah. She'd softened up old man Weatherby to the point where he secretly violated bank policy and lent her $6,000—without collateral. In reality, she was getting it for me. I was going to buy a small saddlery that just went up for sale. Always wanted to be in business for myself. She was to be my silent partner until I could pay her back. Weatherby was never to know what the money was being used for, but she vanished before I got the money from her."

Hiller felt suddenly sick and fumbled his way to a chair, the vision of a no-longer-destitute Clara Simpson flashing through his mind. "What are you going to do now?" he asked weakly.

"I'm clearing out of here in the morning," Kirlin said with bitter finality. "A couple of wranglers from Sulphur Springs Valley are throwing in with me. We got plans." He rolled his spare shirt around a new-looking cartridge belt and Colt and thrust them into his saddlebags. He slung the bags over his shoulder. "The boys tell me there's a bank down in Bisbee that's busting at the seams with cash from the mines and is just aching to share it with an ex-convict down on his luck."

Hiller felt a stab of nausea. How could things have gone so terribly wrong? His mind was in a whirl. Was it too late to untangle the mess he'd made? He couldn't let it go like this. "Kev, I have to explain something . . ."

"Never mind." Kirlin held up his hand. "I appreciate what you've done, but let's face it—I've been snakebit from the beginning. From now on, I make my own luck." He reached for the door latch.

"It wasn't bad luck!" Hiller cried, springing from his chair. "I caused it all!"

Kirlin yanked the door open.

Both men froze.

Framed in the arched doorway of their adobe house was a woman with her hand poised to knock.

"Clara!" Kirlin sounded choked.

Hiller caught his breath, unable to speak.

During several seconds of dead silence, her gaze flicked back and forth between the two of them.

"Well, aren't you going to invite me in?"

Kirlin numbly motioned for her to enter.

"Hope I'm not interrupting anything," she said. Before either man could speak, she went on. "Mister Hiller, I have something that belongs to you." She pulled a coin purse from her handbag and handed it to him. "You must have left this at the bank by mistake the other day. I wanted to return it in person."

Hiller reached for it, his eyes trying to read some expression on her perfect features. He failed. "Thank you." He could feel his face flushing.

"How did you find me?"

"One of the bank tellers trades at your feed store. He told me you lived at the corner of Sunset and Cholla." She glanced sideways at Kirlin. "That address sounded very familiar."

"What's going on?" Kirlin looked suspicious.

"Nothing. Bouncing over fifty miles of ruts in a stagecoach has certainly helped me see straight." She glanced at the saddlebags on Kirlin's shoulder.

"Old man Weatherby said yes to your loan," she announced. "I have a rented rig outside. Want to drive out and take a look at your new tack and saddle shop?"

"Where?" asked Hiller. "Did you say to the site of the saddlery he is buying?"

Kirlin gave a long sigh, and his face relaxed.

"Yeah," he answered, "I guess I do."

TIM CHAMPLIN has authored twenty-seven novels, the latest of which is *West of Washoe* (Thorndike Press, 2009). His short stories and articles have appeared in various periodicals since 1972, including *The American Way,* the inflight magazine of American Airlines. Tim received a bachelor's degree from Middle Tennessee State College and a master's degree in English from Peabody College, Nashville (now part of Vanderbilt University). He served thirty years in the U.S. Civil Service.

Lenses 12
What You See
Is What You Get

DAVID D. JONES

The Telegram

MY PARENTS AND I ARE SITTING IN THE DEN having a before-dinner drink. It's 1961 and the Berlin Crisis is on the front page of every newspaper. Our family has been affected by the crisis because my younger brother has been drafted (just weeks before) and this morning boarded a plane with other army recruits to fly to basic training. He's just twenty-one, a recent college graduate. My mother says she'll worry about him until he returns in two years.

"He'll be all right," my father says. "I've never seen a boy with sterner stuff. He'll go places if he decides to stay in the army . . . why, last year, he was president of his fraternity." He adds with obvious pride, "If he decides to stay in the army, I wouldn't be surprised if he ended up a general."

"Don't talk nonsense," my mother says. "I don't want him to stay in the army."

My father replies as if he hadn't heard my mother. "Larry's a natural-born leader, the only one who takes after me. I couldn't be prouder—he's a chip off the old block, all right, aggressive. He's ready to take on the world. I just wish my other boys were like Larry."

I try to let on I'm not hurt. I lower my eyes and stare at the floor. He's right. I'm not a leader. I just want to edit and write. The remark hurts. Part of me wants to curl up inside myself and hide.

The doorbell rings. My mother quickly moves to the front door and opens it. A young man is standing outside with a telegram in his hands. He thrusts it into my mother's hands with pain on his face, turns, and walks quickly away. Apprehension comes over me. Who would send us a telegram, and why is the messenger upset? Surely nothing has happened to my brother. He's only been in the army for a few days. His flight no doubt landed an hour ago.

I stiffen as my mother opens the telegram. My father can't see my mother from where he's sitting. He's preoccupied sipping beer

Reliquary Guardian Figure (mbulu ngulu).
Gabon/Africa,
wood, copper alloy, bone,
$15\frac{13}{16} \times 4\frac{3}{4} \times 2\frac{1}{8}$ in.,
late nineteenth to early twentieth century.
Cincinnati Art Museum.
Museum Purchase. Gift of Mrs. J. Louis Ransohoff, by exchange.
Photography
© Cincinnati Art Museum, Walsh 10/1999.
(1989.110)

straight from the bottle, thrusting handfuls of roasted peanuts into his mouth. He's had more than a few beers, plus a shot of bourbon, and I can tell by his glazed expression that he's well on his way to his usual state of inebriation before dinner. I dread having dinner with him. Our personalities are like oil and water, and I realize that as soon as dinner starts, he'll get around to arguing with me about politics or other beliefs of mine he disagrees with. Moments before, I had told him I'd developed an interest in astrology and intended to study it at an adult-education class; he'd scowled and rolled his eyes. I already know what tonight's argument will be about.

My mother screams and drops the telegram. My father and I bolt to her. He picks up the telegram, lets out a cry of anguish, and hands it to me. Larry is dead. The plane crashed in its flight, killing all on board. The next few minutes are hell on earth as we return to the den and try to absorb what has happened.

Our first response is denial. "It's a mistake," my father says. "Our boy can't be gone. Why, we saw him board the plane a few hours ago."

Sobbing, my mother turns on the TV. The story of the crash is on every channel. Denial fades, as we know now there is no mistake. Plane down. Everyone dead. We turn off the TV. My mother and I sob loudly. My father looks stricken, but otherwise retains his composure.

Larry was the only member of the family I was close to. He was outgoing, a natural mediator, often joking during family disputes so as to prevent family feuds from erupting. He was the glue that kept the family together. Although I didn't know it then, the family would break into splinter groups. At the moment, I knew only the pain and loss of his passing.

My mother leaves the den without a word and returns with her rosary beads.

"It's my fault," she sobs. "I forgot to pray to St. Christopher. I planned to. I forgot."

She drapes the rosary beads over a chair on the far side of the den, then kneels on the carpet, and begins to pray.

"Jesus, I pray for the soul of my son. I hope he's in your hands. He was a good boy. He always did what we asked. He would have made a fine lawyer some day. He would have done your will. I know this is my fault. I didn't pray to St. Christopher. If I had, he might be safe now."

My father, although stricken, says, "Oh, for the love of God, Theresa, stop that silly praying. His death isn't your fault."

"Yes, yes, it's my fault," my mother insists.

She stands suddenly and rushes over to me, her hands outstretched. We hug each other as we cry. My father stands apart, not joining us. He wipes tears from his eyes with the back of one hand, his expression bitter. I go over to him, wanting to put my arms around him, needing solace from him, too. He doesn't hug me. He grasps my arms and keeps me at arm's length. In that moment, I realize that he has kept me at arm's length my whole life.

"I feel so bitter," he says, sitting down and balling his hands into fists. "Why did this have to happen to us? My boy . . . so much promise, so much life, how could he be dead? My youngest son, gone forever. My favorite son, light of my life, the reservoir of my hopes, the son who gave me the most joy."

He stops suddenly and stares guiltily at me. "I didn't mean . . ." he says, his face dropping.

He doesn't finish the sentence. He knows I know what he means. I sit back down in my chair, tears still streaming. Strangely, or perhaps not so strangely, the hug I didn't get from him the day my brother died has remained as fresh in my mind as the moment it did not happen. It has haunted my dreams and my memories. Even though I'm much older now, time has a way of stopping and snapping a photo of an incident that sums up a relationship, forever etching that image in one's mind.

My mother kneels again, her eyes on the rosary.

"Father, I am heartily sorry for having offended thee. I am no longer. . . ."

My father goes to her, anger and bitterness distorting his features. "Will you stop that nonsense. There is no God. I found that out when I was a boy. I nearly wore out the rug in my bedroom praying when I was hungry and wanted more food. Get rid of the fantasy that this was your fault. It was an accident. For heaven's sake, get your wits about you."

My mother continues to kneel, her eyes on her rosary beads, her hands clasped in front of her. She casts a withering glance over her shoulder at my father.

"Your atheistic ideas poisoned the minds of all our sons. Larry didn't believe in God because of you, and because of that who knows where his soul is now? I don't want him to spend the rest of eternity in purgatory. I want to pray he joins Jesus in heaven. He might still be alive today if he hadn't left the Faith. God takes care of His own. If he'd have had the faith I have, if he hadn't left the Church, he might be alive today. I . . ."

"Don't blame what happened on me," my father shouts, clasping and unclasping his hands.

I go to my mother and try to raise her off her knees. "Mother, let's grieve together. We can't talk while you kneel and pray aloud. You can pray by yourself later."

I gently put one hand on her shoulder, but she shrugs me off.

"You're like your father. You don't believe. What comfort can you be to me? No more of a comfort than he is. I need to pray now, not later, for the soul of my son and for forgiveness for my sins, which are many. I'll never forgive myself for not praying to St. Christopher."

"Oh, leave her alone," my father says. "What is there to say, anyway? Our son is gone."

"Mother, please get off your knees and talk with us."

She ignores the remark and continues to pray.

"God, I'm heartily sorry for offending thee. I'm not worthy to be one of your children. I'm a sinner. That's why you've brought this travail on me. I know I've never been virtuous in your eyes, but I want you to know I've always tried to be as good as you want me to be. Give me strength now to carry on and to face what I must. I want only to embrace Jesus, to be his disciple, to do His will. Ask your only son to help me through this tragedy."

"Oh, for the love of God!" my father says.

He goes behind the bar, opens its small refrigerator and takes out another Rolling Rock. He returns to his seat and takes a long swig. I stare at my mother, worried about her sanity, knowing that she might tip over the edge at any moment.

"Did you take your pills today, mother?" I ask.

"I don't need to take pills," she snaps. "I don't believe in psychiatrists and I never will. I'll never go back to that man. All those people want is to take your money."

My mother lets out an anguished cry. "Only Jesus can make me happy now," she says, performing the sign of the cross. "I know He'll come again and rid the world of sin. I especially pray that He forgives my sins and the sins of those in this family who have tried so hard to make me doubt your existence. Lord, I know only too well that I won't be whole again until Christ comes again. Please let that happen, because He, like you, has all power and can bring my son back to life. I want to be united with Larry, who, unlike me, was innocent and without sin. Oh, if I could only have died in his place! Bring Jesus back to save us, dear God. I praise His name and your name."

"Theresa, aren't you cooking something on the stove?" my father says.

"That can wait," my mother responds, clasping her hands even more fervently. "I want to pray now, for we can only absolve ourselves through prayer. I want to keep praying for the Second Coming of Christ, for only then will I be truly happy again."

My mother wore black for an entire year after my brother's death, going to church frequently to pray for his soul. Death ends a life, but it doesn't end a relationship. In the fifty years that have gone by since my brother died, hardly a day goes by when I don't think of him. No one can know the repercussions of a death in the family. Afterwards, our family, which had once been close-knit, if often dysfunctional, splintered into factions. My father and my oldest brother became close. My mother and I—well—I can't say we ever became close, but we did talk more. In any case, the basic unity of the family was gone. My father became even more bitter about life, and my mother became even more religious. As for myself, I retreated into a self-imposed isolation that lasted for many years. My brother had not only been my brother, he had been my best friend. I felt lost without him. He was the only member of the family I could really relate to. I often wonder how my life would have turned out had he lived. But "what ifs" can cause the sting of loss to hurt even more. We must carry on through our hurt and our tears, for life goes on and waits for no one.

DAVID JONES worked as a technical editor for a Philadelphia publishing company. After retiring in 2001, he became the astrology columnist for a San Francisco newspaper and taught astrology at a community college. He composes hymns for his Unitarian-Universalist church in suburban Philadelphia. David's short stories have appeared in various literary magazines, including *Spitball* and *Dogwood Tales.* His nonfiction has been published in *American Astrology, Horoscope, the Mountain Astrologer,* and elsewhere.

LINDA PASTAN

The Refusal

In this season of endings,
I have started to build a house.
At this time when "goodbye" repeats
its refrain after every verse,
I have chosen a song
without stanzas.
If the earth opens for a grave,
I will use the hole to plant a tree.
If you tell me you must leave,
I will bar the door.

LINDA PASTAN's twelfth book of poems, *Queen of a Rainy Country,* was published by W.W. Norton in 2006. She was poet laureate of Maryland from 1991 to 1995 and has been a finalist twice for the National Book Award. In 2003 she won the Ruth Lilly Poetry Prize.

D. JEANNE WILSON

My Uncle the Failure

I WISH THE RIDE TO THE PARK TOOK LONGER, but in no time we are in the parking lot of Cedar Creek Park, backed up beside Uncle Ken's old green Ford. He is helping Grandmother Cochran from Martin's car and into her wheelchair.

"I'd think Ken would wash his car before the reunion," Mom says.

"It probably looks better hidden under dirt," Dad tells her.

Mom folds down her visor mirror to smile at herself while Dad pats the dashboard of our new Cutlass Supreme like a pet collie.

I look out the back window to see cousins running all over the place. My stomach feels sick. Last year they ran around me as if I had been a ghost. Maybe today they'll play with me since I'm a year older, but I doubt it.

Amy, Uncle Ken's girl, is as young as I am, but we never see her so she doesn't count. I think Uncle had a bad wife who stole Amy away from him, but Mother says we don't talk about that.

If my mother had told Uncle what to wear, he would not be in faded tan pants and a flowered shirt hanging loose. "Well, here's my little Dancy Nancy," he yells, coming toward us with his green shirt flapping. He lifts me, and we whirl about the parking lot. Around and around we go, my hair flying about my face, my breath coming in gasps and giggles, the park spinning by in a fuzzy green blur.

He dances me up to Grandmother Cochran. Her face looks old, even for a grandmother. Her hair is still pretty, soft and white.

"Momsie," Uncle says, "look who I found riding on a bluebird wing. I picked her off so she could come to this grand reunion."

Grandmother smiles, but since her stroke she can't speak. I hug her, but I'm scared. She used to smell like lilacs and be big and soft, but now she smells like our medicine cabinet, and I can feel bones. It would be awful to break one.

The hug over, I look up and see Aunt Olive and Mother coming toward us.

Aunt has stiff black hair and sharp eyebrows. Her gold bracelets jangle when she pats my head. "How are you, little Nancy?" she asks.

I stand as tall as I can and start to tell her I am seven, but she turns away before I can speak. Leaning toward Grandmother, she kisses her. Aunt's shiny red lips make a smacking sound, but they don't touch Grandmother's white cheek.

My mother's hand moves softly across Grandmother's head, her rings sparkling, and her fingers tapping as though they say, "I love you, Mother Edith." My mother loves everyone, even me, some of the time. She works hard to see that I don't grow up a failure.

"Be friendlier," she had said as we drove to the reunion. "Don't wander off by yourself."

I want to be friendly, and sometimes I think up good words to say, but before I get them out someone else talks. This year I will not hide in the restroom but will go everyplace the cousins go. My mother will be proud of me.

Uncle Oshel and Dad come poking up to us and hug Grandmother. My father, a tall man with a closed-up face, often looks past me when I talk to him as if he is trying to see all nine of his computer stores. Now, he looks right at Uncle Oshel. Of course, Uncle is a grownup and says important things. During the week Uncle Oshel flies all over the place and bosses people. Then on Sundays he paints in oils. Uncle Ken doesn't have anyone to boss, and the only thing he paints is his beer joint. That beer joint is part of the reason he is our failure.

Now Uncle Oshel starts to speak to me, but Aunt Olive interrupts by talking about their trip to Hawaii. "Gorgeous flowers. Lovely beaches."

"Fine golf courses," Uncle Oshel adds.

"It was Disney for us this year," Dad says.

I look up past Uncle Ken's drooping socks, rumpled slacks, and flowered shirt to his sad face. He probably wanted to go to Disney World, but failures don't travel much.

"Ken," Aunt Olive says, "I was so hoping to see dear little Amy. Doesn't she enjoy our gatherings?"

Uncle doesn't seem to hear her, for he looks at the ground and doesn't answer. Other grownups gather around until Grandmother and I are in a tunnel of legs. Close by, swings creak and cousins yell to each other. When a cousin jumps from a swing, leaving it to sway above worn-off grass, I slip between the circle of legs and run to grab it. Scooting onto the swing board, I push off, tugging the chains. The swing begins to lift, air cools my face, and with each pull of the chains the words "Dancy Nancy" sing in my head.

Dancy Nancy is not as good as Beet Top, Big Moose, or Stud, names other cousins have, but any nickname helps. None of my cousins play the piano or sew silly flowers on cloth the way I must do. They are into yelling and chasing each other. They also play on the swings, and last year I was the only one who needed a push.

Now, I start the swing by myself and pump until the chains reach out flat as I enjoy the good smell of oil and metal. Cousins swing, laugh, call to each other, and I'm in the middle flying closer and closer to the clouds. As I lean back for a hard pull on the chains, my shiny, black shoes stick out before me.

"I want to wear my Nikes," I had told Mother when we were dressing for the reunion.

"They are worn out, Nancy," she said. "All your relatives will be there. Wear your good shoes."

White canvas shoes sway on each side of me. Only mine shine black in the sunlight for all of the cousins to see. Folding my legs, I hide the shoes under my swing board. The swing begins to slow. I jump while the ground moves beneath me and hope the cousins notice I did not fall.

Men are moving tables into a row so we can eat together—us Martins, the Sweeneys, the Cochrans, the Thurmans, and the Hunts.

Women spread out bright cloths, making the tables look like quilts. I had been too worried about the reunion to eat breakfast and now the smells of fried chicken and baked beans cause my stomach to rumble. Here is a cake, round as the moon with swirls of chocolate icing, but I am not allowed to have any yet.

Uncle Ken puts three cartons of Foodland potato salad on the table. Aunt Olive scoots them out of the way to make room for her bowl of potato salad with its green ruffle of lettuce. When everything is ready, we line up and move around the table to fill plates and then find a place to sit

My mother watches me. "Nancy, don't you want to eat with the other children?"

My cousins sit on the ground in small groups, talking and laughing. A Sweeny cousin throws a grape at a Martin cousin, who catches it in his mouth. If I joined them, someone would say, "Yuck. Here's baby Nancy." I drag my fork through potato salad. "I want to eat at the table," I mumble.

My mother's eyes scrunch up and her mouth looks stiff the way it does when Dad drives too fast. I'm worrying her, so I carry my plate to a patch of shade where Uncle Ken has parked Grandmother's wheelchair. He had asked to be the one to feed her because he doesn't have money to visit often. Now, his flowered shirt floats forward as he leans with a bite of applesauce.

I sit on the grass beside Grandmother's chair, her thin legs—tan sticks. I know she can't stand or talk, but can she still think? Can she still love me? If only my grandmother could talk. "Grandmother," I would ask, "How do you feel when everyone talks around you as if you aren't even here?"

"Nancy, child," she might answer, "I feel like a stick."

"That's how I feel when the cousins don't talk to me," I would tell her. Grandmother might pull me onto her lap and hug me. That's what she used to do.

A row of black ants crawls through the grass at my feet. No one wants ants at a picnic. I know how they feel and lean over to crumble bread in their path.

I'm more comfortable with Grandmother and Uncle Ken than at the table with my mother, who would want me to be someplace else. I take a bite of beans. They are sweet with brown sugar. Aunt's potato salad with boiled eggs and orange stuff on top is good. No one has opened Uncle Ken's Foodland cartons.

On my way to get dessert, I notice the empty swings. If I take time to eat chocolate cake the cousins might grab them all, and I want to swing higher than anybody. A cousin might look right at me and say, "Way to go, Nancy."

I pour iced tea on my shoes, pat on dust to hide the shine, and then walk carefully to a swing. Some dust falls off, so I spit on my shoes and sprinkle more. I start to swing, but the cousins aren't watching. They are holding hands in a circle on a wide space of grass.

Uncle Ken parks Grandmother beside my mother, grabs a piece of cake and while eating it, comes huffing toward me. "Come on, Nancy," he says, swishing crumbs from his shirt. "Let's play dodgeball with the others."

"No." I push hard with my feet to start the swing. More dust falls from my shoes, but I don't care. "I hate dodgeball."

If I played, no one would throw the ball at me. No one would see me standing there like a stick. If they did bother to look at me, they would only see my dumb playsuit with a strip of lace across the pocket.

Uncle's big freckled hands stop the swing. "Come on, Dancy Nancy," he insists.

I follow him across the grass. The kids will not want either of us. My uncle, the failure, will play dodgeball while other grownups talk of important things.

We join the circle and right away Uncle grabs the ball and then throws it at me. "Catch it, Amy," he yells. Why did he call me Amy? There is no time to ask, for I'm in the middle of cousins as we yell, run, throw, slide in the dirt. The lace on my pocket tears. I taste dust, and my sweaty playsuit sticks to me.

"What can we play next?" I ask Uncle when the game is over.

He wipes his damp forehead with the tail of his shirt. His chest goes up and down with fast breaths. "Next, I head for home, Dancy Nancy," he finally says.

A cousin throws the ball toward us. He is almost as tall as Uncle but not as big around. His arm is big, though, and the ball hits the ground hard, sending up puffs of dust. "Hey, Ken Man, don't leave," he yells.

Another cousin, his red hair bouncing, grabs the ball, whirls around, tosses it into the air, and then catches it when it falls. "Yeah, Ken Man," he says. "Play volleyball with us."

Several others circle us, joking, talking, as if they like Uncle Ken. My Uncle Ken. He explains it's two hundred miles down I-79 to the Sand Valley exit and another fifty to his home. Saturday is an important night for the beer joint.

We leave the group, and Uncle Ken shakes hands with Uncle Oshel and Dad, and then hugs Mom. He hugs Grandmother for a long time and then turns to me. Kneeling, he looks into my eyes. That look means something, but I don't know what. His big hands hold my arms tight, and I don't want him to let go, but he does.

His car is the only one dusty enough to write on, and cousins have covered it with names. If only I had written "Dancy Nancy" in big letters so he would not forget me. I swallow, but I don't cry. I'm not a baby. At the car door, Uncle turns to look at Grandmother again. His face is still red from the game; his thin hair almost a Halloween wig. Dirt and sweat streak his shirt. He climbs into the car, and the door clicks shut. The motor chugs, then dies, chugs again, and then dies.

Aunt Olive rolls her eyes. "Leave it to Ken," she says.

"Do you have a set of jumper cables?" Dad asks Uncle Oshel.

Aunt Olive butts in. "Why on earth would Oshel need jumper cables? Our Cadillac came with roadside assistance."

My father sighs. "Well, maybe someone will have a set." He and Uncle Oshel wander off to find cables.

Uncle Ken sits behind his steering wheel trying, again and again, to start the car. My face feels hot, and I begin to cry. I don't want Dad or Uncle Oshel to give my Uncle Ken a start from their cars. I remember how it felt last year to be the only one who needed a push on the swing. It will be one more way for my uncle to be a failure.

I run down the grassy bank, across the sidewalk, and throw myself against the trunk of Uncle's car. I push until my arms shake. I shove with my body. The car will not move.

Push! Push! Push! The words are inside me, for I'm crying too hard to speak. *Push! Push!* I am a mouse pushing a mountain. Furious to be so small, I beat on the trunk until my fists hurt, then close my eyes and try again. "*Push! Push!*" I yell, as if being loud will make me more powerful.

"Way to go, Nance."

I open my eyes to see a Martin cousin pushing beside me. A Thurman cousin appears on the other side. "*Push. Push. Push,*" we call, and now other cousins come running—the rest of the Martins and Thurmans, joined by the Hunts and the Sweeneys. Shoving, chanting cousins cover the back and both sides of Uncle's Ford.

"*Push. Push. Push.*" Our voices are together, like a choir, and on each word we give our best shove. Finally, the car begins to creep forward, slowly rolling, rolling. Encouraged, we yell louder, *push harder.* Fast and yet faster we run, our feet pounding cement, the road a gray blur skimming beneath us. My breath is loud. My heart is loud.

Continuing to run, we finally hear the engine chug. Exhaust fumes sting my nose, and my legs hurt, but I run with the others until the car's speed forces us to stop. Standing in the middle of the road we cheer, clap our hands, and jump up and down. As Uncle disappears around a bend, he blows his car horn again and again. It reminds me of horns blown at a ball game after our high school team makes a touchdown. I rub an arm across my wet face. My legs shake, and I look for a place to sit.

"Come on, Nancy," a Sweeney cousin calls. The others had started back to the reunion, but they turn and wait for me. *Me! Dancy Nancy!* I take a big breath and run toward them.

Because of years as a parent, foster parent, elementary school teacher, principal of a primary center, Girl Scouts and 4-H leader, D. JEANNE WILSON often hears the voices of children when she writes. Her work has appeared in religious and literary publications such as *Seeking the Swan, St. Anthony Messenger,* and *Appalachian Heritage.* Both her fiction and poetry have won prizes in the West Virginia Annual Competition, Scribendi Fiction International, Alabama Writer's Conference, and other competitions.

ARLENE DISTLER

The Case against Mums

I refuse to plant mums,
or set them apron-prim
in pots along my walk.
What have they to say
that hasn't been said before?

I prefer autumn's tawdry mix
of unkempt rows,
sunflower's swollen prose,
stripped-down lily's
arcs of green
turned shadowy wisps,

maple leaves' last fling
with sun,
doomed to fatal swoon
when day's done.

I'd rather not
extend the reign
of the floral domain
with stingy pots
of color spots
when wild fall is all about—
the straggly romance
of late-blooming petunia

twined in Glory blue,
promiscuous phlox
in all its hues,
milkweed's blousy tufts
drifted who knows where.

The day bud's last flower
is all I need of the hour.

ARLENE DISTLER is active in the Brattleboro, Vermont, literary community as co-founder of Write Action, a support and networking organization for writers. A freelance writer, primarily for the arts in Vermont newspapers and magazines, she was a finalist for the James Hearst Poetry Award and has been published in a number of journals, including *Kalliope* and *North American Review.*

Swedenborg Foundation Publishers

BOOKS by Emanuel Swedenborg (1688–1772) have been treasured by countless writers, thinkers, and artists over the past 250 years. Jung, Blake, Goethe, Emerson, Dostoevsky, Helen Keller, Yeats, and Borges, for example, were all profoundly influenced by the Swedish mystic. Founded in 1849, the Swedenborg Foundation fosters broad engagement with Swedenborg's writings. We publish books by and about Swedenborg as well as books (like this Chrysalis Reader) that explore spiritual dimensions of contemporary life.

After almost 150 years of publishing in New York City, the Foundation moved, in 1993, to West Chester, Pennsylvania, where new headquarters were established in a historic building at 320 North Church Street.

The eighteenth-century building (below) is where the Foundation now manages its publishing operations and where we also support translation projects, conferences, lectures, and a research library.

SWEDENBORG FOUNDATION PUBLISHERS, NEW YORK CITY

The Swedenborg Foundation was originally located in New York City. Its offices included a downstairs bookstore (photograph above). Today the Foundation is located in a brick house built about 1773 on a Chester Borough tract (left photograph). The building was used as a residence, Friends Meeting house, offices for the West Chester School Board, and the Chester County Art Center before it was purchased by the Swedenborg Foundation.

SWEDENBORG FOUNDATION PUBLISHERS,
WEST CHESTER, PENNSYLVANIA

Estelle Porter is the first contact that many people make with the Foundation. She discovers what callers want to know and directs them to books that address their particular interests. Visitors to the Foundation's research library, evening lecture series, and annual book exhibits are also greeted by Estelle, who enjoys "selling books, sharing in the excitement of discovering spiritual truths, and helping people on their journeys." Says Estelle: "Being useful in this way is not work: it's a pleasure for me."

Customer Service

By calling 800-355-3222 (ext. 10), inquirers can reach our customer-service specialist, Estelle Porter, to learn about our books or how to join the Foundation in support of our publishing ventures.

In 1996, we embarked on a new—and extensive—publishing project: a completely fresh translation of Swedenborg's eighteen theological books by a team of Swedenborgian scholars. Those works have not been translated in their entirety since the Victorian era, and, unfortunately, the old translations made heavy use of Latinate words drawn directly from the Neo-Latin used by scholars in Swedenborg's day. Thus, as we produce volumes (and this work will be in progress until about 2015)—the "New Century Edition" is enabling first-time readers of Swedenborg to understand what he is saying by saying it as clearly as he does.

Who Was Swedenborg?

An eighteenth-century Swedish scientist and member of the Swedish Parliament, Emanuel Swedenborg's great and defining quest was to find the nature of the body-spirit relationship.

- During the first part of his life, after graduation from Uppsala University, he was an active inventor, a mining expert, a public official, an Old-World traveler, and a prolific writer on scientific subjects. Then he became increasingly interested in spirituality and how matter related to spirit.
- About 1745, in midlife, Swedenborg began having dreams and visions, which he documented in a dream journal. His life and writing took a new direction as he repeatedly entered altered states of awareness in which he vividly experienced the spiritual world—the afterlife.
- Swedenborg's many reports and analyses of these experiences were written in Neo-Latin prose under eighteen titles in some twenty-seven volumes (1745–1771), which he saw through the press in London and Amsterdam.

Many of Swedenborg's insights seem familiar to Western faiths. But Swedenborg was interfaith in a universal sense, unusual for his time.